Bohemia in Southern California

Bohemia in Southern California

Edited by Jay Ruby

San Diego State University Press

2017

Bohemia in Southern California

All efforts have been made to identify and credit sources and artists for images and illustrations included in this book; any omissions or mistakes of attribution should be brought to the attention of SDSU Press, at the address below, for correction in future editions of this volume.

San Diego State University Press publications may be purchased at discount for educational, business, or sales promotional use. For information write SDSU Press Next Generation Publishing Initiative, SDSU, San Diego, California 92182-6020 or email us at memo@sdsu.edu

sdsupress.sdsu.edu
facebook.com/sdsu.press
hype.sdsu.edu

San Diego State University Press
5500 Campanile Drive
Arts and Letters 283, mail code 6020
San Diego State University
San Diego, California 92182-6020

Cover and Book Design by Guillermo Nericcio García
for memogr@phics designcasa

ISBN-10:1-938537-10-6
ISBN-13:978-1-938537-10-3

FIRST EDITION

PRINTED IN THE UNITED STATES OF AMERICA

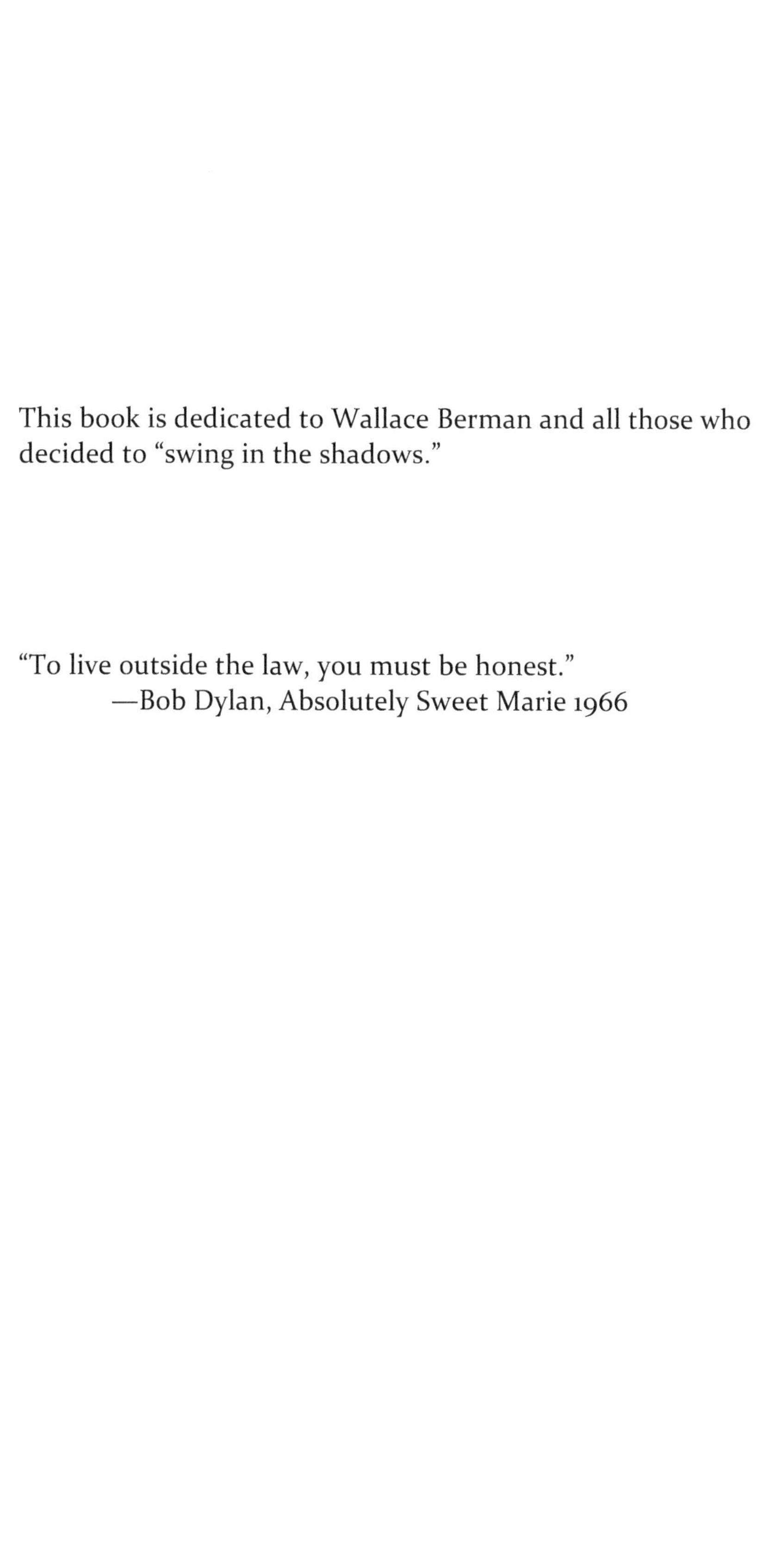

This book is dedicated to Wallace Berman and all those who decided to "swing in the shadows."

"To live outside the law, you must be honest."
—Bob Dylan, Absolutely Sweet Marie 1966

Contents

Malibu/Topanga Beach

Venice

Laurel Canyon

MOUNTAIN DRIVE
PCH
SANTA BARBARA
SOME COASTAL BOHEMIAN ENCLAVES
W
N
S
E
VENTURA
OXNARD
Point Mugu
MALIBU BEACH
COFFEE HOUSE POSITANO
TOPANGA BEACH
L.A.
VENICE

Map 1

Introduction

By Jay Ruby

> California has, as it were a civilization, and an art of its own, independent of the East. It produces its own geniuses, measures them by its own standards, and makes their fame itself, without waiting for the aid or consent of any wiseacre on the other side of the Rockies.
>
> —Isabel McDougall, "Arts and Crafts," *House Beautiful*, 1905

Bohemia in Southern California is a collection of essays that explores some less-well known aspects of alternative life styles and artistic endeavors in the Southland. Taken collectively, they suggest that when *la vie bohéme* arrived in the southland, a unique way of being unconventional was created.

When Midwesterners moved to this region, a complex culture evolved combining elements from the older Spanish, Mexican, and Native American populations with the values of the newer Anglo migrants. One result was that southern Californians seeking to develop their own artistic models were not as burdened with older European models that sometimes impeded eastern Americans from creating a unique form of expression and lifestyle.

There are several additional qualities that make bohemia in the southland significantly different from other such enclaves. Most scholars have assumed that bohemia requires an urban world to exist (Levin 2010:29 and 2010:244; Fairweather 2007). Since Los Angeles, along with other southern California cities, never really developed a serious urban center, it would therefore seem logical to suggest that there cannot be a southland bohemia. However, as will be demonstrated, there is a rich and varied history of alternative communities that thrived outside of urban centers. Their existence is a challenge to the standard definition of bohemia as only possible in an urban environment.

The countercultural communities around Los Angeles in Arroyo Seco, Edendale, Topanga Canyon/Beach, and Mountain Drive in Santa Barbara (see the essays that discuss these communities) were located in rural places sufficiently isolated as to make their accidental discovery improbable. Because Los Angeles lacks a center and is spread over a huge area—one hundred suburbs searching for a city—it was possible for the mainstream to simply be unaware that these alternative worlds existed.

In addition, other factors have contributed to this uniqueness. The sunny, mild Mediterranean climate and a geography with beaches and canyons permitted a lifestyle impossible elsewhere in the U.S. Perhaps nowhere else can one look like and live like a "beach bum" and also be a dentist or business executive.

The existence of the film industry, with its unquenchable need for creative people, meant that southern California became a mecca for the unconventional. As readers will see in Hurewitz's discussion of Edendale, the entertainment industry in California has always co-mingled with southland's bohemia. Those working in the film business frequently live a life of economic uncertainty, making a conventional life often difficult, if not impossible. In addition, people attracted to this world are usually artistically inclined even if they end up working in occupations the public does not recognize as artistic such as set designing or scriptwriting.

A Brief Attempt to Define Bohemia and Provide Some Historical Background

With the advent of the industrial revolution and the rise of capitalism, western countries became fragmented culturally. Craft guilds, organized religion, the state, and the power elite lost some of their control over the artistic, social, and economic lives of their citizens. It became possible for some daring people to subvert mainstream expectations about how one made a living and the lifestyle one chose. Prior to the nineteenth century, most attempts to "live outside the law" were based on religious beliefs, for example, the Amish. In the mid-1800s, secular attempts to lead a creative life emerged. No longer did one have to belong to a guild or be dependent on the patronage of organized religion, the state, or an elite to be an artisan. While it was necessary to conduct oneself outside the awareness of those in authority, that is, to dwell in an underground, one could be an artistic, cultural, and economic subversive. It is at this point, bohemia emerged.

Defining what constitutes a bohemian has been the subject of much debate. However, there seems to be a general acceptance that a bohemian is someone involved in the arts who lives an unconventional life, usually in a community of like-minded persons (Merriam-Webster dictionary 2015).

As a way to contextualize what happened in southern California, a sketchy overview of the development of this concept is offered. The classic form of bohemia (1860-1960) is the most widely recognized form. It conjures up somewhat clichéd images of starving artists dressed in old clothes living in cold-water flats either in the Montmartre section of Paris or Greenwich Village in New York. Involved in unconventional creative endeavors, they were fundamentally opposed to the politics/lifestyle of conventional society (Wilson 2000:24). When not busy creating art, they hung out in cafes or coffee houses drinking cheap wine. In time, they evolved into loosely defined or "imagined" communities (Anderson 1983) that also included some non-artists who were in concert with their approach to living. They chose a life of aesthetic poverty, that is, being poor on purpose, because their artistic ambitions were more important to them than making a good living. As they tended to produce works not understood or liked by the public, there was not much of a market for their work, ensuring that they were unable to make a living from their art.

They lived in an underground world because their attitudes toward sex, marriage, religion, illegal drugs, and alcohol were regarded as immoral, illegal, and positively dangerous. They questioned the foundational assumptions of western politics and society and, as a consequence, were attracted to socialist, Marxist, and anarchist alternatives. Some had the fantasy that they were a true avant garde—the wave of the future—which meant everyone else would eventually convert to their way of life. Others were content to be among the happy few and assumed that most people would not understand or like their work and abhor their way of life. They found themselves in a demimonde inhabited by prostitutes, drug addicts, criminals, and despised minorities—gays, blacks, and so on—people who were involuntarily outside the mainstream.

The underlying causes of the disaffiliation are complex but outside the boundaries of this book. Walter Benjamin (1973) and Pierre Bourdieu (1995) have suggested that the rise of capitalism radicalized artists because their work was transformed into a cultural commodity bought and sold in the marketplace.

Bohemians "pictured themselves as embattled geniuses defending Art against a vulgar bourgeoisie" (Wilson 2000:6).

One could envision an "ideal bohemian" as someone so opposed to the capitalist art market that he/she produces art for which there is no market, an art deliberately offensive, immoral, subversive, incomprehensible, even illegal. The logical consequence of this "ideal" is that one cannot make a living being a "true" artist because there is no market for what one produces. As Wilson points out, "The antagonism between bohemian and bourgeois gave rise to a paradoxical situation in which to succeed was, for the artist, to fail" (2000:18). Scott points out the inherent contradiction of this point of view: "The old phrase 'starving artist' gestures toward an image that is both romantic and pathetic, of a person too pure, and also just too impractical, to make it in the world. When that person ceases to starve, he or she can always be labeled a sellout. You're not supposed to be in it for the money . . ." (Scott 2014).

> She knows there's no success like failure
> And that failure's no success at all
>
> —Bob Dylan, Love Minus Zero, *No Limit*, 1965

Betty Turnbull (1976:3) suggests that some artists involved with the Ferus Gallery in Los Angeles in the 1960s were less interested in making a living from their art than simply exhibiting it. "If you sold a work, so much the better, but the main purpose was to get new ideas and breakthroughs out where they could be seen" (see Hertz, this volume).

There were a few, very few, who refused the "patronage" of the square world. In southern California, a number of Venice West people followed this path, including several poets discussed in William Mohr's essay "When a Coterie Meets the Carnival: The Poets of Venice West as the Neo-Anarchists of a Mid-Century Bohemia" and Wallace Berman as discussed in Harry Polkinhorn's essay, "Space/Time and the Radical Image: Wallace Berman's Semina." Maynard has suggested that these Venice poets were part of "the greatest drive for non-recognition in the history of literature" (Maynard 1991:2).

This classic form of bohemia was more or less recognizable until the middle of the twentieth century when the Beats emerge. While some have argued that the Beats merely continued the traditions and values of classic bohemians, there is one dramatic change that fundamentally alters things. The Beats became the darlings of mass media that caused bohemia to emerge from the underground. While it was gradual, eventually it transformed bohemia into a socially acceptable form of unconventionality, rendering it virtually meaningless. The war with the bourgeoisie is over.

Beats were regarded as less of a threat and more of an amusement. Some individuals were even touted as international celebrities in the New York Times, Time, and Life articles. I am not suggesting that they were the first bohemians to become pop stars. Ernest Hemingway was certainly one of the most widely known of the classic bohemians. However, he might best be characterized as a "socially acceptable" bohemian in that his lifestyle was merely eccentric and his writing hardly avant garde. His way of life was in sharp contrast to the Beat poet Allen Ginsberg—a gay dope-smoking freak whose work was a fundamental criticism of the American Dream.

Until the 1960s, audiences for avant-garde music, theater, film, and literature, and those who went to art galleries or even art museums, were a tiny, select, urban, educated minority. This was particularly true for Los Angeles that did not even have a museum devoted solely to art until 1961. Over the next fifty years, the audience for the avant garde exploded. Today there are genre-bending artists like Jeff Koons, whose work sells for millions of dollars. Bohemian writers have become university professors. Government agencies like NEH and NEA underwrite experimental work that could be seen as positively subversive.

The political fantasies that Communism/socialism, as seen in the Soviet Union, was a serious alternative to capitalism started to sputter with Stalin's pact with Hitler and his 1930s "show trials" and died with Khrushchev's 1956 denunciation of Stalin. While the Beats remained critical of American society, they were mainly liberals or leftists and not revolutionaries. A few like Allen Ginsberg and rock and roll bands like Country Joe and the Fish joined the New Left organizations like SDS in their opposition to the Viet Nam War, but most were in agreement with Lipton when he wrote in The Holy Barbarians (1959), "when the Bomb drops it will find us writing poems, painting pictures and making music."

While there was a brief interlude of bohemian creativity in the 1960s and 1970s among the hippies with musical poets who became pop stars like Bob Dylan, Leonard Cohen, and the Laurel

Canyon folk-rock artists like Joni Mitchell and Crosby, Stills, and Nash, bohemia was destined to become a toothless, socially acceptable version of its old revolutionary self now known as "bourgeois bohemians" or BoBos (Brooks 2000), regarded as an asset for community developers. As a "creative class" (Florida 2000), they are no longer regarded as people who live immoral, illegal, and dangerous lives and who produce unintelligible art that has no market value. They are now an asset that should be encouraged to move into communities in need of being gentrified. "Bohemians had always colonized seedy, marginal districts of cities, but an inexorable law decreed that every Bohemia of the Western world would be subject to gentrification" (Wilson 2000:42). Madison Avenue discovered that sex, dope, and rock and roll could be used to sell products. The revolution will not be televised, as it was now available at Walmart. Torn jeans, once a sign of poverty, have become a fashion item selling for hundreds of dollars. Capitalism can sell rebellion as boho style and hippie-chic.

While the contemporary bohemian or "BoBo" may not be a radical revolutionary force, it would be a mistake to suggest that "living outside the law" is no longer possible. It is simply harder to find an inexpensive place to live and work. Attempting to produce an avant-garde work has become very difficult, some would say impossible. As Susan Sontag is reported to have said, "there cannot be an avant garde anymore; everyone catches up too fast."

Lest I appear to suggest that "Bohemia is Dead"—a clichéd trope that started to appear in the 1880s—I am acknowledging that to predict the future is always a fool's game. The improbable, bizarre relationship between the development of the personal computer and the counterculture suggests that no matter what mainstream culture may be, those wishing to swim against the current can find a way (Markoff 2005 and Turner 2006).

This is the era of DIYs where it is easy to produce all forms of creative expression for little money and to self-distribute—make a feature-length video with your smart phone and place it on YouTube, write a novel or a book of poems and Amazon might distribute it, make a painting or photo or other pictorial work and offer it for viewing and sale on your web site. Perhaps the next phase in the evolution of bohemia is that of the digital amateur who has chosen a new alternative route to the creative world, if he or she can find a cheap place to live.

"It Can't Happen Here" or Southern California as a Cultural Wasteland

There is an extensive literature exploring bohemia that mainly focuses on a particular artist or writer (such as Hopps' 1996 exploration of Keinholz) or a particular time period—1860 to 1920 being the most common (Herny 2008)—or locale—Paris is by far the most popular (Easton 1964) followed by Greenwich Village (Strausbaugh 2013) and then San Francisco (Phillips 1995). Only a few have attempted an overview that encompasses all time periods (Wilson 2000). Curiously enough, there is not an extensive literature devoted to a southern California version of bohemia. In fact, it is often ignored and even dismissed as an impossibility.

In the first history of bohemia in America, Parry (citing an unnamed 1920s source) suggests that:

> I would no more expect to see a group of creative workers gathered about some little sidewalk café in Los Angeles than I would expect to see a Chamber of Commerce bulletin which failed to mention local sunshine. One could imagine how the native citizenry would regard such a group . . . The following Sunday, from every pulpit would thunder denunciations directed at Bohemian indolence which was likely to undermine the celestial props of the City of the Angels . . . this plaint, in the middle and late 1920s, was true not only of Los Angeles, but of any Far Western city, large or small, with the possible exception of San Francisco. (Parry 1933:242)

As late as 1971, when Los Angeles was gaining an international reputation as one of the art capitals of the world, Joseph Masheck, in a letter to the editor in Art Forum, dismissed Los Angeles as being a place incapable of producing anything of artistic value:

> There is that whole shallow, indulgent, Republic of Trivia aspect to Los Angeles which reminds us here in New York that not since the invention of bronze casting has anything of consequence happened in that climate. (Masheck 1971: 71)

Woody Allen in *Annie Hall* (1977), when asked why he didn't move to southern California, said that he did not want to live in a place where "The only cultural advantage Los Angeles has over New York is that you can make a right turn on a red light." The prejudice continues in Holland Cotter's 2011 review of Rebels in Paradise: The Los Angeles Art Scene and the 1960s in which he dismisses fifties Los Angeles as ". . . a boomtown thanks to movies and the aerospace industry, but a cultural backwater." Mike Davis sees Los Angeles as a cultural desert "unable to produce, to this day (1990) any home grown intelligentsia" (1990:17).

It is not too difficult to see why so many have such a negative attitude, particularly New Yorkers who have long regarded themselves as living in the center of everything important. They become threatened when something challenges this position. Saul Steinberg's famous New Yorker cartoon of a map of Manhattan (March 29, 1979) is an excellent example of this cultural myopia. The distance between Ninth Avenue and the Hudson River takes up over half of the cartoon, allowing perhaps one-third of the space for everything between the Hudson River and the Pacific Ocean.

Southern California's clichéd reputation is that of the land of sun-tanned airheads and beach bunnies where nothing complex or sophisticated was ever created—a cultural wasteland, inhabited by plastic people with luxury cars and ultra-expensive beach houses. They produce terrible movies and, even worse, television that lulls the masses into a false sense of contentment.

Perhaps the most important reason why southland bohemia has not gotten the attention it deserves is that when the first bohemians arrived there in the 1880s (see Jessica Holada's "Print Culture on the Arroyo Seco, 1895-1947") a variant of bohemia emerged sufficiently different from bohemian enclaves elsewhere as to be dismissed as insignificant. In addition, many southern California bohemians were more concerned with developing a non-traditional lifestyle than producing art that could compete in the world market. Their life was their art.

But It Did Happen Here . . .

While a comprehensive history of southern California bohemia has yet to be written, there are some references to its existence. Starr's discussion of the Arroyoan culture (1985) is one example. However, Maynard's 1991 study of Venice West is one of the earliest scholarly studies, followed by Candida-Smith's 1995 book Utopia and Dissent: Art, Poetry, and Politics in California:

> In most societies prior to 1960, the concerns of the aesthetic avant garde were of interest primarily to small, select, relatively well-educated coteries whose members claimed personal distinction for their appreciation of the difficult and arcane. California, however, was one of the places where the thinning of the line between bohemianism and popular culture took place earliest, most clearly, and most systematically. (Smith 1995:xv)

It was not until Hurewitz's 2007 study of the bohemian community of Edendale and Warren's 2011 work on the bohemian community surrounding Edward Weston (1906-1923) that the existence of an early twentieth-century southland bohemia was convincingly established.

The following is an attempt to embed the essays that follow in a larger historical and geographical context.

ARROYO CULTURE (Map 2)

In the late 1800s, some *plein air* painters attracted by the southern California sunlight and the rocks, beach, mountains, and desert moved to a rural area between downtown Los Angeles and Pasadena called Arroyo Seco. This is the earliest evidence of bohemians in southern California. Marion Wachtel, Hanson Puthoff, and Franz Bischoff and William Wendt were among this pioneering group (Stern and Gerdts 2002). Jean Stern, Executive Director of the Irvine Museum, has characterized this as "The Great Bohemian Migration" (Stern N.D.).

In addition, a number of other like-minded people lived ". . . on the edge of wilderness" (Starr 1985:107) and looked to the landscape rather than to the city for their inspiration. As Mark Thompson discusses in his essay, Charles Fletcher Lummis's Refuge for Love and Humanity on the Arroyo, the community developed around the marvelously eccentric Lummis and El Alisal, his hand-built stone house, where he held amazingly raucous parties.

These "eccentrics" drew their inspiration from the Arts and Crafts movement as well as Mexican and American Indian art and design (Wilson 2000:39). Lummis was an early advocate for Native American rights and attempted to make Californians

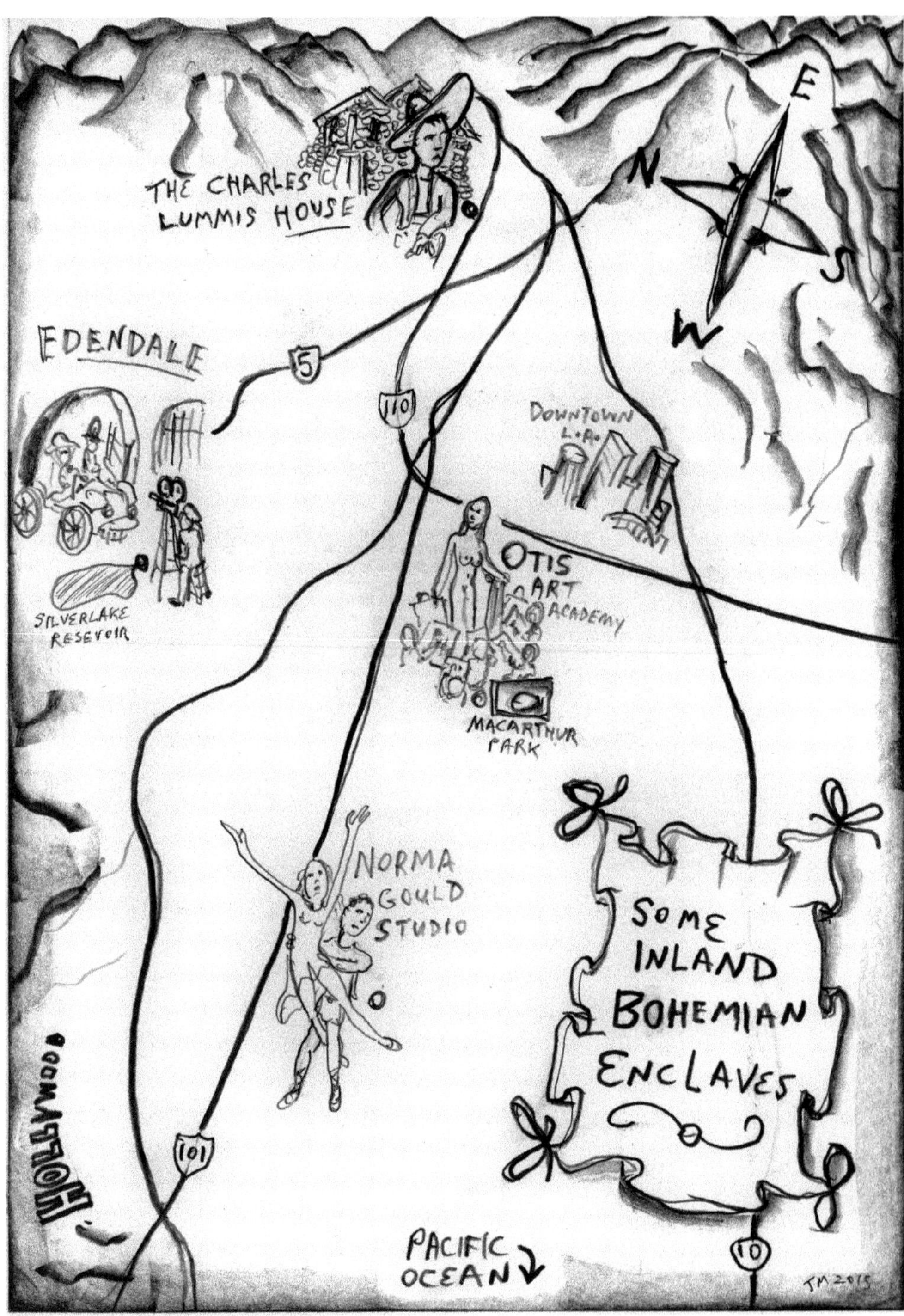
THE CHARLES LUMMIS HOUSE
EDENDALE
SILVERLAKE RESEVOIR
5
110
DOWNTOWN L.A.
OTIS ART ACADEMY
MACARTHUR PARK
NORMA GOULD STUDIO
SOME INLAND BOHEMIAN ENCLAVES
HOLLYWOOD
101
PACIFIC OCEAN
10
N
E
S
W
JM 2015

Map 2

aware of their Spanish and Mexican ancestry and campaigned for the preservation of the missions.

The Arroyoans shared a dislike for modernism and the consequences of capitalism. While unconventional in dress and lifestyle, their main interests lay beyond the creation of art or literature. People crafted a unique way of life. They wore pseudo-peasant clothes and lived in simply-built Craftsman cottages that were filled with hand-made Mission furniture. They sought out a simple lifestyle in opposition to the frills of the Victorian world and the Industrial Revolution and shared in what Kevin Starr suggests was "the Arroyoan ideal: the spiritualization of daily life through an aestheticism tied to crafts and local materials . . . no art would be more important . . . than the art of domestic living" (Starr 1985: 111-12). They were the originators of the southern California Arts and Crafts movement, produced artisan tiles and hand-crafted publications (see Ritchie 1995, Yeoman 2003, Murphy N.D., and Robertson 1993).

Jessica Holada's essay "Print Culture on the Arroyo Seco, 1895-1947" explores some Arroyoan master printmakers like Clyde Browne, who built Abbey San Encino, a structure as eccentric as El Alisal. Browne built workshops and studios in the hopes of creating a colony of artisans. Another Arroyoan, William Lees Judson, was an art glass-maker and founder and dean of the Los Angeles School of Fine Arts, University of Southern California, the first southern California art school (Henderson 2014).

The art produced in this community was not the kind that generally gets discussed in the standard surveys of California art (Moure 1998). Pre-1950 California art has been regarded by many art historians as provincial, having a regional appeal, and therefore not worthy of serious consideration. When the "Cool School" artists associated with the Ferus Gallery emerged in the 1950s, they assumed that there was no significant art tradition in Los Angeles (Moure 1998:407) (for additional discussion see Hertz's "Looking for Bohemia: The Los Angeles Art Scene of the Sixties and Seventies," this volume).

Arroyoan culture flourished from the late 1890s to the 1920s. Traces can be found today; for example, the Judson studio still makes stained glass. It would appear that the Arroyo culture, like the Arts and Crafts movement in general, disappeared around the time that another alternative community was coming into existence, Edendale. "Although there are many ending dates for the Arts and Crafts Movement, ranging from 1916 to 1920 and even up to 1929, it is safe to say that the period had effectively ended by 1916, and its popularity had dramatically declined by 1919" (Ken Lonsinger 2010).

The legacy of the Arroyo culture is difficult to determine, partially because there is so little written about it. Ward Ritchie, a fine-arts printer, wrote a small memoir of "The Arroyo Seco Culture" in 1996 (See Huerwitz, this volume). Sharyn Wiley's unpublished 2003 dissertation, "Messages from the Promised Land: Bohemian Los Angeles, 1880-1920," remains the most extensive study.

EDENDALE (Map 2)

Edendale is an area south of the Arroyo Seco, where another early bohemian enclave was located. It was the place where many unique attributes of southland bohemia were first manifested. Historian Kevin Starr characterized it as Los Angeles' "bohemian quarter of the 1920's and 1930's . . . the closest thing Los Angeles had at the time to an artists' quarter" (1990:329). It was in this sparsely populated, almost rural community that the California film industry started. In 1909, the Selig-Polyscope Company established the first permanent Los Angeles motion picture studio on Glendale Boulevard. Max Sennett bought a studio in 1913 and produced many short films, including those of the Keystone Cops and Charlie Chaplin. Hollywood cowboy Tom Mix had a studio there. The first Walt Disney studio (1926-1939) was located on Hyperion Street. Given the lack of public transportation, many actors, scene painters, and other studio worker had to live close by. As a consequence, they formed an artistic community that lasted beyond the life of the studios. By the 1920s, the studios started leaving. By the 1930s the industry had moved elsewhere, but elements of this community remain to this day.

It is within the Edendale community that an association between bohemians and Hollywood was created. Abrams (2008) argues that an unprecedented number of gays, cross-dressers, and other "so-called deviants" became identified as a part of a glamorous Hollywood lifestyle during this period, perhaps because it was commonly assumed that people associated with the film industry were naturally eccentric. After World War II, there was a resurgence of Hollywood bohemians, beginning with James Dean and then greatly expanded with the actor/directors associated with Dennis Hopper (Russ Tamblyn, Teri Garr, and

Dean Stockwell). Shortly before his death in 2010, Hopper said that he wished to be remembered for his art photography rather than his acting or directing (Leland 2015).

Writers, painters, and others not associated with the film business moved to Edendale because of its reputation for being a place where non-traditional people could live openly. Some students and faculty were attracted to the place because the Chouinard Art Institute was nearby. They formed sketch clubs, others opened galleries, and those who wrote established non-traditional publishing outlets.

Genie Guerard's essay "Jake Zeitlin: Books and Galleries, 1927-1940" explores an Edendale resident who became a nationally known bookseller and confidant of Aldous Huxley, Christopher Isherwood, and many intellectuals and European exiles within the Hollywood community. His bookstore was a space where Edward Weston exhibited and many creative people hung out, such as Ward Ritchie, a printmaker discussed in Jessica Holada's essay "'A Small Renaissance': Arroyo Seco Print Culture, 1895-1947," and Paul Landacre (also a master printmaker and author of a 1996 book on Arroyo Seco).

The architects Richard Neutra and Richard Schindler, responsible for the unique 1950s California hyper-modern houses, lived there. Carey McWilliams (1968) has suggested that Neutra was influenced by the film industry's approach to set construction.

Edendale was one of the national centers for the politically involved folk-song revival. Legendary folk-song writer/performer Woody Guthrie moved here in the 1930s and became close friends with Will Geer, the actor. In turn, Geer was a participant in other aspects of this community. Geer was Harry Hay's lover, who was the founder of the Mattachine Society in 1950, one of the earliest gay activist organizations. Daniel Hurewitz, in "Bohemian Politics and the Edendale Origins of Coming Out," argues that strategies the LGBT community adopted for coming out had their origin in Edendale. Both Hay and Geer were members of the Communist Party. To underscore the marvelously unconventional nature of this community, it should be noted that from November, 1914, to June, 1916, Edendale was also home to a farming commune founded by Mexican anarcho-Communist radicals of the Partido Liberal Mexicano.

This community lasted a long time and probably had a much greater impact on bohemian Los Angeles than the Arroyoan culture. Known today as Eagle Rock, Silver Lake, and Los Feliz, it is an excellent example of how a bohemian community with modest housing costs evolved into a "BoBo" center with cafes, galleries, and high rents.

Norma Gould, the pioneering avant-garde dancer, choreographer, and teacher whom Naima Prevots discusses in "Dancing in the Sun: The Spirited Freedom of Norma Gould (1888-1980)," provides an example of a bohemian so deeply immersed in her own art that she apparently did not become involved with people from outside of her creative world. She worked in a series of studios located in the central Los Angeles/Hancock Park area slightly to the south of Edendale. Even though Gould was most active (1915-1932) at the same time as the Edendale community was flourishing, it appears she had no interaction with that community.

In the late 1960s, painters and other artists trained at the Otis Art Institute and Chouinard Art Institute (both located in the MacArthur Park area south of Edendale) began to produce art that eventually transformed Los Angeles into a center of major artistic importance (See Richard Hertz's essay "Looking for Bohemia: The Los Angeles Art Scene of the Sixties and Seventies" and Peabody, et al., 2011).

Coastal Southland Bohemia–Malibu Beach, Topanga Beach, and Venice

The vast beaches in southern California offer a tantalizing chance to lead a variety of alternative lives from the ultra-wealthy members of the Malibu Colony to the fabled Californian surfer. Katherine Stewart's essay "Mountain Drive: Santa Barbara's Iconoclastic Experiment in Living" discusses how a few World War II veterans decided to create an alternative community on Mountain Drive in Santa Barbara. Bobbie Hyde purchased fifty acres of land and, in turn, sold plots to his friends and colleagues. Eventually a community of hand-made houses was born. Like the Arroyoans before them, the main interest of these folks was developing an alternative way of life. The art they made was of secondary importance. Ron and Phyllis Patterson, founders of the Renaissance Pleasure Faire, claim that their visit to one of the community's "Pot Wars" heavily influenced their thinking about the character of the Renaissance Pleasure Faire (see Rubin, thus volume).

While much has been written about the surfer as a quintessential part of southern California pop culture, it is Pablo Capra's essay about his life at Topanga Beach, "Idlers of the

Bamboo Grove," that suggest that this form of unconventional living can be viewed as another unique manifestation of bohemia in the southland.

Only one mile from the surfers at Topanga Beach was Coffee House Positano. Jay Ruby's essay "Bohemia in Malibu—A Hidden Treasure" suggests that Positano was unlike the many other 1960s coffee houses in southern California. Located on a cliff above the Pacific Coast Highway, it was yet another example of the rural character of bohemia in the southland. It was where some legendary surfers like Miki Dora lived (see Lawler, this volume) and where those interested could mingle with the famous and not so famous while enjoying music, poetry, theatre, political discussions, and, of course, drink coffee. Jake Zeitlin (see Guerard, this volume) was among the many who made presentations at Positano.

Venice West is undoubtedly the first name that pops up when most people think about bohemia in southern California. For some, it is the first and only manifestation of la vie boheme there. This is partially the result of the tireless self-promoting efforts of Lawrence Lipton and his book The Holy Barbarians (1959:20). By the end of World War II, Venice was in a sorry state of derelict houses and abandoned businesses, which meant that the poor, college students, and bohemians could rent apartments and spaces easily converted into studios very cheaply. As Venice was easily accessible, the bohemian enclave became a major tourist attraction and the source of much conflict between those wishing to develop Venice into a commercially viable and expensive place and those who did not. While there is a vast literature already devoted to this place, two essays in this collection shed new light on Wallace Berman and his groundbreaking publication, Semina—Harry Polkinhorn's "Space/Time and the Radical Image: Wallace Berman's Semina" and William Mohr's "When a Coterie Meets the Carnival: The Poets of Venice West as the Neo-Anarchists of a Mid-Century Bohemia." Mohr also explores some Venice West poets whom he feels have not been given the attention they deserve. It seems ironic that these artists appear to have succeeded in their struggle for anonymity or as Mohr characterizes it "their ideals of non-success." Maynard has suggested that they represent "the greatest drive for non-recognition in the history of literature" (Maynard 1991:2).

Given the general sense that southern California is the land of make-believe, it seems only logical that the Renaissance Pleasure

Faires should have originated there (see Rachel Rubin's "'I Think That Maybe I'm Dreaming': Southern California Gives Birth to the Renaissance Pleasure Faire.") Phyllis and Ron Patterson, the creators of the faires, lived in Laurel Canyon, famous as a bohemian enclave populated by folk rockers like Joni Mitchell and Jackson Browne. The Pattersons were, at least partially, inspired by a visit to the Mountain Drive community discussed in Katherine Stewart's essay.

The essays in Bohemia in Southern California provide an opportunity to enlighten readers about the innovative ways in which those seeking an unconventional life were able to create a home.

Arroyo Seco

"A Small Renaissance": Arroyo Seco Print Culture, 1895–1947

By Jessica Holada

In the 1880s, a visitor to southern California's Arroyo Seco would have discovered an austere landscape shaped by a seasonally dry watershed, accentuated by mature sycamores, scattered live oaks, and stunning river rock. It cut a course from the San Gabriel Mountains to the north, meeting the Los Angeles River to the south. The eminent Los Angeles printer Ward Ritchie described the area as a sort of Nile of the West (Ritchie 1996: 1), providing a place for colorful personalities to flourish and fantasy-build along its unpopulated banks. Over sixty years after he and Lawrence Clark Powell rented a studio at the Abbey San Encino to print poetry pamphlets and play the pipe organ for $1 on Sundays, Ritchie recalled his encounters with a number of prodigious eccentrics in his book *A Southland Bohemia: The Arroyo Seco Colony as the Century Begins* (1996). It provides a portrait of a vibrant if scattered enclave of nonconformists that represented an emergent print culture, most notably Charles Fletcher Lummis, Margaret Collier Graham, Idah Meacham Strobridge, George Wharton James, William Lees Judson, Clyde Browne, Alice Millard, and Olive Percival. Their homes, gardens, and studios were locations for music-filled "noises," moon-viewing parties, "dungeon" meetings, and Guildhall gatherings, as well as sites of self-assured writing, skillful printing, irrepressible book collecting, and tenacious book selling.

Arriving from out-of-state, the Arroyoans sought improved health and the year-round climate where in winter "house-plants never froze and ... ripe oranges hung on the trees" (Apostol 1992: 1). Moving to Pasadena, South Pasadena, Garvanza, and Highland Park, they brought their diverse talents, progressive opinions, voracious curiosity, and developed wit—drawn to the area for its rural appeal and affordability. Architecture historian Robert Winter termed this corridor of sophistication "Arroyo Culture" (Winter 1998: 1), and it was comprised of artists, architects, photographers, naturalists, educators, craftspeople, collectors, writers, printers, publishers, bookmakers, and booksellers. Many adopted their new environment with cultish enthusiasm, relishing the proximity to the deserts and mountains for adventure and fresh subject matter, and to the not-too-distant waters off San Pedro for regular boating and primitive wikiup camping.

Above: Bartered for job printing, Clyde Browne had the Judson Studios fabricate this stained glass window for his pressroom (Apostol 1997: 23). The Mission Indian working a wooden hand press and the friar checking a printed sheet is a scene of historic fiction.

Despite their perpetuation of Spanish Mission- and Mexican Rancho-era romanticism, Arroyoans possessed relatively enlightened views. Their output placed an early value on multiculturalism, gender equality, and a sensitivity towards the natural setting in which they lived and worked, well before the Arroyo Seco Parkway was built and the perennial stream was channeled with concrete to control wild winter run-off.

As progressive tastemakers and idiosyncratic place-makers, Arroyoans were not guided by a unifying manifesto or influenced by the European avant-garde (the arts colonies of Carmel and Taos were closer in spirit). As ardent regionalists, these outdoorsy bohemians helped reshape the prevailing notion that southern California was a "cultural wasteland." While their activities were marked by a native self-consciousness, they took aesthetic cues from elsewhere, adopting the values of simplicity, integrity, and happy labor espoused by William Morris of the Kelmscott Press and T. J. Cobden-Sanderson of the Doves Press in England, later championed in America by Elbert Hubbard and Dard Hunter of the Roycrofters shop, and Gustav Stickley, whose furniture fame launched the influential *Craftsman* magazine.

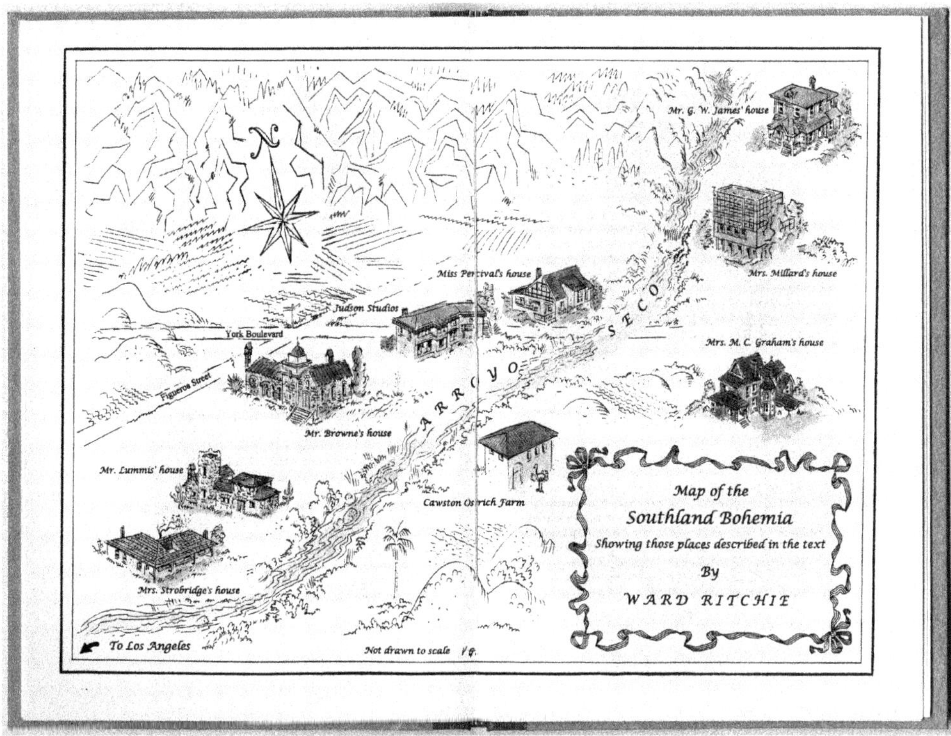

Fig. 1 The houses of colony dwellers are clustered around a swift-moving Arroyo Seco in this playful map drawn by Vance Gerry. Courtesy of the Vance Gerry Estate

A charming map forms the center of Ward Ritchie's book of reminiscences, depicting the unique homes associated with the main characters who contributed to Arroyo Seco print culture [Fig. 1]. With the exception of the plain Victorian owned by George Wharton James, the houses, cottages, and bungalows of Margaret Collier Graham, Olive Percival, Idah Meacham Strobridge, and Alice Millard were custom-built to fit their budgets and tastes, ranging from American Queen Anne to Mayan modern. Inspired by craftsman, mission, and medieval styles, Charles Lummis and Clyde Browne designed and fabricated their own dwellings using the most abundant building material at hand—Arroyo stones. These properties were embodiments of personal identity, stages for mingling and myth-making, and the subjects of self-authored publications that located their craft and showcased the objects of their delight.

Just as the map humorously notes, the history that follows is "Not drawn to scale." The deeply diverting biographies of the key figures are only cursory for this concise treatment. A concentrated timeline begins with Charles Lummis as editor of the literary magazine *The Land of Sunshine* in 1895, and ends with *Our Old-Fashioned Flowers*, Olive Percival's meticulous assembly of colloquial plant names, posthumously printed in 1947 by Ward Ritchie. Between these fitting bookends are various descriptions of people and printed matter, and those moments when the spheres of influence they inhabited overlapped.

The Arroyoans

When **Charles Fletcher Lummis (1859-1928)** encountered it, the Arroyo Seco was still untouched—a landscape of hillside chaparral and riparian flora. The area would eventually become the site for El Alisal, his "ostentatiously primitive" (Winter 1999: 6) "castle" situated around a magnificent sycamore tree. From 1898 to 1910, he labored as a stonemason and carpenter creating an unforgettable oasis and rendezvous point for notable artists, authors, musicians, and scientists.

Lummis [Fig. 2] first arrived in Los Angeles from Ohio in 1885—on foot. His famous cross-country "tramp"—designed as a newspaper stunt for the *Los Angeles Daily Times*—not only sold papers and earned him a job as editor, but established his bold persona, made more flamboyant with his signature costume—a green, wide-wale corduroy suit.

During his travels through the southwest, Lummis encountered Native Americans, and these indelible experiences profoundly changed him. Eventually, he would build the Southwest Museum of the American Indian and help reverse government policy he called "Remote, Uninformed, Unhuman, and Unsatisfactory" (Thompson 2001: 27). Describing native customs and lore became his primary subjects in stories compiled by Century, Scribner's, A. C. McClurg, and other publishers. Only a few of Lummis' books were ever printed in California that were not under the auspices of imprints connected to associations or periodicals he conceived or transformed, including The Landmarks Club, The Sequoya League, The Southwest Society, or *The Land of Sunshine* (later *Out West*) magazine.

His first and only foray into printing was in 1879 with *Birch Bark Poems*, a miniature printed directly on birch bark on a small press given to him by his grandfather. This little novelty was so popular it went through multiple printings, selling over 14,000 copies. (Lummis 2012: 3). A triumph like this could have served as inspiration, but the value of creating a local identity through a fine press under his creative control was never an objective. Ordinary, reliable commercial printers would suit his needs and torrential output. With a few exceptions, the Arroyoans tended to follow the same low-risk model.

In addition to his own contributions to Western literature, Lummis acted at various times in the role of impresario and interpreter of genre-defining authors and artists, among them Mary Austin, who lived for a time in the Arroyo and received mentorship from Lummis before the publication of *The Land of Little Rain* (1903).

In January of 1895, Lummis assumed editorship of the Los Angeles Chamber of Commerce magazine *The Land of Sunshine* [Fig. 2] (renamed *Out West* in 1902), moving it from a strict marketing tool flaunting the advantages of the southland climate to a provocative pictorial literary magazine. While images of "cherubic children in the buff surrounded by flowers enjoying the balmy delights of Los Angeles in winter" (Thompson 2001: 180) endured, *The Land of Sunshine* became a serious testing ground for Arroyo Seco-based prose, poetry, photography, and illustration, and an outlet for established and fresh voices from California and neighboring states. During the eleven years Lummis was editor, he assembled a pool of over six-hundred contributors, writing as many as 250 pieces himself (Bingham 1955: 73). "In the Lion's Den," his uproarious opinion column, was just one example of his "volcanic outpouring of journalism" (Starr 1985: 346).

Lummis considered South Pasadena pioneer **Margaret Collier Graham (1850-1910)** to be a gifted regionalist and a leader of western letters. Her monthly piece, "The Angle of Reflection," which ran in *The Land of Sunshine* from 1898 to 1899, provided "refreshing counterpoise to the bristling, often extreme utterances of [the] editor" (Bingham 1955: 70). Her evocative, humorous, closely observed tales of ordinary people brimming with vernacular dialogue and sublime descriptions of nature were gathered into two volumes published by Houghton Mifflin, *Stories of the Foot-hills* (1895) and *The Wizard's Daughter, and Other Stories* (1905). She also wrote passionately in defense of women's suffrage, making "her point by an appeal to logic and a sense of the absurd," (Apostol 190) in the posthumous compilation of her feminist writings, *Do They Really Respect Us? And Other Essays* (1912).

Fig. 2 Lummis reading in the company of his pet parrot (left). Lummis hired Sierra Madre artist Gutzon Borglum, later of Mount Rushmore fame, to design a new cover for the magazine. Braun Research Library Collection, Autry National Center; P.3618

Fig. 3 Strobridge was a self-taught bookbinder. Much of her equipment, including her sewing frame, was custom built by her father, who illuminated copies of her first book. Braun Research Library Collection, Autry National Center; OP.393

Another strong-minded woman who occupied the Arroyo Seco was **Idah Meacham Strobridge (1855-1932)**. Having experienced personal trauma after the loss of her husband and children, Strobridge quit a career in ranching and mining in Nevada to take up writing and bookbinding full time. In 1898, her photo-illustrated editorial "A Neglected Corner," about San Francisco's decaying, overgrown Mission Dolores, was printed in *The Land of Sunshine*. She was also the subject of "A Sage Brush Oasis," a glowing piece by Lummis, who presented her as a binder of "staunch and honest" books, not "as a fad, nor yet commercially; but, so far as can be seen, for the pure love of work worth while" (Lummis 1901: 28). The article provided glimpses of her Artemisia Bindery [Fig. 3] and a most unusual self-portrait of Strobridge confidently leaning against a doorframe, dress sleeves rolled, forearms exposed, and clutching a backing hammer at her glue-stained hip.

Not long after the 1901 profile appeared, she returned to California (the state of her birth)—a decision that refocused her bookbinding business and propelled her writing and publishing efforts. She had a bungalow built in Highland Park called "At the Sign of the Sagebrush." In addition to housing the Artemisia Bindery, it contained the "Little Gallery of Local Art," an exhibit space for "The Best of the Best" (Borg papers: MS.677) by emerging artists. Like many others creative souls, painter Carl Oscar Borg fell under the spell of the Arroyo Seco, observing, "As artists know color and poets know it, the most colorful corner in the world" (Sherrell 1992: 12).

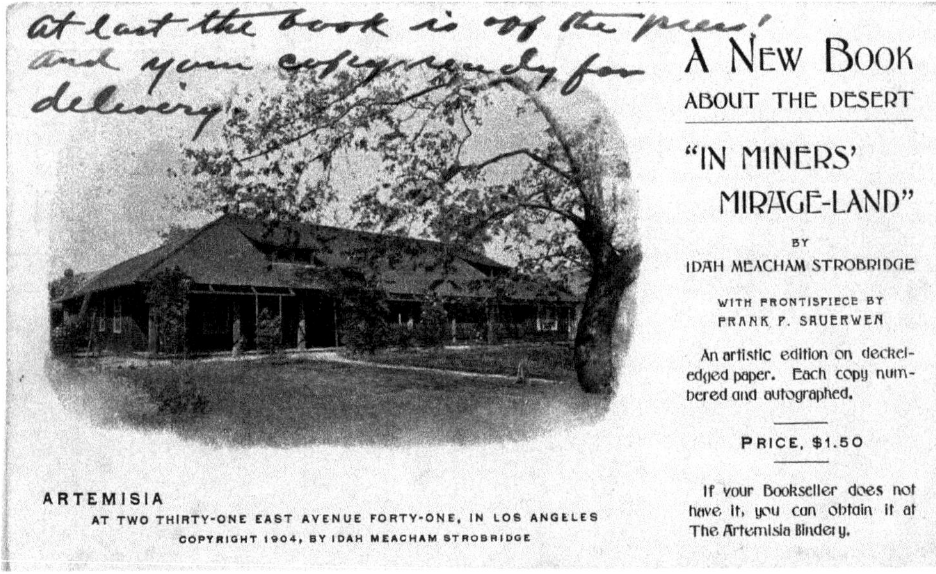

Fig. 4 An inscribed postcard announcing Idah Meacham Strobridge's first book. The William Andrews Clark Memorial Library, University of California, Los Angeles

Strobridge wrote three books about the daring and resourcefulness that the "Desert" required—a vast, enigmatic territory she was the first to dignify with capitalization. A mood-setting passage from Mary Austin's debut novel provided the foreword to Strobridge's first book, *In a Miners' Mirage-Land* (1904) [Fig. 4]. The success of this book was followed by *The Loom of the Desert* (1907) and *The Land of Purple Shadows* (1909)—both containing dynamic illustrations by Maynard Dixon. Together, the three books comprise the "Sagebrush Trilogy." Originally issued in illustrated paper wrappers, advertisements indicate Strobridge also offered autographed and numbered editions on heavy paper limited to 1,000 copies, for

$1.75. Deluxe leather binding options included three-quarter morocco with illuminated chapter heads for $6.75 and full morocco for $10.00 (*Out West* 1909: 992).

In 1906, Strobridge managed to publish several books via the short-lived Arroyo Press, including *Hieroglyphics of Love: Stories of Sonora Town and Old Mexico* by Amanda Mathews Chase. It is considered one of the earliest books of fiction printed in Los Angeles. Since the typography and general layout of the Arroyo Press books are consistent with others by Strobridge, the presswork was likely by Baumgardt Publishing Company, the Los Angeles firm responsible for Strobridge's first two books, or R. Y. McBridge Press, which printed *The Land of Purple Shadows* (Schneider 2014: 7). Some would dismiss the books for their commercial lineage, but the late writer and UCLA Librarian Lawrence Clark Powell said they represent "the beginnings of fine book production in Los Angeles, in which content, format, and illustrations, join harmoniously" (Powell 1959: 105).

An Arroyo Seco transplant from England with equal interest in book design and a flair for self-promotion was **George Wharton James (1842-1928)**. He later settled in Pasadena after a humiliating divorce and removal from the Methodist ministry on a charge of adultery. He may have been cut from different cloth than Charles-Lummis-corduroy, but he was equally unconventional [Fig. 5], correspondingly curious, and shared a passion for identical topics that suggested an undeclared competition was underway. Like Lummis, James also shared an enormous capacity for work. He was responsible for over 80 books and pamphlets, nearly 200 articles, countless bits of ephemera, and assumed editing duties for magazines such as *Out West* after Lummis stepped down. James, who was a teetotaler, a vegetarian, and a zealous outdoorsman, had manic tendencies that prompted rounds of mammoth productivity followed by periods of recuperation for "mental congestion" (Larson 1991: 76) at health resorts, sanitariums, and hot springs. James once likened the sensual pleasure of hot springs to bathing in champagne, exclaiming "The whole being seems exhilarated; you want to run and shout and work" (James 1906: xxxvi). Exuberance was one of James' characteristic modes, but he gave much of the credit to the remarkable weather in the state, a personal perspective that became an expansive thesis in *The Influence of the Climate on the Literature of California* (1909).

Fig. 5 George Wharton James at Cawston Ostrich Farm (left). He would form a more intimate friendship with another bird–Scraggles, a lame song sparrow that was the subject of two books. Braun Research Library Collection, Autry National Center; P.13114 and P.36101.

James leveraged his skill as an orator and former preacher, becoming an itinerant illustrated lecturer. The public adored his educational entertainments, which were billed as refined and high-class. He traveled with an elaborate, multi-lens lanternslide projector called the Malden Trinopticon that produced dissolving and rolling views that required flammable gas for illumination. The showmanship and promotional savvy he brought to his lectures translated fluidly into his publishing style. Marketing techniques included announcing a cascade of forthcoming publications and incorporating fervent testimonials to garner interest and bolster his status as a high-volume specialist. James paid meticulous attention to production quality, sometimes in ways that exceeded a book's intended use. One example is *The Itinerary of the Hotel Men's Mutual Benefit Association of California, April 10-20, 1896*, bound in Mexican hand-tooled leather with gilt edges, a hand-tinted map, and profuse illustrations. Another, *The House Blessing Ceremony and Guest Book* (1917), is a striking western adaptation of the Navajo hogan blessing ceremony filled with hospitality quotations and blank pages for signatures. These books communicated excellence, uniting subject and design in ways similar to Strobridge's best efforts.

James' eclectic bibliography, which spanned over thirty years, presents a dizzying assortment of descriptive travel guides, commissioned promotional pieces, inspirational literature laced with personal philosophy, and serious studies of Native American ethnography. Drawing from his ample reference library, field notes, photographs, significant study collections, and copious imagination, James quickly became a voice of authority on Native American basketry and southwestern exploration. Between 1914 and 1922, the Page Company of Boston published his books on the scenic wonders of Arizona, California, New Mexico, and Utah as part of the "See America First" series. These were geared towards a national audience, but James would also self-publish locally, starting The Radiant Life Press imprint in 1916 for his unabashedly spiritual, self-help-tinged writings like *Quit Your Worrying!; Living the Radiant Life*, and *Your Memory! A Delightful and Profitable Servant*.

Books and articles on "modern mission" architecture tied James to the Arts and Crafts ethos. Partnering with his artist friend and temperance sympathizer, **William Lees Judson (1842-1928)**, they established a home for the Guild of Fellow Craftsmen at the Garvanza-based USC School of Fine Arts where Judson served as dean. The School, which continues today as the Judson Studios stained glass atelier, expanded in 1909 to include an adjacent Guild Hall for "an association of expert workers in the applied arts" (James 1909: cover). The purpose was to exhibit wares by Guild members, present public lectures, and house the Arroyo Guild Press, which would print the Guild's organ the *Arroyo Craftsman*.

James orchestrated a publishing-first campaign to build Guild membership. In the journal's one and only issue, he presented a tantalizing agenda: to channel the spirit of William Morris and Gustav Stickley, bringing together area architects, furniture builders, and others to elevate so-called humble materials like wood, leather, metal, glass, and paper. He articulated the Guild's aims of "simple living, high thinking, pure democracy, genuine art, honest craftsmanship, natural inspiration, and exalted aspiration" (James 1909: 1). Like other exponents of the Arts and Crafts Movement, James called for higher standards of beauty in design and fabrication, adopting the motto "We Can!"—a confident variation on the tentative mottos of William Morris and Gustav Stickley—"Si Je Puis" (If I Can) and "Als Ik Kan" (The Best of My Ability). Consistent with James' inflated tone, an advertisement in the journal for the Arroyo Guild Press promised "extra choice, or *de luxe*" printing in "one or ten colors" on "first class" equipment.

In 1910, the School was destroyed by fire, and although it was quickly rebuilt, James' ambitious program to promote local handcrafts and California literature came to an end. The Arroyo Guild Press did succeed in printing a handful of titles in 1909—a mix of tasteful pocket-size poetry books like Charles Warren Stoddard's *Apostrophe to the Skylark*, the first and only volume in the "California Classics Series devoted to the life and work of California authors." One example from a more utilitarian line of printing was his syllabus to lectures on California writers, a canon he endeavored to define and interpret—from nature writers to satirists. "For many years I have believed and taught that California is destined to become the radiating center of the artistic, literary, and inspirational powers of the world," he said in the introduction to *In Love's Garden, and Other Verses* (James 1909: 7). While he was given to overstatement, his passing attempt to nurture a center for print culture in the Arroyo Seco is in evidence.

Located nearby on a sloping lot in Garvanza was the home of **Clyde Browne (1872-1942)**, a career pressman who left the Los Angeles *Examiner* to start his own business. In 1910, he assumed the unofficial title of printer to Occidental College, a busy post he relished. With an "appreciation for monastic life as a model for working and living in a disciplined, productive, communal fashion" (Hurd 1999), he built the Abbey San Encino (1915-25), as a scaled adaptation of mission and medieval Scottish architecture, ingeniously constructed of Arroyo Seco stone, on-site eucalyptus timber, and reclaimed materials. Along with a pressroom for the "master printer and his smocked assistants" (Browne 1932: xvii), the compound included family living quarters, cloisters, a wedding chapel, artists' studios, and a basement "dungeon" that served all manner of festivities [Fig. 6]. Like El Alisal, the Abbey was an extension of Browne's personality and deepest fancies (the plan was laid out in printer's picas rather than inches), and may have overshadowed his significance as a printing educator and supporter of typesetters, designers, publishers, and printers who formed the next wave of fine press printing in the 1930s.

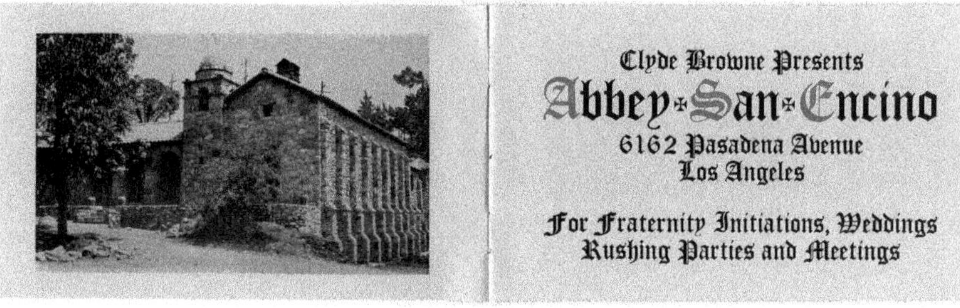

Fig. 6 "Clyde's Castle" was a social extension of the Occidental College campus. Occidental College Special Collections and College Archives

With commercial job printing in greater demand, fine-press books like *Cloisters of California* (1917), with poetry and illustrations by Browne, became a rarity in his limited bibliography. Between his regular work for Occidental College (the weekly newspaper; the humor, literary, and alumni magazines; issues of the yearbook; events ephemera), and mostly one-off journals like *The Anti: Being Peculiarly the Ideas and Observations of One Clyde Browne* (1910) and *Abbeygram: A Week-end Potpourri of Information, Approbation and Dissent* (1932), Browne produced several florid pamphlets on the Abbey's construction. Their design sensibilities seldom diverged from the Roycrofters formula he admired [Fig. 7], but it suited his "neo-Franciscan" (Starr 1985: 86) press identity and matched his amusingly effusive writing style. His last book, *Tiburcio Vásquez: The Life, Adventures, and Capture of the Great California Bandit and Murderer* (1941), was an anomaly of conventional fine printing in collaboration with his son Jack (father of singer-songwriter Jackson Browne).

Throughout the 1920s and into the depression years, the Abbey San Encino Press operated as a collective hub, creating a stimulating setting for many significant individuals. House Olson, Browne's chief assistant and designer from 1923 to 1931, co-founded The Castle Press with Roscoe Thomas. They printed the firm's first announcement, a play, and a catalogue for the Huntington Library at the Abbey before moving to Pasadena. Helen Sloan, Browne's long-time linotype operator, would also join The Castle Press (Davies 1982: 19).

CLYDE · BROWNE · BUILDER

THE ABBEY FANTASY

AN IDYL OF SAN ENCINO'S MAKING ❋ *By* THE BUILDER

DONE IN THE ESCRITORIUM OF THE HOSPICE AT THE TIME OF HALLOWMAS UNDER THE BENIGN SWAY OF ALL SAINTS AND IN THE YEAR OF THE CLOISTER THE TWENTY-FIRST

ABBEY HANDSET PRESS AND BINDERY
GARVANZA OLDTOWN • LOS ANGELES
ANNO DOMINI MCMXXIX

Fig. 7 *The Abbey Fantasy* is a "good example of Browne at his most lush" (Carpenter 1948: 59) with wide decorative borders reminiscent of William Morris. Occidental College Special Collections and College Archives

Once Browne built hillside studios to rent, some of his neighbors furthered their artistic and vocational aims with access to a press. Noted landscape designer Warner Lincoln Marsh, who created a far-fetched rendering of the Abbey as a pueblo with added side streets and a plaza (Hurd 1999), made woodcut illustrations for Abbey publications. Scott E. Haselton [Fig. 8] used the Abbey as headquarters for *The Journal of Cactus and Succulent Society of America*. The layout and typography were done there, as well as typesetting for several sumptuous color-plate books on cacti and succulents, before he started his own press. Ward Ritchie and Lawrence Clark Powell enjoyed the genial, boisterous atmosphere of the Abbey, with Ritchie putting his newly acquired typesetting skills to work on a handful of simple poetry pamphlets in 1930, like *Nut-Brown Beer: Being a Very Careful Analysis of Life's Major Joy*; *Stars* by fellow Occidental graduate Robinson Jeffers; and *The Booklover's Litany*—the first item Ritchie printed for the newly formed bibliophilic group the Zamorano Club. A prospectus for *Laughter in the Dark: A Symphonic Poem in Four Movements* by Dee Verlaine was printed at the Abbey, but this more elaborate publication went unrealized when Ritchie ventured to Paris to apprentice under François-Louis Schmied. Gregg Anderson, who would later join forces with Ritchie, printed *Body's Breviary* at the Abbey for the Zamorano Club, along with the elusive broadside *Two Whippersnappers*, printed with his former roommate, avant-garde composer John Cage (Browne collection: MS.2007.016).

Fig. 8 Scott E. Haselton (second from right) in the Abbey's "dungeon" with Society officers. Courtesy of the Cactus and Succulent Society of America

One indisputable contributor to the development of taste and refinement in the Arroyo Seco was **Alice Parsons Millard (1873-1938)**. In 1914, she and her bookseller husband George moved from Chicago to South Pasadena, bringing their shared love of the British Arts and Crafts, their knowledge of rare books, and their experience importing them from abroad. Samuel T. Clover adapted a popular Southern Pacific railroad slogan to describe their discriminating in-home shop, calling it "The Book Room of a Thousand Wonders" (Clover 1914: [2]). George, who was considerably older than Alice, died in 1918, but she seamlessly continued the business, aspiring to the highest end of the trade. She augmented sales with fine art and antiques, and with her competence and assertiveness, acquired manuscripts of real magnitude and superlative copies of books (Rosenthal 1985: 12). "Crowned with a glorious burst of white hair delicately tinted bluish" (Ritchie 1995: 654) to match her eyes, Millard left a memorable impression, which extended to the ambiance she created for her stock. Millard shrewdly commissioned Frank Lloyd Wright to build La Miniatura (1923), a modernist gem on the northeast bluff of the Arroyo Seco [Fig. 9]. Although she would leaden the design with heavy velvets and tapestries, the space matched her desire for a live-in showplace that elevated books and manuscripts so they were "seen as undeniable opportunities for those who wanted to possess fine things" (Powell 1954: 143). The house also served as an exotic backdrop for teaching "The Gospel of Beauty," the title of one of her instructive lectures on the book as an art form. A year after Henry E. Huntington opened his library gallery to the public, Millard began to assemble public exhibitions, adding a small wing to La Miniatura—"The Little Museum of the Book." Exhibits consisted mostly of books on loan from her affluent clients, including Estelle Doheny, whom Millard determinedly molded into a world-class collector (Cloonan 2006: 171). Even with finances constantly on edge, Millard was indulgent, sparing no expense on finely printed invitations and exhibit catalogues. *A Catalogue of an Exhibition of the 53 Books Printed by William Morris at His Kelmscott Press 1891-1898: A Loan Collection* (1929) was printed by Bruce McCallister for the Zamorano Club. *Order Touched With Delight* (1933) presented a nearly complete sequence of bindings by T. J. Cobden-Sanderson. For the catalogue, Ward Ritchie referred to the first page of Cobden-Sanderson's elegant five-volume Bible, featuring a purely modern adaptation of red initial capitals from the manuscript tradition.

Fig. 9 Alice Millard displaying an early Bible inside La Miniatura.
Papers and addenda of Alice Parsons Millard, Huntington Library, box 2 (6)

As the entries in her drolly-titled house book "The gueste bookes of Mistresse Olive Percival, Spinster" attest, Alice Millard frequented the home of **Olive May Percival (1869-1945)**, who was a friend and inveterate bibliophile. In 1899, Percival had a half-timber, English-style cottage built on an acre lot she called Down-hyl Claim. Perennially single, her scant free time was spent gardening, collecting, reading, writing, crafting, defending women's suffrage, and playing hostess. Through a combination of ingenuity and self-discipline she amassed 10,000 books on a meager insurance clerk's salary that never exceeded $150 per month. A portion of her collection now forms the core of the children's literature collection at UCLA. "It was the children's books she thought of when floodwaters threatened the Down-hyl Claim in 1914. Warned to evacuate, she filled two baskets to take with her if forced to leave. In one she packed her cherished Kate Greenaway books. In the other she placed a mother cat and five kittens" (Apostol 1992: 15). Her diaries spanning 54 years are an engaging mixture of self-concern and perceptive reportage. There are many entries about book finding and book buying, including this rousing account from 1896: "When I go into a bookstore these days, my heart beats wildly, my cheeks burn and I hardly breathe until I am outside again . . . How splendid a thing it would be to have one thousand dollars to buy books with! Ah! Me!" (Apostol 1992: 13).

Despite being an active contributor to leading magazines on a range of topics, such as Japanese decorative arts, Percival never achieved the financial success as a writer enjoyed by her friend and neighbor Idah Meacham Strobridge. She prospered, however figuratively, as a promoter of bookplate collecting and design [Fig. 10], organizing the first exhibition of bookplates in southern California at the Friday Morning Club in 1901 and writing pieces like "Some Los Angeles Bookplates" for *House Beautiful* in 1914.

She would only have two books published during her lifetime, the first being *Mexico City; an Idler's Note-Book* (1901). Charles Lummis, whom Percival considered a braggart and a tippler, dismissed her recollections on foreign travel in his review column, "That Which Is Written." Her second book, *Leaf-Shadows and Rose Drift: Being Little Songs from a Los Angeles Garden* (1911), was modeled after Haiku poems and intoned the sensory pleasures of her back yard. The binding with green cloth and decorative hearts could conceivably have been a tribute to the creator of one of her most cherished bindings—a copy of *Sentimental Journey* by T. J. Cobden-Sanderson, which she described as "full crushed levant, green, with all-over design of tiny gold hearts." Percival bought it from local bookman Irving May, and later loaned it to Alice Millard for her Doves Press exhibition.

Fig. 10 Although she was playful and possessed childlike enthusiasm, Olive Percival was a serious and discerning collector and critic (left). Her most ubiquitous bookplate depicts Down-hyl Claim (right). Olive Percival Collection, Ella Strong Denison Library, Scripps College

Abiding by the wishes laid out in her will, Ward Ritchie printed a collection of poems, *Yellowing Ivy* (1945), and her compilation of plant names, *Our Old-Fashioned Flowers* (1947). Entries for the pansy—Little-thoughts, Heart's Ease, Three-faces-under-a-hood, Cupid's Fancy, and None-so-pretty—underscore her whimsy, which is revealed in another posthumous book, *The Children's Garden Book: Instruction, Plans & Stories: a Voice from a Gentle Age* (2005). In it she advises the young gardener to have "patience, faith, and you ought to have a little make-believe (that is needed now, because everyone seems so practical, so calculating and so nervous, so self-centered!), and a great deal of stick-to-it-iveness" (Percival 2005: 17).

Conclusion

Legendary Los Angeles bookseller Jake Zeitlin dubbed the feisty achievements of Pasadena bookseller Alice Millard part of a remarkable little Renaissance (see Guerard, this volume, and Zeitlin 1982: 7), but it could easily extend to the whole Arroyo scene. Although the colony's brightest had an uneven relationship with fine printing and book production, their pluck, imagination, and drive carried print culture forward on a promising, if sometimes halting course, not unlike the Arroyo Seco itself. The bohemians of the Arroyo Seco, whose interior climate was no doubt influenced by the exterior one (Stern 1985: 151), demonstrated that place-making was central to fostering community. They linked themselves and others to life's simple splendors, which were often in the form of books. They also foregrounded the next generation of print bohemians, Ward Ritchie among them, who would emerge in the nearby Edendale neighborhood of Silver Lake.

Arroyoans thrived in this region, whose geography and beauty had attracted a significant population that insured most of the comforts and culture of western civilization, but had yet to threaten the natural features that stimulated the migration (Larson 1991: 71). Through their phenomenal individuality, they modeled courage and invited others to collect, to write, to publish, to print. Alice Millard brought "the world to Southern California, to seek out the symbols and artifacts of older civilizations so as to possess and re-express them locally" (Starr 1990: 334). Today as yesterday, this local impulse is a characteristic that defines southern Californians.

Charles Fletcher Lummis's Peculiar "Refuge for Love and Humanity" in the Arroyo Seco

Mark Thompson

Charles Fletcher Lummis, though just 33, was already a legend in Los Angeles when he moved back to town in December of 1892. Except for occasional return visits, he had been away for nearly five years. Seven years earlier, he'd been a star reporter for the *Los Angeles Times*, who had walked all the way from Cincinnati to Los Angeles to take the job, writing a widely reprinted, weekly newspaper column about his adventures along the way. After three years of, as he told it, relentless toil at the paper, he was felled by a stroke that left him partially paralyzed and retreated to New Mexico to recuperate, where he got back on his feet and resumed reporting for the *Times* and the leading eastern magazines of the day. His stories exposed a string of politically motivated murders, showcased the rich cultural traditions of the Hispanic and Native American inhabitants of the Southwest, and inveighed against government oppression of the Pueblo Indians, with whom he lived in the village of Isleta on the Rio Grande for three years. He survived an assassination attempt, which garnered national press coverage. Lummis also dumped his first wife, a doctor whom he had left behind in Los Angeles, and married the pretty school teacher who nursed him back to health after the shooting in New Mexico, the first of many sexual scandals that also assured he was talked about. Lummis spent the better part of 1892 accompanying the famous archaeologist Adolph Bandelier on a dig in Peru.

His return to Los Angeles at the end of that year should have been a personal triumph for Lummis. It was anything but. He had a few adventures, but for the most part, he had been miserable in Peru. Bandelier never got over his not-unfounded fear that Lummis would steal credit for any discoveries in the field by writing swashbuckling magazine stories exaggerating his role so he left Lummis, for most of his ten months in the country, cooped up in gloomy Lima, crating artifacts and pining for his wife. He spent most of his final paycheck from Bandelier on rare books, an heirloom flintlock rifle, and other artifacts. Now, he was back in Los Angeles, without a real job and practically penniless. While he was away, he had arranged for his wife, Eve, and an infant daughter to receive just enough money to scrape by in a two-bedroom house that he had purchased before departing on the trip. It was too small now that he was back, trying to work from home. Under the circumstances, the joy of his reunion with Eve—to whom he had written daily letters running over 50,000 words a month from Peru—was short-lived. A terse entry in his diary for the day after Christmas of 1892 summed up the state of his marital life. He and Eve had engaged in a "peleo tremendo." Lummis did not say what the big fight was about, but a good guess is that it was about money.

Figure 1: Charles Lummis in the early 1890s, around the time when he moved back to Los Angeles. Braun Research Library Collection, Autry National Center, Los Angeles; N.42477

Lummis was a driven man, with manic depressive tendencies. At that highly charged point in his life, with no need for help getting motivated, he commenced a frenetic scramble to make a living. Restarting one side venture that he had launched during his bivouac in Isleta, he cranked out hundreds of postcard-sized prints of his photographs of the Southwest and sold them to Wilbur Campbell, a prominent pioneer-curio dealer in town. He also sold Campbell some woven blankets and pottery from the Acoma and Zuni pueblos in New Mexico for five or ten times what he had paid. Meanwhile, he continued to land assignments from the leading magazines of the day, ranging, at various times, from *The Cosmopolitan, Scribner's Monthly,* and *Harpers Illustrated Weekly* to *The Atlantic Monthly, Drake's, Punch,* and *Puck*. He repackaged some of his magazine stories into books, nine of which he published in the 1890s. They generated a modest but steady stream of royalty income.

It would take more than a year for him to save up enough to make a purchase, but Lummis began scouting out possible home sites within weeks of his return from Peru. The search suddenly took on new urgency in April of 1894 when Eve announced that she was pregnant with the couple's second child. The next month, Lummis made a $100 down payment towards the $650 purchase price of a lot in the Arroyo Seco, six miles from downtown Los Angeles.

The lot was two and a half acres in size, large enough to absorb the torrent of ideas for a dream home that Lummis had been storing up in his head for years during his travels to pueblos, missions, forts, and homes throughout the Southwest. Over the next decade, with the assistance of helpers, some of whom came from Isleta to live with the Lummises for a while, he proceeded to build a castle out of stones collected in the nearby arroyo, framed with hand-hewn timber. While the main part of the house was finally ready for occupancy in January of 1899, he continued to build a place large enough for the sort of family and social life he wanted. It would ultimately have 13 rooms, with a courtyard and fountain and an encircling garden of native plants. He called it El Alisal, an old California-Spanish word for sycamore, after the grove of sycamores that shaded the property.

Fig. 2: El Alisal on May 21, 1900. The main part of the house was completed the year before, but Lummis continued to add rooms for years. His son, Amado, is standing in front of the house. Braun Research Library Collection, Autry National Center, Los Angeles; N.13690

The Arroyo Seco by the early 1890s was beginning to fill up with the homesteads of writers, artists, musicians, photographers, eccentric entrepreneurs, and other free-spirited bohemian types. There was an ostrich farm a couple of miles up the arroyo, a quirk Lummis liked. At the upper end, in South Pasadena, Horatio Nelson Rust, a legendary abolitionist and noted archeologist, was developing one of the region's first large-scale commercial citrus orchards. Rust was one of a number of like-minded neighbors who would become collaborators in Lummis's crusades and regular visitors to his home.

Indeed, El Alisal fit right in to the vibrant, offbeat intellectual and artistic community that was emerging in the arroyo. In the considerable wake that Lummis created, other artists and writers moved in. By the first decade of the twentieth century, El Alisal had become the cultural haven's epicenter. As Ward Ritchie, a book printer and publisher who set up his shop in the arroyo after Lummis's death in 1928, put it in a memoir he wrote about life in the bohemian enclave, "The dominant figure in the Arroyo Seco culture was undoubtedly Charles Fletcher Lummis" (Ritchie 1996: 21).

His penchant for flaunting societal conventions, and standing out in a crowd, was apparent throughout his life in the array of flamboyant and peculiar outfits that he trotted out for different occasions. He had first arrived in Los Angeles, at the end of his "tramp across the continent," with a red Pueblo sash around his waist, the skin of a rattlesnake for a hatband, and a coyote hide draped around his neck. The *Times*' publisher, Harrison Gray Otis, who met his new reporter at the San Gabriel mission, walked the last ten miles with him into town, could tell on sight that he had landed a showman who could help put his paper on the map. Lummis's outfit, Otis noted, clearly admiring his audacity, was "calculated to excite the curiosity of the police" (Otis 1885:1).

Lummis favored scantier attire while at work on El Alisal, as visitors couldn't help but note. Even when receiving friends on Sunday, he wore "a pair of white jean overalls, a jacket of the same, and only an undershirt half-concealing, half-revealing his muscular form," observed Henrietta Keith in an admiring article for *The Booklovers Magazine* about her visit to the construction site (Lummis Scrapbooks: undated clipping). Grant Wallace, a reporter for the *San Francisco Bulletin*, added that Lummis's gauze undershirt was "cut decollete to the point of immodesty, from which his sinewy neck rose like a bronze pillar, crowned with a leonine head, thatched with a tumble of gray hair." Wallace reported that some commentators had taken Lummis to task for his intentionally revealing garb. Reflecting a sharp split in opinion about the iconoclastic journalist that followed him throughout his life, Wallace declared, "I would walk a good ways any day to see a wholesome man who has shocked conventionality by 'committing the crime of being unusual'."

El Alisal was "the most remarkable house in California, if not the world," Wallace went on to assert. It is "so utterly out of the ordinary, particularly in its interior arrangement and decoration as to proclaim it the work of a genius—and a very sane and artistic one at that. Here is one of the few homes that I have seen that really means something. Every stone and timber and door in it spells comfort—permanence—rest—individuality" (Lummis Scrapbooks: undated clipping).

When Lummis purchased the lot in the arroyo, his newfound, and uncharacteristic, sense of financial security was undoubtedly bolstered by a job offer he was mulling at the time. The Los Angeles Chamber of Commerce wanted him to edit a promotional magazine it launched in July of 1894 called *Land of Sunshine*. It extolled the glories of life in southern California, the better to stoke the inflow of immigrants looking to buy a piece of the paradise for themselves, which the real-estate developers in the chamber were happy to offer.

Lummis had no reservations about that mission. Indeed, since his arrival, in much of his own writing, he had been effusive in his praise for southern California and its climate. But in negotiating for job of editor, Lummis insisted from the outset that he would not be "a hireling promoter" and demanded latitude to slip some challenging stories in with the syrupy pieces. He didn't take the job until November, when he got the assurance he needed from Charles Dwight Willard, secretary of the Los Angeles Chamber of Commerce. Willard had some qualms of his own about Lummis, but was delighted with his catch. As he put it in a letter to his father shortly after Lummis took the job, "He has certain oddities but you soon forget them." He is a "tireless worker and is throwing his whole soul into the undertaking" (Bingham 1955: 65).

Indeed, Lummis was indefatigable in the decade he spent editing the magazine, which was renamed *Out West* in 1902. By Edwin R. Bingham's count, he personally contributed more than 250 articles, not including a monthly column called "In the Lion's Den" that he wrote for more than a decade, and book review column, "That Which Is Written," which he cranked out for five years. Meanwhile, he shepherded a flock of more than 600 other writers, and dozens of photographers and artists who contributed to it in those years (Bingham 1955: 73).

The Chamber was delighted with Lummis, at first. His knack for drawing attention to himself rubbed off on the magazine, its contributors, and the causes it espoused. As the *Los Angeles Times* observed in a report on his appointment as editor, "Mr. Lummis belongs not to Los Angeles alone, for already his name has become a household word throughout the land" (attributed to Lummis 1895: Vol. II: 145). The *New York Daily Dispatch* also gushed about "the bright and famous young American author" who had taken charge of the *Land of Sunshine*. Success was the foregone conclusion of "every effort made by this indefatigable intellectual athlete," the New York paper said (quoted Lummis 1895: Vol. II: 146). Sure enough, the 5,000-copy press run for the January, 1895, issue, the first that Lummis edited, sold out in three days, according to Lummis, who boasted in his second issue that the two leading newsstands in the city had sold 527 copies, compared with 385 copies of *Harper's, Century, Scribner's, McClure's, Cosmopolitan,* and the *Overland Monthly* combined.

Over the years, Lummis published plenty of content of the sort that kept trainloads of Easterners heading towards Los Angeles. But early on, as promised, Lummis also offered his readers more provocative fare. "We believe it a magazine's duty to teach as well as to tickle," he wrote in a letter to one of his contributors (Bingham 1955: 54). It would show that "Southern California grows brains as well as oranges," he vowed in his third issue (attributed to Lummis 1895: Vol II: 71).

Indian rights was one cause that was especially dear to Lummis, and was doggedly covered in his magazine. His deep personal opposition to prevailing government policies dated back to his days in New Mexico, when he helped liberate 36 Pueblo children from Isleta from captivity in a government boarding school. During his time as editor, the magazine ran dozens of pieces extolling Native American culture and lambasting Bureau of Indian Affairs policies that were bent on forcibly assimilating the tribes and obliterating their traditions.

Lummis had an equally fervent interest in counteracting the anti-Spanish and anti-Catholic sentiment that was reaching a fever pitch in the run up to the Spanish American War. He sought to do so by highlighting in his magazine the cultural contributions left by Spain and Mexico in California and the Southwest.

In unflinching detail, Lummis also eloquently denounced grisly lynchings of blacks in the South, and in some of his most impassioned columns, he railed against the imperialistic foreign policies of President William McKinley and his successor, Theodore Roosevelt. That required considerable rhetorical dexterity on his part. Lummis had known Roosevelt since they had crossed paths at Harvard years earlier, and had occasionally corresponded with him since then. As president, Roosevelt invited Lummis to the White House on several occasions to offer advice on western affairs. Perhaps because Roosevelt, who had famously led the Rough Riders in Cuba in the Battle of San Juan Hill, admired his bravado, Lummis was somehow able to maintain a drumbeat of criticism of the president's foreign policy without losing his place among a group of informal advisers on policies affecting the west that came to be known as the Cowboy Cabinet.

Lummis's anti-imperialist rants did not sit as well with some of the businessmen who were bankrolling his magazine. W. C. Patterson, president of the Los Angeles National Bank and by then of the Land of Sunshine Company, had apparently become a lightning rod for criticism of Lummis. In a letter in the summer of 1900, he tried to get him to tone down his "rabid but conscientious notions" about U.S. foreign policy. Lummis would hear nothing of it (Patterson, W.C. Letter to Lummis, Aug. 2, 1900, Charles Fletcher Lummis Papers, Braun Research Library Collection, Autry National Center, Los Angeles). By 1902, the Chamber of Commerce had ended its sponsorship of the magazine. A year later, on the brink of insolvency, *Out West* was saved by a loan from Phoebe Hearst, the mother of newspaper publisher William Randolph Hearst, whose newspapers, ironically, had led the drumbeat the Spanish American War.

Lummis's magazine gained respect in the process. "Courage has a permanent berth in the office of the *Land of Sunshine*," the New York weekly *The Nation* editorialized (quoted in *Land of Sunshine*, Nov. ,1899, Vol. XI: 369). *The Dial*, published in Chicago, praised the "brave little magazine" and the "sober and fearless words" of the editor, who "keeps up a running fire of comment on the literary and political happenings of the day" (attributed to Lummis, 1899: 369). As a writer and editor, the University of Santa Clara awarded Lummis an honorary Doctor of Letters degree in 1903. Three years later Harvard, from which he had been suspended several time and where he fell two math tests short of graduating, used the occasion of the 25th reunion of his class of 1881 to awarded him the Bachelor of Arts degree.

At the magazine, he took pride in cultivating local writers and in giving a break to those who had never been published before. He found some of his most feted contributors that way. But from the outset, he also began seeking and getting contributions from the most famous writers in the West, including veterans of California's pioneer literary era, such as Joaquin Miller and Ina Coolbrith.

John Muir responded to a solicitation from Lummis with an encouraging note about the magazine six months into Lummis's tenure. "I have read your little plucky magazine and I like it," Muir wrote. "It has the ring and look of true literary metal . . . I doubt not you will be successful" (Muir, John. Letter to Lummis, June 11, 1895, Charles Fletcher Lummis Papers, Braun Research Library Collection, Autry National Center, Los Angeles). Muir was already on his way to becoming famous, thanks to his well-received first book *The Mountains of California*, published the year before. But he wrote occasionally for Lummis's magazine, the two men corresponded for years on a range of personal and political topics, and Muir was an occasional visitor at El Alisal.

Jack London was unknown and barely scratching out a living when *Out West* accepted two short stories of his in 1902. In one letter to Lummis, London complained about an associate editor's delay in responding to a submission, while begging forgiveness "for bothering you in this, my everlasting chase of the glimmering dollar." In another letter, he wondered why he was paid $15 for his first story but only $10 for the second (London, Jack. Letters to *Land of Sunshine* associate editor Charles Moody, July 2, 1902, and Dec. 15, 1902, Charles Fletcher Lummis Papers, Braun Research Library Collection, Autry National Center, Los Angeles). The next year, London became a national sensation with the success of *Call of the Wild*. He never again wrote for Lummis, though the two men corresponded from time to time.

Mary Austin, who eventually made a name for herself as a novelist, playwright, and essayist on topics ranging from mysticism to Native American culture, was an aspiring writer trapped in a failing marriage in the town of Independence in the remote Owens Valley when she first started corresponding with Lummis. They each immediately recognized in the other a kindred spirit, and commenced a prickly friendship that would play out over 30 years. She, too, raised eyebrows with her unconventional views and lifestyle, which was all the more scandalous because she was a woman. When her daughter was an infant, she was expelled from her church in Independence and charged with child desertion for taking part in Indian dances and starting a community theater.

One of her first pieces to make it into print was a poem called "Little Light Moccasin" in the April, 1899, issue of *Land of Sunshine*. Encouraged by that breakthrough, and Lummis's praise, she moved to the Arroyo Seco that summer, frequently visited El Alisal, and borrowed furniture from Lummis to use in rented quarters two blocks away. Over the next five years, Lummis published more than a dozen of Austin's stories, poems, and essays, and touted her as one of his magazine's best finds. As he put it in May, 1901, issue, she was "another voice crying out in the wilderness, and not in vain. With her close touch of nature, her refinement, and an often surprising strength, she has much promise of growth and a more tolerable success (attributed to Lummis, 1901: Vol. XIV: 392). Her best-known work, *The Land of Little Rain*, a collection of short stories and essays about the Southwest, was first published in 1903 and has been reissued a number of times since then, most recently in 2014.

Austin, at various times, expressed gratitude and some affection for Lummis. In a letter seeking to curry favor with a publisher, she described him as her "first and warmest friend in the West" (Overton, 1918: 164). But her conflicted feelings about the man were reflected in the fact that she dedicated the book not to him but to his beleaguered wife, "Eve, comfortess of our unsuccess." Austin offered a caustic assessment of him in her autobiography, *Earth Horizon*, published in 1932 four years after his death. He drank too much, slept too little, and leaned on his wife's translation of Spanish historical documents, she said. She also mentioned in passing that Lummis had attempted to add her to his long list of sexual conquests.

The thrice-divorced Lummis had a long history of troubled personal relationships with women. In his personal correspondence, he occasionally lashed out at "sufferjets," or as he once put it in the bitter aftermath of one of his divorces, in a note signed in the name of his ten-year-old son, "do-funnies that we ought to spank." At the same time, he clearly respected and liked tough, smart women. Indeed, all three of his wives were accomplished and strong-willed— qualities that perhaps both drew him into the marriages and doomed them from the start. He helped a number of talented women get a start in their careers.

Lummis's many admirers included Caroline Severance, one of the leading women's suffrage advocates in Los Angeles. In one letter that she sent to him when opposition to his diatribes about the Spanish-American and Philippine wars was building, Severance declared, "You are amazing! Pray God your courage never wavers and your strokes cut to the bone as they must in high places" (Severance, Caroline. Letters to Lummis, April 13, 1900, and July 26, 1900, Charles Fletcher Lummis Papers, Braun Research Library Collection, Autry National Center, Los Angeles). Charlotte Perkins Gilman, another prominent feminist, who had dumped her husband in Connecticut in 1888 and had decamped for Pasadena, was another of the numerous advocates for women's rights who contributed to Lummis's magazine.

Lummis was also an important mentor to a number of emerging painters, illustrators, photographers, and other artists, a number of whom lived in the arroyo or nearby. John Gutzon Borglum, who lived in Sierra Madre above Pasadena, designed the cover logo for *Land of Sunshine* in 1895, depicting a mountain lion sprawled on a ledge. A couple of decades later, he would begin work on his most famous work: the monumental sculpture of U.S. presidents carved on the side of Mt. Rushmore.

Maynard Dixon, who lived in Garvanza, a neighborhood overlooking the arroyo, also produced illustrations for Lummis's magazine at the start of what would become an illustrious career as a Southwestern artist. Dixon, then just 22, is "earnest, sympathetic, with a vein of genuine poetry in his nature," Lummis proclaimed in the April, 1898, issue. He has "an intimate touch for Western subjects; and the rapidity with which his technique improves augers very handsomely for his future as an illustrator (Lummnis, 1898: Vol. xiii: 214). Lummis and Dixon remained close personal friends for 35 years, and Lummis presided at Dixon's marriage to the photographer Dorothea Lange in a ceremony at El Alisal in 1920. "Lummis was the first man to give me counsel, advice and encouragement. He was completely honest and of impeccable integrity," Dixon said of Lummis after his death (Gordon, 1972: 258).

His hyper-enthusiasm was off-putting to some, but he could be an inspiring leader and savvy organizer. He managed to put his magazine, his home, and his large circle of friends and associates in the arroyo and beyond to good use in the service of a succession of advocacy groups that he launched and promoted. Early on in his tenure at the magazine, he took over and revitalized a moribund organization called the Landmarks Club, which sought to raise funds to restore crumbling Spanish missions. The group was instrumental in restoring the famous Mission at San Juan Capistrano and other vestiges of California's Spanish and Mexican past, as numerous articles in *Land of Sunshine* and *Out West* noted.

Another organization that he ran from El Alisal, the Sequoya League, was an advocate for Indian policies that respected native traditions. He hastily launched it when he was suddenly summoned to White House, just a month after the assassination of President McKinley, to offer the newly sworn President Roosevelt advice about western affairs. The magazine proved to be a propitious platform for the League and its crusades. Of the many articles and columns on Indian rights in the magazine over the years, one of the most sensational, which got the president's attention and got a Bureau of Indian Affairs edict reversed, was a multi-part series titled "Bullying the 'Quaker Indians'," about a ruthless Indian agent's abuse of the Hopi and Moqui tribes of Arizona. The writer of the articles was a Pasadena resident, Gertrude Lewis Gates, who was discovered by Lummis. The wife of a lumber baron and a would-be anthropologist who had befriended the Hopis when she spent two summers treating a respiratory ailment by camping in the high desert near their pueblo, she agreed to go undercover for *Out West*. Her articles about the cruel agent and his victims were illustrated with stark photographs taken by Adam Clark Vroman, whose studio was a few miles away in Pasadena. In yet another of his personal crusades, Lummis and his magazine were instrumental in launching a Los Angeles chapter of the Boston-based Archaeological Institute of America, called the Southwest Society, and setting a goal of raising funds to build a world-class museum in Los Angeles for Southwestern artifacts. Lummis persuaded many of the most prominent business leaders in southern California to contribute to that cause. Launched with twelve members in the fall of 1903, it had grown, according to Lummis, more than ten-fold by the time of the first annual meeting, a gala Spanish dinner at El Alisal a year later. The society's efforts culminated in the construction of the Southwest Museum, on a hillside in the arroyo near El Alisal, which opened its doors in 1914.

In the first decade of the twentieth century, dinners and parties were a regular occurrence at El Alisal, featuring a shifting array of fascinating characters from Lummis' vast circle of friends, colleagues, and pen pals. He had a March Hares party each March, featuring rabbit stew and a singing of the March Hares Hymn, in honor of those, like him, who were born in March. He had another set of amusing rituals for a party he hosted on Christmas day. For visiting dignitaries, Lummis would hold what he called a Court of El Alcalde Mayor, an elaborately staged event at which the guest of honor would be put on trial for the crime of "Not Knowing an Old California Good Time When You See It." The notables who were thus feted at El Alisal included John Muir, Joaquin Miller, John Burroughs, Ernest Thompson-Seton, John Philip Sousa, and Frederic Remington.

When there was no special occasion for a party, Lummis would convene one for no particular purpose and call it a "noise," featuring music by a performer who was visiting town or by one of El Alisal's house musicians, such as Rosendo, a blind Mexican virtuoso of a one-stringed harp, and Francisco "Pancho" Amate, a guitar player from Andalusia who lived at El Alisal for six years. The parties at El Alisal in its heyday were one of the hottest tickets in town. "No one invited ever failed to come," the singer Edith Pla reminisced years later, "and there were people who wanted to come for years but were never invited" (Fiske 1975: 164).

Figure 3: Charles Lummis on Oct. 30, 1904, dressed for work on the grounds of El Alisal. Braun Research Library Collection, Autry National Center, Los Angeles; N.13716

Guests were asked to sign a giant ledger, called the House Book, which was on display in the entry hall. According to Dennis Harbach, who has deciphered many of them, it contains more than 7,000 signatures. The names and clever inscriptions bear testimony to the diverse range of guests. Prominent artists, including Dixon, Remington, Borglum, and Ed Borein, drew sketches next to their names. The composer, Sousa, who first came to El Alisal on the recommendation of friends to listen to Lummis's recordings of Spanish songs, signed his name beneath a few measures of music. Marguerite Zitkala Noni, one of the few Sioux survivors of the 1890 massacre at Wounded Knee, was an honored guest at one event. Actors Douglas Fairbanks, Mary Pickford, and Harold Lloyd turned heads at other parties at El

Alisal. Leaders of the Los Angeles establishment, including the prominent lawyers Henry O'Melveny and Isidore Dockweiler, were also there on a regular basis, mingling with the avant-garde artists and bohemian intellectuals, who could, in turn, hobnob with the likes of humorist Will Rogers and attorney Clarence Darrow.

Lummis ran El Alisal in what he proclaimed to be the spirit of old Spanish hospitality that he fondly remembered from his earliest days in the Southwest when he began a lifelong friendship with families in New Mexico and California whose roots in those places ran well back into Spanish colonial times, and who had welcomed him into homes filled with food, song, and dance. There weren't many such homes left, he lamented, and offered El Alisal to help fill the void. As he put it in his last book, *The Flowers of Our Last Romance*, his home was "hog proof (if barbed wire, a bull-dog and certain 'company manners' of my own could make it so), but with its latch-string out for Love and Humanity." It was "the last ditch of the old California patriarchal days" (Lummis 1929: 274).

His high-minded defense of his frenetic socializing notwithstanding, life at El Alisal was not optimal for his wife or his children, four of whom were born and one of whom died at the age of 6 of pneumonia at El Alisal. Amidst the constant bustle and revelry, they sometimes were an afterthought. Eve, in particular, came to resent the endless succession of parties, visitors, temporary and long-term house guests. The brunt of the work of running the household and staging the parties fell on her, as did the responsibility of buying all of the provisions on a very limited budget. Some of the wealthy regulars would sometimes quietly pass a hat among themselves to help cover the costs. But there was never enough money to pay the bills. The children recalled that their father would often reduce Eve to tears with his sharp questioning about the grocery budget at the end of every month. But she had to put on a happy face as the crowds arrived. It was Eve's job to welcome the guests— who invariably included fawning young women— and make sure their needs were met.

None of the throng at El Alisal gave Eve more grief than the endless procession of secretaries and stenographers. The more assertive among them sized up the pecking order at El Alisal, realized the wife was well down in the pack, and let her know it. As Turbese, Charles and Eve's eldest daughter, observed of her mother, "As her husband gained importance, he relegated her to an inferior position in the household. Always there were at least two secretaries inclined to treat her as a prudish and backward country girl" (Fiske 1975: 168).

Many of these assistants happened to be pretty young women who doted on her husband and were willing to stay up late at night with him up in his Den on the second floor of El Alisal to take dictation or help him with all his paperwork. She had reason to be suspicious that some of the secretarial relationships went beyond paperwork. Some of the young female artists, poets, and writers who were given shelter at El Alisal over the years were also suspiciously cozy with Lummis.

As early as 1902, Eve's patience with her husband of eleven years had worn thin. She spent Christmas that year with Phoebe Hearst in Berkeley, explaining in a letter to him in early December why she had no intention of being anywhere near the festivities at El Alisal on the day, which happened to be the second anniversary of the tragic death of the couple's six-year-old son Amado. "I do not grudge you your relaxation," she wrote. "But I do not like to celebrate that terrible anniversary with a noisy crowd." She added, "I do not know of any other woman who would so continuously surround you with women you care for, working hard herself to do it, and getting for herself very little courteous attention," she wrote. "I have not the strength to cook for the crowd" (Lummis, Eve Douglas. Letter to Lummis, Dec. 7, 1902. Charles Fletcher Lummis Papers, Braun Research Library Collection, Autry National Center, Los Angeles).

The marriage would last for the rest of that decade. The final straw was Eve's discovery in 1909 of a ledger in which Charles had recorded, in Spanish code words rendered in the Greek alphabet, a record of his extramarital sexual conquests. She could not determine exactly how many other women there had been, but in the divorce proceedings that soon followed, her lawyers suggested that the indefatigable Charles Lummis had engaged in extramarital sexual relations with somewhere between twenty and fifty other women. Taking two of the three children with her, she retreated to the San Francisco Bay area and moved back in with Phoebe Hearst. Lummis responded with a bitter fusillade of accusations against Eve, and he threatened to file a suit against Phoebe Hearst, his erstwhile benefactor, seeking $100,000 in damages for the "millionaire kidnapping of my children."

The ensuing divorce cost Lummis many of his friends and supporters, and was the beginning of the end of the prime years of his life in the arroyo. Many of the artists and writers in

Lummis's circle adored Eve, who became a well respected English translator of Spanish language novels. Some never forgave him for his treatment of her in the divorce proceedings. He slipped into periods of depression and alcoholism after the divorce, though he rallied from time to time, and was married for a third time for a few years. But Lummis never again had any semblance of financial security. The divorce had cost him one of the unlikeliest, but steadiest jobs, he ever held, as Los Angeles city librarian for a tumultuous but intermittently inspired stretch of five years.

Charles Lummis had plenty of critics in his own time. He was eccentric to a fault, and the taint of personal scandal always hovered over him. But there were plenty of others who were not put off by his peculiarities and who could see that there was method in his oddness. As David G. Hogarth, a distinguished British archaeologist and Fellow of the Royal Geographic Society, put it, "I was prepared for a poseur but found too much reality behind the pose to care whether it were there or not. I found a man of real taste and power." Lummis had "the real temperament of the artist and superabundant energy and natural ability, expressing itself in all sorts of strange ways."

He was a showman, as he had to be to sell books and freelance magazine articles to make ends meet. His highly unconventional dress and behavior were also a form of personal protest against silly prejudices towards people who are different, which was at the root of the racism and xenophobia that Lummis spent his career very effectively fighting. His iconoclastic lifestyle undoubtedly was also an inspiration to other bohemians in the Arroyo Seco, who were marching to their own drummers and promoting their own artistic, literary, and intellectual endeavors.

EDENDALE

Bohemian Politics and the Edendale Origins of Coming Out

Daniel Hurewitz

A Genealogy of Coming Out [1]

Twenty years before gay liberation, at the end of 1950, the Mattachine Society, the first long-lasting gay rights organization in the country, began to form in a corner of Los Angeles known earlier as Edendale, now called Echo Park and Silver Lake. This was at a time when homosexual characters had been driven from the stage and screen, when homosexual socialization in a bar would cause its owner to lose the license, and when same-sex sexual activity could lead to arrest and multi-year prison terms. Even as it entered such treacherous waters, Mattachine nonetheless deliberately followed a strategy of what Milk would call "coming out," even if they did not use that language for it. Indeed, this belief that a politics of self-revelation could be transformative was part of what marked Mattachine as thrilling and revolutionary.

Two of the earliest Mattachine actions made clear the centrality of that ethic for them. The first of these was the acquittal of Mattachine founder Dale Jennings on an indecency charge in 1952. Jennings was one of the earliest members of Mattachine, and he was arrested by a police officer he had met in a park and who had followed him home. Jennings was convinced by Harry Hay, perhaps the central founder of Mattachine, to fight the charges. As part of his defense, Jennings not only claimed that he had been entrapped by the officer, but perhaps most importantly, he told the jury that he was homosexual. He "came out" in the hope that attention would focus less on him as a potential "deviant," and more on the officer's behavior. Coming out was at the center of his defense, and when he was acquitted that was what was celebrated and inspired a steep spike in new memberships.

This work was carried further later that year when the organization began to solicit local political candidates for their positions on laws criminalizing homosexual behavior. They mailed questionnaires that were nothing if not "out" in terms of their public expression of homosexuality, and of course they were political in exactly the way that Harvey Milk later argued that being out could be. That is, by standing up and saying, "*We* are your homosexual neighbors and constituents," they humanized a question that seemed only theoretical or abstract and legal. As Los Angeles *Daily Mirror* columnist Paul Coates rightly noted in 1953, their determination to ask such questions and reveal themselves in this way marked them as a "new pressure group" that appeared "to represent the homosexual voters of Los Angeles" and that was "vigorously shopping for campaign promises" (Coates 1953). In other words, Mattachine not only represented humanized homosexuals, but demonstrated them to be a viable and potentially politically significant voting bloc and public constituency.

Historians have bemoaned how the sudden and dramatic visibility initiated by the questionnaires and Coates' columns triggered an anxious response by some Mattachine members, who took over the group's leadership in the spring of 1953. While they certainly diminished the level of "out" activity Mattachine pursued for the next dozen years, they hardly diminished the organization's real achievements in these early actions: it launched the simultaneously cultural *and* political work of shifting sexuality and homosexual desire directly into the public sphere in order to make claims for legal protections and civil rights. Coates very astutely saw Mattachine as the leading edge of the "new pressure group" that would ultimately come to be called the "LGBT rights movement." A decade before SDS began, and nearly two decades prior to any meeting of the Gay Liberation Front, Mattachine began the cultural-politics of self-revelation, following an ethic of exposing the authentic emotional and desiring self, and framing that self as a political subject.

The Bohemian Roots of Coming Out

Significantly, Mattachine did not invent the idea that there was an authentic self that should be revealed. Even as there lay a fairly clear line from Mattachine to Gay Liberation, the idea of self-revelation grew directly from Mattachine's deep ties to Los Angeles' bohemian center in Edendale, where local artists and leftists dramatically explored the public meaning that should be given to the inner life and identity. The history of how those explorations yielded a Mattachine ethic of coming out unfolded in three significant stages in a process that began with artists.

Edendale was a quiet corner of Los Angeles that remained underdeveloped during the early twentieth century while much of the city was being transformed into housing and business. Particularly because of its hilly geography, Edendale literally sat off the rest of the city's omnipresent grid, with streets winding up and over hillsides, some of them simply coming to a dead end and then turning into a staircase to give access to the homes above, and while the streetcar lines did find their way to Edendale, it remained for many decades a rural outpost with panoramic views of downtown Los Angeles. The neighborhood possessed simple homes surrounded by trees, bushes, wildflowers, and even occasionally unpaved streets. Indeed, early in the twentieth century, when William Selig sought a home for what would be his burgeoning movie business, he placed it in the heart of Edendale. One of the key reasons for this decision in 1908 was that it gave him easy access to the hilly topography that his Westerns would require, and there were enough yards with chickens and goats to make that corner of Los Angeles feel like small-town America. Indeed, within a few years, Mack Sennett, Tom Mix, Pathé, and Vitagraph were all shooting movies in the area, making Edendale, as one contemporary wrote, "one of the most unique villages in America" (Bartlett 1938).

While the movie studios eventually moved on, finding large, flat, open lots in places like Burbank and Culver City, the appeal that Edendale had as a residential neighborhood for creative folks did not diminish. Across the 1920s, 30s, and 40s, the hilly streets of Edendale remained homes to cinematographers and set decorators, along with painters, photographers, sculptors, writers, and the aficionados who adored what they did. The fine arts and film arts were hardly deeply segregated then, and so with the Disney Studios at one edge of the neighborhood, the city's major art school at another, and a host of private studios sprinkled across it, the creative life was a widely shared endeavor across Edendale.

Much can be said about the vibrant, self-sustaining communal life that these folks developed: the shared life-drawing classes and Shakespeare readings; the avant-garde concerts and subscription art clubs; the regular gallery openings and collaborative art projects. Historian Kevin Starr (1990:329) deemed Edendale, Los Angeles' "bohemian quarter of the 1920's and 1930's," and described it as "the closest thing Los Angeles had at the time to an artists' quarter."

In the first phase of developing what became the "coming out" ethic, a host of Edendale artists set out to develop a Californian art that offered something new and novel: many focused their efforts on depicting what might be called "the inner life." Their central aspiration was to convey to their viewers and readers their internal dreamscape, the vistas of their thoughts, fantasies, and fears; they sought to unlock their own internal lives and put them on display. One local artist, painter, and sculptor, Lorser Feitelson, described the significance of these goals in a letter to an art critic.

> Unlike the almost anonymous artists of the past, who gave form to the thought-world of the group, the contemporary creative artist is often concerned uncompromisingly with externalizing a completely personal world, which he expects the group to make the effort to enter. Since his work is untraditional in its methods and imagery, his comprehending audience is often limited to a few friends and "initiates" (Feitelson 1950).

Feitelson helped drive this shift into expressing the inner life of the "personal world."

He was joined in that project by painter Grace Clements. Clements, who arrived in Los Angeles in 1931 and settled in Edendale not long after, gained national attention a few years later when she, Feitelson, Helen Lundeberg, and Knud Merrild began exhibiting as the "Post-Surrealist" group. For many years, Clements later wrote, she embraced Feitleson's position and insisted that good artwork was a statement of self, an unrepentant ego-document. Even as a twenty-year-old art student, she wondered about choosing between the traditional codes of communication that spoke to the group, and the particular and idiosyncratic ones that she alone could create. She recorded the question as:

> Was art a matter of *feeling*—of what the artist could "say" about his response to things outside himself? Was art *interpretation* rather than *imitation*? The affirmative to these questions provided my first conviction that I had the answer to the puzzle. I defended the distortions that began to appear in my work on the ground that this was the way I *felt* about it (Clements 1968: 15-16).

Quite self-consciously, Clements proposed that her paintings were canvases on which to inscribe *her* feeling, her inner life, her ego. Reading Freud in the 1930s convinced her that "man" was "a psychological being, subject to all manner of hidden forces which impelled him in contradictory directions" (Clements 1968?: 19), and Clements pushed steadily for art that examined and articulated that individual psychology.

This insistence on individual expression circulated widely among Edendale artists in the years between the two world wars. In 1917, painter Mabel Alvarez's notes from a lecture at the Los Angeles Academy of Modern Art contained several aphorisms on expressing the "inner life" that she rewrote for herself: "Create everything from the inside out"; "Listen to the *inner* self all the time"; and "Listen to the Master within" (Smith 1995:6-7). Even master printmaker Paul Landacre, whose artwork today seems fairly representational, told a journalist in 1936 that individual expression remained for him the ultimate goal. Art, he said,

> finds its real value in self-expression for the person doing it, and for the person re-experiencing it . . . We can examine it closely, line by line, concept by concept; but the real essence eludes our critical faculties. It escapes analysis because it has an emotional basis. Real art is the simple expression of the self, and the self is expressed by feeling (Wilkins 1936:38-9).

Ego-documentation was the shared Edendale project.

By 1934, when Clements joined Lorser Feitelson and Helen Lundeberg as Post-Surrealists, they framed their goal as giving artistic expression to the emotional challenges brought on by central life dilemmas. Unlike Surrealists, they decided that they did not want to focus on dreams or the unconscious; instead, their interest lay with how the conscious mind sorted through various experiences, making connections and building analogies, and, importantly, they also wanted their art to be fundamentally legible.

The technique they developed was to offer viewers a sequence of images that would guide them along an emotional path. For instance, one representative painting moved from large hands interlocked, to a smaller couple, a man adrift, and an iceberg. They were trying, according to Feitelson (1941), "to direct an ordered movement of flow of the observer's attention through a planned series of objects, or configurations of objects, which unfold and develop a universal idea." By guiding the viewer through these "series of objects," the Post-Surrealists hoped to convey their own emotional journeys, and for some viewers they succeeded. "Post-surrealistic beauty," reviewer Harry Kurtzworth (1937) wrote, "deals with the splendors of the inner world of thought and feeling . . . explaining the classics, those vast queries, hopes and fears which constitute life." Even critics of the Post-Surrealists and others who suggested they were "expressing nothing but the frayed tassels of near-neurosis" nonetheless understood that the psychological self was now the focus of their art (Macdonald-Wright 1944). The inner life was being fashioned for public display.

Bridging the Emotional and Political

Even as Edendale artists came to believe that their task was to plumb the depths of their conscious or unconscious lives, many simultaneously believed that artists also had to speak to a wider public; that is, they had to look *outward* as well as inward. Indeed, Edendale artists launched a second phase in the development of the "coming out" ethic by starting to emphasize the goal of political engagement. They rejected, as it were, Feitelson's idea of the artist awaiting a small audience. Instead, especially while living through the depths of the Depression, many of these artists clamored for art that demonstrated public and political engagement.

Clements argued in those years that, "the artist's lot was inevitably bound up with the lot of his fellow man; that all together they were affected by the health or disease of the social structure of which they were a part." Thus, although she did not reject the subjective and psychological challenges that the Post-Surrealists had addressed, she felt that the additional task of the artist was "to find his place in the present social upheaval and to become the revolutionary instrument to carry on the tradition of great creative art." Clements felt called to abandon what she called art's "Ivory Tower" and instead enter the "Class Struggle," in the social and political world. Art must, she announced repeatedly, be socially relevant and politically engaged (Clements 1968?: 30-1, 55-7).

That need and desire to engage with the public showed up in various Edendale artists' work of the 1930s. In fact, as many Edendale artists found jobs in the collaborative undertakings of the Public Works of Art Project and the Federal Art Project, they, like many American artists of the 1930s, began to make "message" art. This was art that tried to be as explicit and transparent as possible in delivering a socially or politically meaningful idea. For many of the artists in Los Angeles, Mexican muralist David Siqueiros was an important inspiration in this regard. Siqueiros worked in the city during 1932, and several Edendale artists joined forces with him to help complete multiple murals, such as *Workers' Meeting* and *Street Meeting*, that offered radical messages denouncing American imperialism or framing racial conflict.

One local artist who shared his goals was dancer and choreographer Lester Horton, who ran a studio on the edge of Edendale. His dance style seemed designed to deliver political messages, often described as severe and without flourishes: hands were kept flat or balled into fists. "To be decorative was to be corrupt," recalled Bella Lewitzky, one of Horton's principal dancers and co-creators. Horton developed dances on topics ranging from the Warsaw ghetto to the Ku Klux Klan, and, in the midst of the Depression, he even choreographed a piece on the plight of Dust Bowl families. As Lewitzky (1985) said, "Lester made dances about the things we were very concerned with, that dealt with our lives."

While Siqueiros and Horton set a high bar for how political art could be, for many local artists, the art that they created for the PWAP or FAP rarely had such radical messages. What is more, determining a way to create artistic "ego-documents" that were *also* politically meaningful was a difficult goal to achieve. For many area artists, while they could articulate their aspirations, forging connections between the psychological self and political life proved elusive for them. That task was reframed, however, by a new group of Edendale residents who much more successfully forged connections between the internal and political worlds.

Starting at least as early as 1931, a cohort of Communist Party activists and their families began to move into Edendale and build a community there, and a wide swath of area residents began to follow and support their efforts. Indeed, just as the artistic communities of Edendale can be described by the life-drawing groups, gallery openings, and publication parties they enjoyed, in a very similar way Edendale began humming with a rich variety of Party activities that constituted new yet vital threads in the communal fabric of the neighborhood.

Party activities drove two dramatic shifts in reframing what counted as political and public. Firstly, the Party, in surprising ways, succeeded at the artists' second goal of constructing a bridge between the inner life and the political arena. Although the Communist Party tends to be remembered for its political and ideological positions, the Party made politics a full life experience. Being a Party member in Edendale was closer to living and working in a particular ethnic or religious community: communal ties were constantly being reinforced and elaborated through a host of seemingly non-ideological activities. Parties and sing-alongs were as meaningful in this regard as planning meetings and rallies, and the communal connections that they developed infused Party activities with deeply emotional meanings, so much so that membership in the Communist Party became an entire way of life, shaping families, marriages, and love affairs even as it called people into engagement with wider public issues. Politics for them became a zone where ideology was reinforced by feelings of friendship, empathy, identification, love, and lust.

This mixture of emotion and politics was evident in multiple ways. On the one hand, Communist activists have consistently spoken of the deep love that developed between fellow members. Dick Nikowsski, for instance, a "lifelong" Party member, explained that when he discovered Marxism and was thrilled with its political insights, he also found that through the shared work he was doing, he "loved everybody! . . . When we were in the middle of some intense analysis of the Russian Revolution at three in the morning and we all had to be up on our feet and at work at seven, I'd look around the room at these guys, and they were my comrades, and I loved them so hard I thought I'd burst with it" (Gornick 1977:65). The political work was infused with emotional value and feeling.

Additionally, this emotional politics was also evident in the centrality of marriages inside of the Party. Miriam Sherman, one of Edendale's leading organizers, pointed out how frequently local Party members fell into affairs and marriages with one another. Perhaps that was to be expected with so much passion circulating in Party activities. What is surprising, however, is that the Party itself took those marriages seriously and treated them as a vital part of Party life. When someone's marriage became strained—as often occurred because of the demands of Party work—the local leadership took it upon themselves to work as marriage counselors and try to facilitate reconciliations.

According to Sherman, it was not "unusual at all for the Party to intervene and [say] . . . 'Let's have a discussion and see what's happening'." Party leaders got involved in just such a way when her own marriage was deteriorating. "Sometimes that went over, and sometimes it didn't go over." But, she pointed out, the Party believed that resolving marital disputes "made it possible for people to function better, both within the Party and outside as individuals" (Sherman 2000). Thus, the Party not only engaged people's hearts, and their desires for love, affection, and connection; it took seriously that that was an important part of their political project that had to be tended.

Thus, if Edendale artists were working hard to make their emotional lives public yet struggling to show how doing so contributed to the political issues of the day, Edendale Communist activists had a much easier time of fusing their emotional and political worlds. Love, lust, and affection were rolled right into the political work that Party members did, and they created a political culture that celebrated that fusion.

Forging a Politics of Racial Identities

Importantly, in the third piece of constructing the "coming out" ethic, Edendale Communists also focused enormous political attention on issues of race and racial identity. While the Party is typically portrayed as emphasizing class consciousness and economic inequality, in truth, in Los Angeles some of the Party's greatest impact came from their work on racial inequality and racial discrimination. For many Edendale and Los Angeles activists, this was what drew them to the Party initially. As Dorothy Healey, who became the organizational secretary of the L.A. Party said, "there was never anything in the Party that compared with the attention that was given to the question of African Americans" (Healey 2000). For her and other activists, fighting racism was the central task they took up. Importantly, this effort entailed not simply working to challenge discrimination against already clearly defined and recognized racial minorities, but also involved fundamentally developing a framework of understanding for what it meant to be a racial minority in the modern United States. Indeed, in a profound way, Communists and leftists in the early and middle decades of the twentieth century helped to forge and create the very notions of shared "minority rights" and analogous "minority identities" (Naison 1983, Kelley 1990, Solomon 1998, Sides 2006).

In multiracial Los Angeles, African American, Mexican American, and Japanese American activists had long tried to bring political attention to the discrimination they suffered. They did so, however, largely independent from one another and without a clear framework of their shared oppression. Across the 1930s and 40s, however, L.A. Party activists began to view African Americans as not occupying a unique and solitary position in the social and political landscape of the city. Rather, they argued, Mexican Americans, Japanese Americans, and Jews were experiencing the same things—housing discrimination, police harassment, employment exclusion, and more—and those seemingly different groups were actually radically similar.

Central to their thinking was that the Party viewed these racial groups as individual nations. Repeatedly, even into the 1950s, Party educational materials stressed treating African Americans as meeting "the Marxist definition of a nation." This meant that they were "a historically evolved stable community of language, territory, economic life, and psychological make-up manifested in a community of culture" (SEC 1946). Because of that status, they argued, they also possessed a "right to self-determination" (LAED 1950), and while at the national Party level, much of the racial thinking focused on African Americans, in Los Angeles, where African Americans were far less visible prior to World War Two than Japanese Americans and Mexican Americans, that framework was easily applied across racial categories. Leftists in Los Angeles began to portray the city as made up of a variety of similarly oppressed analogous "race nations."

Describing racial discrimination as attacks on analogous race-nations allowed L.A. leftists to treat seemingly disconnected events as evidence of a broad system of political and social oppression against a wide constituency. This approach was expressed vividly by the Civil Rights Congress (CRC), a Party offshoot that started nationally at the end of World War Two and quickly formed chapters inside of Edendale. The CRC rallied Angelenos to see local acts of racial hostility, even against different races, as part of a shared national phenomenon. For example, in 1952, when two African-American homes were bombed in the West Adams neighborhood of Los Angeles, the Edendale CRC argued that the attacks were directly connected both to the recent assassination of an NAACP secretary in Florida and to local police brutality against Mexican families: the oppression was the same. A leaflet announcing a meeting about the bombings demonstrated how the CRC saw these multiple groups as analogous: "Such attacks have a special meaning for the Jewish people in our community as well as the Mexican people and other minorities. To permit this example of growing Southern terrorism to go unchallenged and unpunished is to encourage its spread by Ku-Kluxers and white supremacists" (CRC 1952a). For them, these groups and their oppressions were alike. In fact, the CRC regularly used the relatively new word "genocide" to describe anti-black and anti-Mexican police violence: they were building a framework in which all minority oppressions were the same (CRC 1952b).

For many Angelenos, the experience of World War Two did much to push their thinking about racial groups in the direction that Communists had mapped out. In wartime Los Angeles, where Japanese residents were rounded up for evacuation and Mexicans were subject to widespread violence, it felt as though race-nations were battling in the city, and by war's end, many Angelenos began grudgingly to endorse some very watered down idea of racial co-existence. In 1944, the city established a first Human Rights Commission to address racial discriminations, and by summer 1945, Mayor Fletcher Bowron called on local residents to recognize that "our country is, in a sense, composed of minorities; it is the United Nations on a continent." Because of the war, he suggested, Angelenos had begun "to understand that our civilization can be saved only when groups, as well as nations, learn cooperation in inter-dependence." (Bowron 1945)

Here was the Communist and CRC framework at work, arguing that American society was constituted by multiple distinct nations and implying that political effort was necessary to keep those nations at peace. Of course, these ideals of racial similarity were not universally embraced. But for a cohort of Edendale locals, the leftist strategy of identifying multiple racial groups as analogous and suffering analogous oppressions provided an opening for them to make claims for their own minority status. Indeed, this was the strategy that Mattachine embraced.

From Race to Sexuality and Identity

This was the moment and context in which Mattachine was born. The first meetings occurred at the end of 1950 and start of 1951—at the same moment that the Civil Rights Congress was rallying Edendale residents to respond to the West Adams bombings across town, and to see them as connected to the genocide that had been waged against Jews in Europe and to the police brutality against Mexican Angelenos. Neighborhood homosexuals stepped forward to add themselves to the list of analogous groups. Their primary goal, they said, was to speak to the "thousands of homosexuals [who] live out their lives bewildered, unhappy, alone—isolated from their own kind," and offer to them "a consensus of principle around which all of our people can rally and from which they can drive a feeling of 'belonging'." It is no surprise, however, that in the Edendale context where the early Mattachine founders slowly drafted their mission statement, they identified the growth of a "homosexual culture" as "paralleling the emerging cultures of our fellow-minorities—the Negro, Mexican, and Jewish peoples" (Hay 1996: 131-2). This was the very thinking of the local CRC and Edendale leftists; Mattachine was embracing their idea of analogous oppressions and peoples, and placing homosexuals on the list of oppressed race-nations.

That Mattachine drew on this framework can be attributed to the fact that the group's leading founder, Harry Hay, was himself a Communist Party activist in the neighborhood, one of the key players on the Party's local education team. His deep immersion in Party thinking shaped Mattachine's early structure and framework. But in truth, *several* of the early founders came out of leftist and Communist activism, and so they readily adopted the analogous nations framework as well. As Konrad Stevens said about himself and his then-lover, Jim Gruber, both early members of Mattachine, "We had been very progressive in our thinking: the Negro question, discrimination—we had been in tune with that sort of thing. And this went right along our line of thinking. We thought, 'Well, it's the same thing, only we hadn't really thought of it before'." Indeed, when Stevens worked with later Mattachine members to explain the idea that homosexuals constituted a similarly oppressed minority, he regularly made analogies about African Americans and Irish Americans (Stevens 1977). Seeing men and women who organized their desires around same-sex activity as an oppressed social minority was an essential part of the legacy of Edendale leftists.

But for Mattachine, the Edendale lesson was not simply the leftist one that American society was carved up into similarly oppressed minorities. The lesson was also that emotions and desires—the psychological self—mattered in the political arena. This was a repeated teaching. The Communists relied on desire to fuel their political work, and indeed they cared who their members fell in love with and built their lives with: that carried political weight for them. That was true for Mattachine as well, only more so: for Mattachine, desires and relationships were central to their political agendas.

But in putting desire at the center of their politics, Mattachine members were also following the lead of the Edendale artists who said that their emotions and fantasies were the primary thing that needed to be expressed. The inner life, they insisted, was central to who they were and needed to be given a public airing. This was their essence, and importantly, Hay, the Communist, was also steeped in the local artistic culture, as were many of the other Mattachine founders. Hay was an actor, who had been introduced to the Party by fellow actor Will Geer, and later became a music and musicology instructor. He took his daughter to dance classes at Lester Horton's studio. There he met fashion designer Rudi Gernriech, who became another early key member of Mattachine. They developed Mattachine in conjunction with people like Dale Jennings, who was also a leftist and novelist; Chuck Rowland, a former Communist organizer and soon-to-be theater producer; and Bob Hull, a Party member whose passion was piano and who had taken a music history class with Hay (Timmons 1990). In other words, Mattachine emerged out of the artistic circles of Edendale as much as out of its leftist circles. Indeed, those overlapping circles constituted a single bohemian world, and the Mattachine founders and the organization they constructed expressed the bohemian fusion of culture and politics that was central to life in Edendale.

Where Mattachine went beyond the Communists' analysis of racial groups was in insisting that their emotional lives mattered politically. They built on the artists' commitment to the importance of the inner life and argued that their consistent romantic and sexual desires were the very thing that defined them as a group and made them a "nation." This was true, in part, because their desires triggered state-sponsored oppression, and therefore their desires marked them as much as racial minorities were marked. But their commitment to the public expression of the inner life was the fullest expression of what Grace Clements and and Lorser Feitelson had been pushing for years, and it placed the emergence of Mattachine at the cutting edge of a new phase of American politics, one that several decades later was deemed "identity politics." In all their subsequent "coming out" activism—whether defending Dale Jennings at his trial for indecent behavior, or asking political candidates their views on homosexual criminalization—Mattachine enacted that cultural-political ethic.

As has been well-documented, the understanding that the bohemian founders of Mattachine possessed—namely, that their desires marked them as an oppressed social minority—was not one that was instantly embraced by men and women who shared same-sex desires. In truth, even at the turn of the twentieth century, many individuals who have same-sex experiences do not view themselves as possessing a particular identity, let alone belonging to a particular minority; the acceptance of Mattachine's minoritizing view of homosexuality has hardly been universal. But within twelve or fifteen years after Mattachine's emergence, a rapidly growing cohort of thousands of American men and women began embracing their framework.

In the grand scheme of things, that seems a fairly short period of time for a new idea about sexual desire, authenticity, and identity to take hold. In fact, even tracing that idea of the authentic emotional self to 1920s Edendale, the speed with which this concept took hold in American culture still seems breathtakingly rapid. What is more, its impact on American lives continues to unfold with profound implications. If the success of the marriage equality movement rests on the last few decades of "coming out" campaigns in both popular and private American culture, that call to "come out" itself was a product of the cultural and political work done inside of bohemian spaces like Edendale. That attention to the authentic self was not invented by the New Left or the Counterculture of the 1960s and 70s. That was an interest emerging among Edendale artists in the 1920s and 30s, and given political overtones by them and their leftist collaborators in the 1930s and 40s. The cries for a politics of authenticity or even a policy interest in the psychological concept of "self-esteem" in the last decades of the twentieth century was the outgrowth of that much longer trajectory, and it is a trajectory that has demonstrated vividly the power of cultural effort— of paintings and songs and dances—to shape minds and political attitudes in the most profound ways.

Endnote

[1.] Much of the research in this essay draws upon my book on *Edendale* (Hurewitz 2007), and can be assumed to come from there unless otherwise specified.

Jake Zeitlin: Books and Galleries, 1927-1940

Genie Guerard

In 1927, Jake Zeitlin set up shop in his first bookstore on Spring Street, downtown Los Angeles. It was a tiny shop, measuring about eight feet by twelve feet. Despite its size, there was a space within it set aside as an art gallery. There would be more and larger bookshops for Jake, each of which contained at least a small space for displaying art works. Although in some cases, the space was too small to be referred to as a gallery, it held a place of great importance within his bookshops. Curiosity about these galleries became the focus of an exploration within the voluminous archives of the UCLA Library Special Collections. [1] What emerges is a portrait of a young, aspiring poet whose intellectual inquisitiveness and steadfast pursuits of fostering new creative expression among kindred spirits led him to spearhead activities that eventually formed a community of artists and writers whose voices defined the culture of Los Angeles during its formative years, with Jake himself at its center.

Reading through the Festschrifts that were written around his landmark birthdays (sixty-fifth – eighty-first) and bookstore anniversaries, one begins to form a picture of the forces that moved Zeitlin into a leadership role among those who had what he liked to refer to as "bookish" interests. Tributes were written by printers, typesetters, book collectors, librarians, physicians, lawyers, poets, journalists, literary critics, painters, sculptors, ceramicists, printmakers, and photographers, each of whom had collaborated creatively in some way with Jake.

Jake was more inclined to thank his friends and associates for contributing to his successes than toward self-praise. Perhaps the term "catalyst," borrowed from Ward Ritchie, best describes him. Ritchie noted Jake had a talent to "gather around himself kindred souls to foster myriad projects," and, "Constantly he was encouraging and stimulating the artists, the printers, the poets, and writers of those days when the rise of the Depression was just beginning to surge in. And, incidentally, he was also trying to sell them books" (Ritchie 1967:50).

Fig. 1: Max Yavno. Portrait of Jake Zeitlin. Photograph, c. 1946 Los Angeles County Museum of Art, The Marjorie and Leonard Vernon Collection, gift of The Annenberg Foundation, acquired from Carol Vernon and Robert Turbin

Zeitlin's later successes are well documented by many who also credit him with providing them with their first opportunities, inspiration, and moral support during those early days in Los Angeles. But what is lesser known is what inspired him to include art galleries in his bookshop, an unusual practice at the time. What relationship did the galleries have to his interests in the book arts, fine printing, and other ways in which he displayed an appreciation of aesthetic surroundings in his bookshops? Where did this talent for orchestrating collaborative works come from? A look at his early years begins to shed light on some of the ideals he brought with him to Los Angeles in 1925, along with characteristics of his that were, as his son David would say, "Just Jake" (D. Zeitlin 1997).

Early Years

Jacob Israel Zeitlin was born in 1902 in Racine, Wisconsin. He moved with his family as a boy to Fort Worth, Texas, and lived there with his mother, father, and brother until 1925, when he moved to Los Angeles. The Zeitlin family were conservative, Orthodox Jews who struggled to make ends meet by running a condiment business. Both Jake and his brother, Sam, were forced to drop out of high school in order to help out with the family business. Jake had a tremendous curiosity about a wide range of topics, including the natural sciences, poetry, literature, and music. Lacking support from his family to pursue these interests, he sought out experts, such as eighty-year-old Albert Ruth, one of Texas's outstanding botanists of his time. Whether he was simply not self-conscious, or whether the possession of "a curiosity bump larger than normal" (Zeitlin 1980: 3) drove him beyond his shyness, is not known. In Zeitlin's words:

> I never thought anybody was taller than I was, so that if I heard of somebody that was an authority on geology or botany and that I wanted to learn something from, I would just go and knock on their front door and then tell them I was interested, would like to talk to them. (Zeitlin 1980: 3)

When Carl Sandburg came to Texas for a poetry reading, Zeitlin drove through a snowstorm to see him. After the presentation, Jake introduced himself to Sandburg, told him he was a great admirer of his poetry and that he knew some folk songs that Sandburg might not have heard of. Three or four of these folk songs later appeared in Sandburg's "American Songbag," and a lifelong friendship between Zeitlin and Sandburg began. (D. Zeitlin 1997)

Jake sometimes followed his impulse to escape the dreary, book-less routine of working for the family business, like the time he hopped on a train and ended up near Austin, Texas. There he took jobs on nearby farms while devouring books at the Austin public library, but soon he was found and returned to the condiment business. (Kugelman, n.d.). Fate met fate, however, when he met a young man, Ben Abramson, who was assigned to work on the delivery truck with Jake. Abramson had worked in a bookshop in Chicago, McClurg's, with the famous Saints and Sinners Corner written about by Eugene Field. There he had met some great writers, such as Sherwood Anderson, and had seen Amy Lowe smoke a cigar. He also knew about *Poetry* magazine, which interested young Jake greatly, as he was writing poetry himself (Zeitlin 1980: 4-7). This meeting with Abramson left a strong idea in Jake's mind that what he wanted to do was to become a bookseller. (Zeitlin 1980: 458).

Zeitlin described himself during these early years in Forth Worth as not fitting in with the ordinary social group. He was not very athletic and didn't play team games because he didn't like to lose. Instead, he chose activities that were non-competitive, like swimming, bird-watching, reading, and writing (Zeitlin 1980: 454-55). Zeitlin's social life grew out of the recognition he had gained as a writer, leading him to participate in a couple of informal literary clubs and publishing reviews and poetry in his local newspaper. He enjoyed being recognized by established journalists in the area (Zeitlin 1980: 18). While still a teenager, Zeitlin was invited to join the Cosmos Club, through a man named Peter Molyneaux. Molyneaux, the chief editorial writer for the *Fort Worth Star-Telegram,* and Franklin Wolfe, who ran another local newspaper, gave Jake writing assignments for their papers. It was later at Molyneaux's home that Zeitlin saw a private library for the first time, and was introduced to a book by Edward Newton titled *Amenities of Book Collecting and Kindred Affections,* which he described as having "inoculated me with the virus of book collecting" (Zeitlin 1980: 14).

Moving to Los Angeles, 1925

In 1925, at the age of twenty-three, having secretly married Edith Motheral, who was pregnant with his child, Zeitlin made the decision to move to Los Angeles. With twenty-five dollars borrowed from Franklin Wolfe, Jake put his wife on a train to Los Angeles then began to walk and hitch rides, arriving himself about three weeks later. He was literally down to his last dime (Zeitlin 1980: 23).

Despite the difficult economic times during which Jake and Edith arrived in Los Angeles, and the fact that they had only one friend (of a friend) in the city, cultural and social forces were at work in favor of a person with Jake's interests and personality. Book collecting was among the first serious cultural activities to emerge in Los Angeles and was well on its way by the time Zeitlin arrived, eager to establish himself as a bookseller with fresh ideas about how to inspire and bring together its citizens.

In fact, though, he had a very difficult time getting started. Coming to the city at age twenty-three, a high-school drop-out whose only credentials were writing literary reviews for the *Fort Worth Star-Telegram*, it was difficult to get (and keep) a job. He was hired (and fired) by the *B'nai Brith Messenger* to do a story on Marco Newmark as part of the history of Jews in L.A. A series of odd jobs followed, including working as a gardener for the Doheny estate. When the manager of the apartment Zeitlin was renting insisted he enter the building through the back door because he always smelled of fertilizer, Jake and Edith refused, and rented a house near USC instead. Then he finally got a job working for a bookstore—Holmes Bookstore on Sixth Street (Starr 1990: 305-7). In June, 1925, though, Zeitlin was fired from that job, too, and the following night their house burned down. A friend of Edith and Jake's from Texas, Bates Booth, was staying with them at the time. Bates said to them: "Well, Jake, I guess we've had it. We're licked. I think the best thing to do is to get in touch with our folks back in Texas, and they'll send us money, and we can all come home." To which Jake Zeitlin replied:

> No, we can't do that. If we go back, we'll be defeated for the rest of our lives. We give up, and we're done for. We'll be captives. I'm going to stay here, and someday I'm going to have a bookshop, and it's going to be a bookshop where you'll find first editions of the classics and the great names in literature, and beautiful art books, and etchings of Rembrandt and Dürer on the walls, and hangings and carpets on the balconies. And I'm going to stay here till I get it. (Zeitlin 1980: 461-62)

Within a few weeks, Edith was in a mental institution, the baby, Judy, came down with scarlet fever, and Jake was in the Barlow Sanitarium with tuberculosis (D. Zeitlin 1997). When he left Barlow, having had brief careers in the book departments of May Company and Bullocks, he was able to garner support from other bookstore owners and publishers to build a stock of books and at first just make a living on the returns. Pedaling books to collectors was not what he had envisioned. Nevertheless, it did introduce him to the world of the antiquarian book trade, special-edition, and fine-press printing.

The Book Trade in L.A., 1920s

During the 1920s, the book-collecting elite of Los Angeles represented the cultural elite of the city. In its infancy as a city, Los Angeles lacked cultural forms and institutions, such as the Music Center, that might have competed with book collecting as its cultural identity (Starr 1990: 308). Los Angeles businesses were centered downtown, and it was common practice then for the doctors, lawyers, and businessmen to frequent the local bookstores after lunch, on their way back to their offices (Ritchie 1967: 50-51).

The basis of the book trade had been set around the turn of the century by Adam Clark Vroman and Ernest Dawson. The Vromans had come to Pasadena in 1880 in an attempt to settle in a healthy environment for the tubercular Mrs. Vroman. Established in 1894 (after his wife's death), by the 1920s Vroman's had become the largest bookstore in the West. Catering to Pasadena's bookish population, Vroman's specialty was current trade imprints.

Dawson's, on the other hand, was founded in 1905 as the first antiquarian bookstore in Los Angeles. By the time Zeitlin had arrived in Los Angeles, Dawson's had established a clientele interested in special edition and antiquarian books. Although Ernest Dawson brought in the tradition of the Continent—holding afternoon tea at his shop, for instance—he made it clear that snobbery and pseudo-Anglophilic attitudes were inappropriate in L.A. Highly influenced by his background in retail, he had a tradition of regularly marking down the prices of books to keep a constant turnover of stock, while encouraging browsers to return (Starr 1990: 309-10).

The book business established in Los Angeles during the first twenty years of the twentieth century, then, was modeled after Dawson's, and an area which came to be known as "Booksellers' Row" emerged. It established downtown Los Angeles as *the* cultural center of this new city, adjacent to its public library. It has been estimated that one-half million books were offered for sale on Booksellers' Row through the 1930s (Starr 1990: 310).

The main stem of Booksellers' Row was Sixth Street, beginning with Fowler Brothers off of Pershing Square. "Father" Dawson (so named because of his "Methodist-inspired utopian streak") provided Zeitlin with his start-up stock at ten percent above cost (Starr 1990: 310). A pen-and-ink drawing depicting a map of Booksellers' Row, with an original woodcut of Jake by

Paul Landacre, was commissioned and printed as an announcement for the opening of Jake Zeitlin's Bookstore.

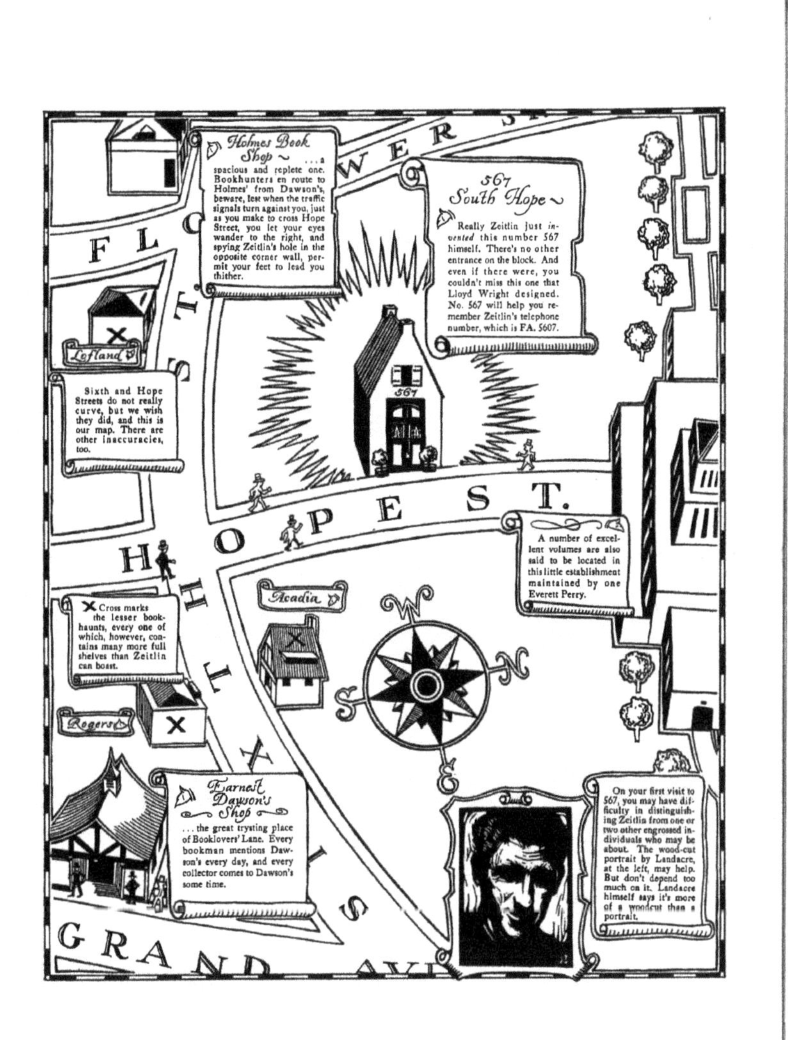

Fig. 2: Paul Landacre. Woodcut, c. 1927 In *An Unofficial Map of Booklovers' Lane & Environs* Jake Zeitlin Papers. UCLA Library Special Collections

It included sketches depicting Holmes Bookshop, Lofland & Russell, Acadia, and terminated with Dawson's at the northwest edge, at Sixth and Grand (Zeitlin 1927).

Zeitlin's friend Lloyd Wright, son of Frank Lloyd Wright, designed the interiors of his first two bookstores, including small galleries. Every detail of the shop reflected an aesthetic choice made by Zeitlin, deliberated to inspire a particular intellectual, cultural, and political atmosphere. His logo was that of a grasshopper, rendered in art deco style. The grasshopper represented the protagonist of Aesop's fable, who fiddled and sang in the summer and therefore froze and starved in the winter. His cable address, "Jabberwock," supported two of his loves—poetry and nonsense.

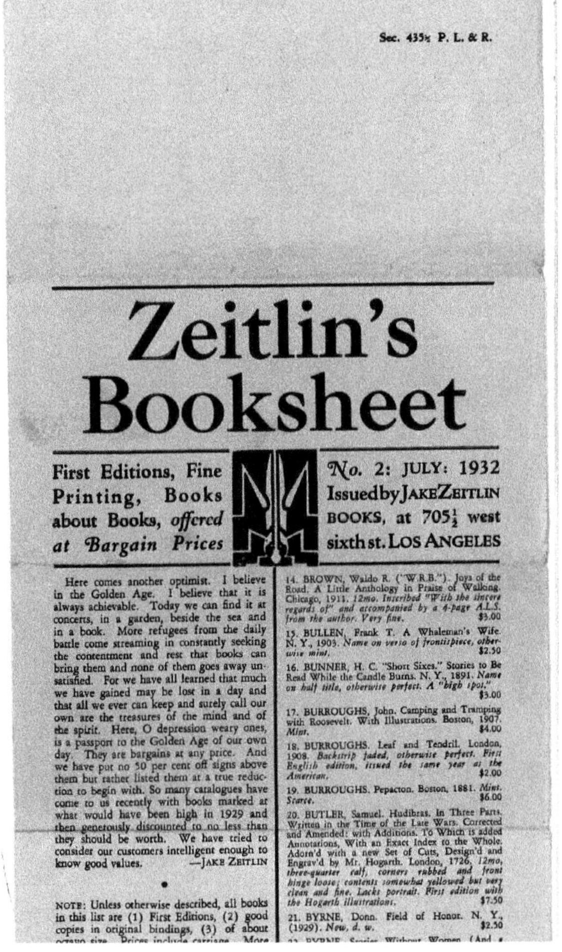

Sec. 435½ P. L. & R.

Zeitlin's Booksheet

First Editions, Fine Printing, Books about Books, *offered at Bargain Prices*

No. 2: JULY: 1932 Issued by JAKE ZEITLIN BOOKS, at 705½ west sixth st. LOS ANGELES

Here comes another optimist. I believe in the Golden Age. I believe that it is always achievable. Today we can find it at concerts, in a garden, beside the sea and in a book. More refugees from the daily battle come streaming in constantly seeking the contentment and rest that books can bring them and none of them goes away unsatisfied. For we have all learned that much we have gained may be lost in a day and that all we ever can keep and surely call our own are the treasures of the mind and of the spirit. Here, O depression weary ones, is a passport to the Golden Age of our own day. They are bargains at any price. And we have put no 50 per cent off signs above them but rather listed them at a true reduction to begin with. So many catalogues have come to us recently with books marked at what would have been high in 1929 and then generously discounted to no less than they should be worth. We have tried to consider our customers intelligent enough to know good values. —JAKE ZEITLIN

•

NOTE: Unless otherwise described, all books in this list are (1) First Editions, (2) good copies in original bindings, (3) of about

14. BROWN, Waldo R. ("W.R.B."). Joys of the Road. A Little Anthology in Praise of Walking. Chicago, 1911. *12mo. Inscribed "With the sincere regards of" and accompanied by a 4-page A.L.S. from the author. Very fine.* $3.00

15. BULLEN, Frank T. A Whaleman's Wife. N. Y., 1903. *Name on verso of frontispiece, otherwise mint.* $2.50

16. BUNNER, H. C. "Short Sixes." Stories to Be Read While the Candle Burns. N. Y., 1891. *Name on half title, otherwise perfect. A "high spot."* $3.00

17. BURROUGHS, John. Camping and Tramping with Roosevelt. With Illustrations. Boston, 1907. *Mint.* $4.00

18. BURROUGHS. Leaf and Tendril. London, 1908. *Backstrip faded, otherwise perfect. First English edition, issued the same year as the American.* $2.00

19. BURROUGHS. Pepacton. Boston, 1881. *Mint. Scarce.* $6.00

20. BUTLER, Samuel. Hudibras. In Three Parts. Written in the Time of the Late Wars. Corrected and Amended: with Additions. To Which is added Annotations, With an Exact Index to the Whole. Adorn'd with a new Set of Cuts, Design'd and Engrav'd by Mr. Hogarth. London, 1726, *12mo, three-quarter calf, corners rubbed and front hinge loose; contents somewhat yellowed but very clean and fine. Lacks portrait. First edition with the Hogarth illustrations.* $7.50

21. BYRNE, Donn. Field of Honor. N. Y., (1929). *New, d. w.* $2.50

Fig. 3: Jake Zeitlin's bookshop logo In *Zeitlin's Booksheet.* No. 2: July, 1932. Jake Zeitlin Papers. UCLA Library Special Collections

The galleries helped to create a sense of place within Zeitlin's bookshops—a conscious and considerable area of importance to Zeitlin—because for him, the bookstore should not only be a business; it should also function as a community center where intellectuals—scholars, lawyers, authors, teachers, journalists, poets, artists, printers, librarians, typesetters—could come to inspire and encourage one another in an exchange of ideas and ideals.

Fig. 4: Will Connell. Photograph, c. 1935 Interior of Jake Zeitlin's bookshop at 614 W. 6th Street, designed by Lloyd Wright.

A shift in the political climate between the 1920s and 1930s also contributed toward Jake's shops becoming a natural gathering spot for L.A.'s literati. Carey McWilliams was a lawyer whose practice was originally centered around oil rights and securities. In the early 1930s he made a transition to the left. His legal practice came to focus on labor law, and he became a journalist and editor of *The Nation.* This shift in political views from the right or center to the left was typical during the Depression era, when the unbalanced economy of the 1920s became the unprecedented disaster of the 1930s. As McWilliams stated, "The literary radicals of the 1920s . . . later became the political radicals of the 1930s" (Starr 1996: 262). Spending time in the bookshop with Jake also appealed to McWilliams because it was a place where one could spend hours "chatting with him about books and politics and swapping lies" (McWilliams 1967: 4-5).

Fig. 5: Paul Landacre. Wood engraving, c. 1935 In *New Places & New Faces*. Invitation to bookshop house-warming, 1935. Jake Zeitlin Papers. UCLA Library Special Collections

Kevin Starr also speaks to the bookshop's role in the formation of L.A.'s cultural identity when he states, "Zeitlin raised bookselling to a civic art form, a way of relating, not just to books, but to the broader concerns of Los Angeles as well. He was committed to liberal politics, to city planning, to a myriad of projects having as their goal the betterment of the city he so loved. Aspiring young men and women in other cities might hang out in cafes or bars. In Los Angeles, they hung out at the bookstores run by Jake Zeitlin" (Starr 1989: 34).

The very quality that cost him his job in working for other bookstores, taking too much time to talk to the customers, turned out to be one of Jake's greatest strengths as a bookshop owner. The reputation Jake's shop gained for providing stimulating conversation and good books worked together with the carefully-designed environment of Lloyd Wright to create a sense of place for its frequenters.

McWilliams points out that he, Zeitlin, photographer Will Connell, journalist Phil Hanna, bookman-turned UCLA Librarian Lawrence Clark Powell, and others were consciously attempting to give form to a particular cultural atmosphere for this emerging city, when he states:

> We did our best, along with some of our friends—Will Connell, Phil Hanna, Larry Powell and others—to conjure into being the kind of intellectual atmosphere and interchange which the community needed and which we never doubted it would someday enjoy.

As for Jake's role:

> In all such efforts, Jake was the prime mover and the foreordained treasurer . . . Jake has always had a genius for relating talent to opportunity, of seeing to it that those who had an idea met those who could help them make it work. (McWilliams 1967. 5)

Zeitlin's politics had always been "a little left of center" as can be seen in the book titles, events, and art displayed or offered for sale in his bookstore (D. Zeitlin 1997). Jake Zeitlin was not afraid of being involved in controversial issues. Lawrence Clark Powell plainly states in one of his many tributes to Jake:

> You were an artist, a tough-minded, realistic one . . . You lived by what you thought was right, and you were not afraid of being in the minority. (Powell 1967: 37; 1997)

Nor did a fear of failure deter him from pursuing the creative endeavors he believed in, and indeed, not all were perfect successes.

"Opinion"

In 1929, a group of intellectuals of a variety of political persuasions met at René and Jean Restaurant with the purpose of organizing the production of a magazine titled *Opinion*. Zeitlin always felt that Los Angeles needed a periodical in which scholars could air opinions, and would serve as a basis for intellectual dialogue and education. New art works by emerging local artists were also featured in each issue. Unfortunately, the members of this creative group were unclear about just what it was they were to produce (Thompson 1975: 47). Zeitlin himself stated, "*Opinion* collapsed because too many of its editors had opinions" (Starr 1990: 305). The journal folded after a year and only six publications. Most importantly, though, the attempt was made, however unsuccessfully, to utilize *Opinion* as a medium to express the hope of this group that Los Angeles had intellectually and artistically come of age, and its contributors went on to establish a creative identity for Los Angeles through other artistic avenues. Some of them were graphic designer Grace Marion Brown, photographer Will Connell, art collector and critic Walter Arensberg, impresario, collector, and critic Merle Armitage, art critic and artist Arthur Millier, artist and printmaker Richard Day, publisher and essayist Phil Townsend Hanna, attorney and journalist Carey McWilliams, author Louis Adamic, architect Lloyd Wright, author and historian W.W. Robinson, novelist and critic Paul Jordan-Smith, and Judge Leon Yankwich.

December, 1929

OPINION

The New Salesmanship
Chaplin's Pilgrimage
The Farmer in Town
Damn the Women
Poems and Groceries

Cover Design by Grace Marion Brown

Fig. 6: Grace Marion Brown. Cover design, *Opinion,* October 1929. UCLA Library Special Collections

December, 1929 Page Seven

Dancing for the Rain,
a new wood cut by
Barbara Morgan

Fig. 7: Barbara Morgan. *Dancing for the Rain.* Wood engraving, 1929. In *Opinion,* December 1929, p. 7. UCLA Libray Special Collections

The Primavera Press

Ward Ritchie cites 1928 as being the "heyday of press books" (Hart 1970: 40). By the time Zeitlin opened his first shop in 1927, Los Angeles's book lovers had already been introduced to fine printing, typography, and illustrations found in English books by those specializing in the antiquarian book trade, such as Dawson's. First-edition and private-press books from England—those of Ashendene, Golden Cockerell, Cresset, and Nonesuch—were found in Zeitlin's shops.

The works of the Primavera Press, so optimistically named by Zeitlin after the original name for Los Angeles's downtown Spring Street (Hart 1970: 42-43), not only spawned the opportunity for many of Los Angeles's talented printers during the early 1930s, but contributed greatly to what would later be seen by Zeitlin as a "small Renaissance" in southern California, including the flourishing of libraries, book clubs, printers, and collectors (Zeitlin 1972: 15). The Primavera Press was originally established by Zeitlin alone in 1929, but was later incorporated with Phil Townsend Hanna and Ward Ritchie as directors (Ritchie 1987: 22-23). It was dedicated to publishing the literature of California and to do so using only the finest of typographic and book design (Barker 1982: 288).

Fig. 8: The Primavera Press logo. Alexandre Dumas, *A Gil Blas in California* Los Angeles. The Primavera Press, 1933, c. 1934. UCLA Library Special Collections

In 1936, in the midst of the Depression, the Primavera Press was forced to close its doors, as were many others. However, many of those who contributed to the resurgence of fine printing in Southern California found their first opportunities and inspiration through Jake Zeitlin. Ward Ritchie's first commission from Zeitlin was to design and print two Carl Sandburg poems (Ritchie 1982: 295). He also gave Saul Marks one of his first commissions, a catalogue of Zeitlin's books titled *The King's Treasure of Pleasant Books & Precious Manuscripts.* Marks took such care in creating and hand-setting the type for this catalogue that by the time it was printed, most of the books it listed had already been sold. It was also Jake who helped Grant Dahlstrom set up his Albion press, imported from England. The "Ampersand Press," named by Zeitlin and run by Dalstrom, was the first hand press to operate in Los Angeles.

Art Galleries

During the 1920s, the politics of the art culture in Los Angeles were decidedly conservative. There were print collectors, oriental art collectors, and individuals such as Huntington and Harrison, who had very clearly defined goals. In 1927, when Robert C. Vose, a Boston art dealer, visited Los Angeles, he made a profound impression on local art patrons. He was extremely critical of any endeavor in the area of modern art. Arthur Millier, art critic for the *Los Angeles Times*, an artist and good friend of Zeitlin, noted that Vose did much to foster the antiliberal art movement in Los Angeles (Higgins 1963: 92-100).

During the 1930s, while those who contributed works to the L.A. County Museum of History, Science, and Art (predecessor to the L.A. County Museum of Art) were collectors of conservative painters or old masters, some of Zeitlin's friends—Merle Armitage, Madame Galka Scheyer, the Arensbergs, and Aline Barnsdall—collected modern works of art. Modern American, French, and German artists became familiar and popular during this decade, and great collections were acquired by Joseph von Sternberg, George and Alice Millard, and Mr. and Mrs. Edward G. Robinson, to name a few.

Despite the status quo, Zeitlin's interests in art were more progressive. As was suggested by Merle Armitage, Zeitlin wrote to Carl Zigrosser, then manager of the print department at Weyhe Gallery in New York, in hopes of making acquisitions of the type of art that met Zeitlin's own criteria. Some of the artists shown in Zeitlin's bookshops were procured on a consignment basis. Among them were Rockwell Kent and Marie Laurencin. Many artists were selected by Zeitlin because he wanted to promote local, living artists who otherwise had very little opportunity to exhibit (Zeitlin 1980: 153, and x: Introduction by Ward Ritchie). He often exhibited works by the younger painters as well (Moure 1978: xix). The L.A. Museum of History, Science, and Art showed very little contemporary art, and there were only about four or five local galleries dealing in contemporary art.

He always had an appreciation for prints—lithography, woodblock prints, and etchings. Many of the contemporary artists in this area were also illustrating books as well as making their works available for sale and exhibition. It follows, then, that some of the early exhibits at Zeitlin's Book Store were of graphic artists and printmakers. Some of the exhibition announcements found in the archive are: Grace Marion Brown, Peter Krasnow, Aries Fayer, Franz Geritz, Paul Landacre, and Richard Day. Others were painters such as Thomas Craig, Buffie Johnson, Millard Sheets, and Arthur Millier (who also wrote reviews of many of the exhibits at Zeitlin's bookshop.) Zeitlin also dared to exhibit photographers, such as Will Connell and Edward Weston (Zeitlin papers, box 8). Although photography was only beginning to be recognized as a "serious art," Zeitlin exhibited photographers out of his own conviction. He said:

> I didn't know much about Stieglitz. I simply knew that in my opinion photography could be an art in the hands of men who had the right eye. And I decided to show and offer for sale prints of photographers along with prints by wood engravers, lithographers and etchers. (Zeitlin 1980: 65)

Many of these artists hung their first exhibitions on the six-foot-by-eight-foot wall that comprised the gallery of Zeitlin's bookshop (Zeitlin 1980: x). Jake enjoyed the support and enthusiasm generated by the art exhibits. It drew people to the shop who were aware of new developments in the arts, and he had the feeling that although it was a small effort, it was a unique one and it was a way of contributing to the success of the shop (Zeitlin 1980: 63-67). He stated:

> . . . I had a lot of encouragement from people like Arthur Millier, who was the art critic of the *Times,* Merle Armitage, who was the manager of the Los Angeles Opera at the time and a collector of prints and graphic arts. And very soon this little shop of mine was a very busy place. I started getting out little brochures. I would send out postcards in which I reproduced an artist's work and announced that I had an exhibition. (Zeitlin 1980: 64)

The fact that very little money was made from the art gallery did not deter Zeitlin. Once he decided it was a matter of importance, he continued to exhibit artists despite the financial strain it placed on him. As Zeitlin describes in an announcement of Grace Marion Brown's show, "Financially, one month's rent out of the year could not be paid with its earnings. However, as I now look back over the years, I see the names of many artists whose first showing in a downtown gallery occurred in my shop. Doris Deutsch, George Stanley, Leopolod Mendez, Grace Clements, Phyllis Shieldds, Richard Day, Paul Landacre, Edward Weston, Ione Robinson—these are only a portion of what I suddenly realize is quite a long list. And many of this list are now of considerable significance in the local and national art firmament."

THE

LITHOGRAPHS OF

RICHARD DAY

Jake Zeitlin

presents

BUFFIE JOHNSON

in her first Exhibition

March 22 *to April* 17

at his Gallery

614 West Sixth Street, Los Angeles

Reception Monday, March 22 at 8 p.m.

Figs. 9-12: Page previous + this page (from lower left): Announcements of artist exhibitions in Jake Zeitlin's bookshops: *Lithographs by Richard Day, Pen Drawings and Water Colors by Andre Duranceau* (original artwork for announcement), *Woodblock prints by Leopoldo Mendez,* and *Paintings by Buffie Johnson ("Buffie").*

Edward Weston

The second art exhibit at Zeitlin's shop, photographs by Edward Weston, provides further testimony to his determination to show local and modern artists. In this case, the discovery was made by Zeitlin purely based on his eye and ability to trust his instincts. Zeitlin went into the local hand laundry in the downtown area one day to pick up his shirts, and saw what he thought were some marvelous prints on the wall. He asked the proprietor who had done them. The owner explained that they belonged to someone who couldn't pay his laundry bill, so that they were selling his prints on consignment. Zeitlin then contacted the photographer, Edward Weston, and offered to exhibit his photographs.

This was the beginning of a lifelong friendship, and years of exhibitions for Weston in Zeitlin's bookshops. Very few prints were sold during the early years, despite their usual price of around $10 or $15. Zeitlin would arrange sittings for Weston as well as the exhibitions, but Weston usually ended up owing rather than making money because he was constantly trading Jake books for credit on his prints. In some cases, Weston paid off his debts to Zeitlin by taking family photographs. (D. Zeitlin: 1997). Although both Weston and Zeitlin were quite concerned with making ends meet during that time, one can see from the letters included in the archives that their resolve to create and appreciate the arts of photography and books overrode the financial incentive.

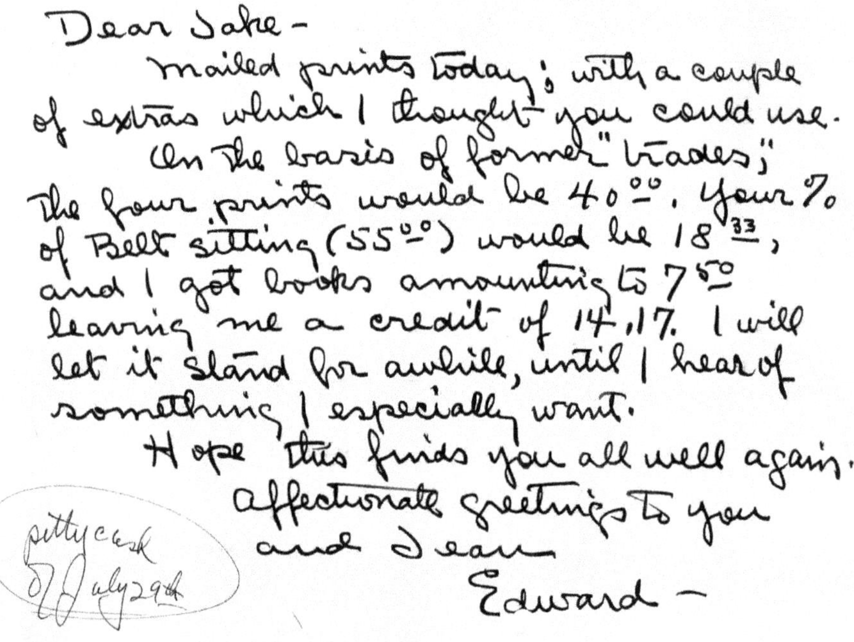

Dear Jake –
mailed prints today; with a couple of extras which I thought you could use.
On the basis of former "trades;" the four prints would be 40^{00}. Your % of Bell sitting (55^{00}) would be 18^{33}, and I got books amounting to 7^{50} leaving me a credit of 14.17. I will let it stand for awhile, until I hear of something I especially want.
Hope this finds you all well again.
affectionate greetings to you and Jean
Edward –

petty cash
July 29th

Fig. 13: Letter from Edward Weston to Jake Zeitlin, c. 1933 Jake Zeitlin Papers. UCLA Library Special Collections

Paul Landacre

Zeitlin had a great deal of admiration for Paul Landacre and his works. Landacre's wife, Margaret, worked for Zeitlin as a secretary in 1929, and introduced the two. His early works were linoleum prints, and later he became an exceptional woodblock artist. Landacre was exposed to the work of old master and modern printmakers through Zeitlin, and thus developed an interest in studying the fifteenth-century woodcuts of Dürer and others. From then on he determined to master the ability to create textures in woodblock prints. Exhibitions of Landacre's works were shown in Zeitlin's bookshop in 1930, 1935, and 1939. It was also through Zeitlin that Landacre met and collaborated with Grant Dahlstrom, Saul Marks, and Ward Ritchie on a book for the Primavera Press, *A Gil Blas in California,* which Zeitlin believed to be the "best-designed, printed, and illustrated book ever published in Southern California" (Zeitlin papers, box 250).

Zeitlin was very proud of the fact that Carl Zigrosser discovered Landacre through the exhibitions in his bookshop, and that later Zigrosser exhibited his prints at the Weyhe Gallery in New York. Zigrosser later went on to become the curator of prints at the Philadelphia Museum of Art (Zeitlin 1980: 202).

During extremely tough financial times for the Landacres, Zeitlin and screenwriter/director Delmer Daves partnered to insure an income for them. They created the "Paul Landacre Foundation." Twelve members were solicited for the purpose of ". . . helping an important artist to live by his work and leave him free to develop his art to a greater expression." For the annual fee of $100, members received a new Landacre print each month. Some of these members were Estelle Doheny, Kay Francis, Carl Zigrosser, Ruth Chatterton, Mrs. Samuel Goldwyn, and Frank Borzage (Ritchie 1980: 19, 77).

After Landacre's death, Zeitlin continued to promote his work. In 1982, Zeitlin held a fifty-year retrospective of Landacre's work at Zeitlin & Ver Brugge, Booksellers, and encouraged the L.A. County Museum of Art to exhibit them as well (Zeitlin 1983: 5-6). The prominence of Landacre's work at the recent exhibit at the Norton Simon Museum, *Proof: The Rise of Printmaking in Southern California,* serves as further testimony to Zeitlin's recognition of important artists when they were emerging, and on the fringe.

VII : THE PLACERS

NOW THAT we had acquired the amount we had fixed as our goal, that is, when I had 400 & Tillier 600 piasters, we decided to leave San Francisco & push on to the placers. What remained was to choose between the region of the San Joaquín & the Sacramento. The advantages & disadvantages of both locations were debated, our final decision falling on the San Joaquín as being closer than the Sacramento. Its mines, moreover, were reputed to be equally rich.

This trip proved epochal. For one thing, the local steamers —this traffic, which has not heretofore been mentioned, was one of the most important enterprises in California—made a rate, exclusive of food, of fifteen piasters each for the trip up to Stockton. Moreover, since the most accessible placers, which almost invariably follow the course of the small subsidiary streams of the San Joaquín or the Sacramento, were,

[59]

Fig. 14: The Primavera Press logo Alexandre Dumas, *A Gil Blas in California* Los Angeles. The Primavera Press, 1933, c. 1934. UCLA Library Special Collections

Käthe Kollwitz

In 1936, the Reich Chamber of Fine Arts, under direction of Chancellor of Germany, Adolf Hitler and his appointed Director of Propaganda, Joseph Goebells, had taken control of public art exhibitions in Germany, and had declared Käthe Kollwitz's work degenerate because of the subject matter her works portrayed. Her art strongly portrayed anti-war themes, depicting suffering German women and mothers. (CSULB).

Herbert Klein and Mina Cooper, friends of Jake who were living in Berlin, sent him a Kollwitz lithograph on the occasion of his marriage to Jean Weyl in 1933. Profoundly moved by her work, he wrote to Kollwitz in Berlin, and she subsequently asked the Hudson D. Walker Gallery to be in touch with him. He was then able to arrange the exhibition of her works in his bookshop. This was a landmark first exhibition of Kollwitz on the West Coast.

A strong anti-fascism movement in Los Angeles had developed at the time, which was looked upon by many as dangerous and Communistic. Nevertheless, Zeitlin decided to hold the exhibit for the benefit of the League Against Fascism. He was able to procure the sponsorship of the anti-fascist organization, with Melvyn Douglas chairing the opening. Modernist musical composer George Antheil and Expressionist playwright Ernst Toller were guest speakers at the opening as well.

Zeitlin strongly opposed censorship of any kind, and stood up publicly to state so, not only in exhibiting Kollwitz's work, which he loved, but also in offering for sale banned books such as Henry Miller's *Tropic of Cancer*, which he admired less. [2] (*Library Journal* 1965: 2480).

After the exhibit, Zeitlin sold some of Kollowitz's works to the San Diego Museum of Fine Arts and the Museum of Fine Arts in San Francisco. He also wrote to Ms. Kollwitz following the exhibit opening, describing the event to her in detail, and the positive recognition for her work. He also wrote, "I assure you that I would be glad to do everything in my power to spread the knowledge of your work and sell it to those who love it" (Zeitlin papers, box 249).

The Kollwitz exhibit may have been a turning point in the galleries, for beginning when he moved to 624 Carondelet Street, names of more established artists, such as Georges Braque, begin to appear in gallery invitations, with an emphasis on master works and older prints in the later years, at Zeitlin & Ver Brugge's Big Red Barn on La Cienega.

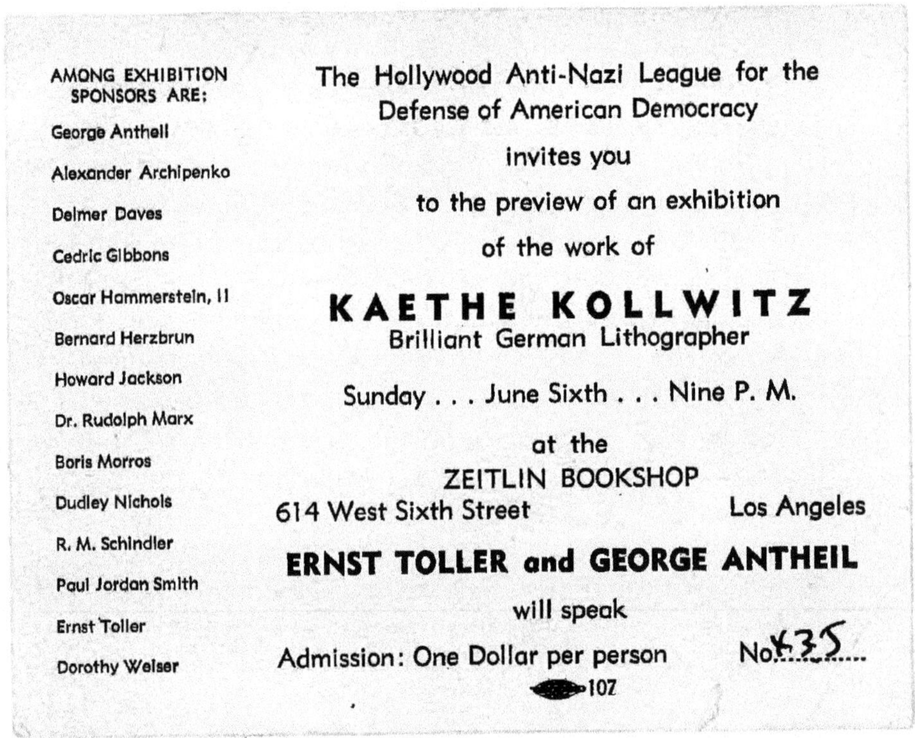

AMONG EXHIBITION SPONSORS ARE:
George Antheil
Alexander Archipenko
Delmer Daves
Cedric Gibbons
Oscar Hammerstein, II
Bernard Herzbrun
Howard Jackson
Dr. Rudolph Marx
Boris Morros
Dudley Nichols
R. M. Schindler
Paul Jordan Smith
Ernst Toller
Dorothy Weiser

The Hollywood Anti-Nazi League for the Defense of American Democracy
invites you
to the preview of an exhibition
of the work of
KAETHE KOLLWITZ
Brilliant German Lithographer
Sunday . . . June Sixth . . . Nine P. M.
at the
ZEITLIN BOOKSHOP
614 West Sixth Street Los Angeles
ERNST TOLLER and GEORGE ANTHEIL
will speak
Admission: One Dollar per person No. 435
107

Fig. 15: Original Invitation, 1937 Käthe Kollwitz Exhibition at Jake Zeitlin Bookshop and Gallery. Jake Zeitlin Papers. UCLA Library Special Collections

Conclusion

In 1980, Zeitlin was interviewed by Joel Gardner, UCLA Oral History Program, for the purpose of creating an oral history. He was asked why he was beginning to pull away from the contemporary art scene. By that time, his bookshop was on La Cienega Boulevard, a street that had become the contemporary art gallery center in Los Angeles. His reply reminds us of his son David's remark noted earlier, that along with all of his great accomplishments and ability to be actively involved in numerous, diverse areas, he was also "just Jake." The response was:

> Well, yes, of course it's always been my policy to pull away from competition. If the competition gets too strong, I left the field to them and carved out another area. And I've always been able to discover new areas, where the competition was less, into which I could go.

> That's been true throughout the history of my bookselling and my art selling. (Zeitlin 1980: 537)

One suspects that there was more behind it than this, even though it does echo his own recollection of avoiding competition in his social life as a young man in Fort Worth. Perhaps competition in an area was an indicator to Jake that it had become popular and made him restless to discover new territory. Jake never waffled about the artists' or authors' works he wanted to promote in his shops. Whatever sparked the change in his art collecting, though, the result was merely one of evolving iterations of the bookshop gallery, still based on his original vision of a bookstore with first editions, great literature, beautiful art books, and etchings on the walls. Jake understood the power of community and arrived in Los Angeles with an appreciation for his mentors and the doors that had been opened to him along the way. He wanted to give emerging, local, progressive artists the opportunity to show their works, and for his shop to be a place where the ideas behind those works could be praised, criticized, and debated, and would not only stimulate new works, but a mutually supportive, open-minded community.

This all folded into the mini-utopia now commonly referred to as "Zeitlin's circle." He had a sense of the connection between art forms that are hung on walls and those that appear in books, and through his galleries and publications, he encouraged artists to cross over and contribute their works to both realms. The result was a series of stunningly crafted publications, bookshops, and galleries that flourished as focal points in Los Angeles during a period when the boundaries of photography, art, architecture, design, and literature were being defined anew, and where there was a collective creative pulse toward a Modern aesthetic.

End Notes

[1] Among the treasure troves of archives at UCLA reflecting the history of L.A.'s Moderns, which happen to coincide with many of the UCLA Library's foundational special collections (many of which are in the archives at UCLA by Jake's doing) are the personal papers of Jacob Israel Zeitlin (389 linear feet) and his circle: Librarian (and fellow book tradesman) Lawrence Clark Powell, architect Lloyd Wright, authors Aldous Huxley, Freida Lawrence, Henry Miller, Anais Nin, and Lawrence Durrell, journalist Carey McWilliams, the papers of musician Sol Babitz and of his wife, artist Mae Babitz, the records of Dawson's Book Shop and the Zeitlin & Ver Brugge archives. The William Andrews Clark Library, UCLA, houses the papers of many of the printmakers and typesetters whose works adorn fine press books of the era: Gregg Anderson, Grant Dahlstrom, Saul and Lillian Marks, William Cheney, and Paul Landacre.
Where personal papers of those in Jake's circle are not present, many of the library's oral interviews reveal their associations and overlap into the areas of the art, architecture, design, and literature of Modern L.A., including Merle Armitage, Galka Scheyer, Fred Grunwald, Paul Jordan-Smith, Phil Townsend Hanna, Arthur Millier, Dalzell Hatfield, Earn Stendahl, Carl Zigrosser, Fred Grunwald, Will Connell, Edward Weston, Buffie Johnson, Rockwell Kent, Paul Landacre, and many more.
Jake Zeitlin also helped private collectors build personal libraries. Among them is the renowned collection on Leonardo da Vinci and the Italian Renaissance, donated to the UCLA Library in 1961 by Dr. Elmer Belt.

[2] This paper was presented by Zeitlin at the California Library Association conference in Detroit in 1965 and addressed the issue of censorship. He stated, "My role as a bookseller is not the least among those who must defend the right to read. The bookseller is usually the first object of legal action in censorship cases. I feel that we must do battle on the ground where the battle is posed, whether we like it or not. My personal tastes are secondary. When I filed as a plaintiff to clarify my right to sell *Tropic of Cancer,* I did not do so because I think it is a great or brilliant book, nor because I have any great regard for Henry Miller. Our City Attorney is alleged to have reported before a public meeting that I said *Tropic of Cancer* is an obscene book. I did not say that; I said it is a dull book.

Dancing in the Sun: The Spirited Freedom of Norma Gould (1888-1980)

Naima Prevots

Norma Gould lived a life of spirited freedom while dancing in the sun, literally and symbolically. Growing up at the turn of the century and defying the usual expectations for young women to marry, have children, and stay at home, she forged a life of independence and creativity. She chose to work and live outside the mainstream of middle-class society, and the world of artists was her realm. She danced as she wished and where she wished, and became an image of possibilities for countless scores of other young women. Los Angeles was a small town when she was born and grew up, with few formal arts institutions and very little in the way of dance training or performance. Her story over the years is that of a woman who created her own pathways, and lived a life of art that was enormously productive and unusual.

Gould forged her life patterns in several unconventional ways. Her work in dance moved away from accepted conventions of classical ballet and ballroom dance, as she explored new ways of expressing ideas and feelings in movement. She travelled on her own as performer and teacher, and was the first Los Angeles dancer sponsored by that city's impresario, L.E. Behymer. She took it upon herself to bring people together in dance who came from different traditions and aesthetic persuasions, as she created a Dance Theatre where Native Americans, Spanish, African, and Indian dancers all showcased their work. A notable example of her work with composers was her dance creation *Lenox Hill.* This was done to an original score by African American Los Angeles-based composer William Grant Still, and her choreography was accompanied by the Hall Johnson Choir, an African American group. Her activities at the Dance Theatre and collaborative work for *Lenox Hill* will be analyzed in greater detail later on in this essay, as the culminating activities of her adventurous and unconventional life.

Most of the information on Norma Gould has come from her scrapbooks, manuscripts, programs, school brochures, costumes, and class notes. These were retrieved from the garbage in 1968 by another Los Angeles dancer/teacher, Karoun Toutikian, who happened to visit Gould at the Arizona Convalescent Home in

Santa Monica. I began my research on dance in Los Angeles in 1980, and after interviewing Toutikian, she gave me all the Gould material. This made it possible to illuminate her contributions to the arts in Los Angeles, as very little was known or written about her. Most recently, I donated the entire collection to the Music Division, Library of Congress, and it is catalogued as "Norma Gould Papers."

Fig. 1: Norma Gould, 1933 (Norma Gould Papers, Music Division, Library of Congress)

There are a few hints of Gould's private life in these scrapbooks and other materials, but we still do not know a great deal. It is most likely she was a lesbian, and her lover and partner was a woman named Marjorie Dougan. Her name appears on several scripts that Gould produced, and she was also on the Board of Directors of the Dance Theatre. Dougan apparently was also an unusual woman. Articles in the *Los Angeles Times* talk about her owning several cars and tinkering with them, and also indicate that in 1927 she was Fashion Editor for the *Los Angeles Examiner*.

Fig. 2: Norma Gould and Ted Shawn, 1912
(Personal Collection, Naima Prevots)

The context of dance in Los Angeles and America during the period around 1900-1940 is an important component in understanding Gould, her life and work. In America we had no tradition of classical ballet, as this was an art form developed in the courts of Europe with support from kings and queens. What little training or performance that existed came from some ballet masters who had been immigrants, and occasional visiting dancer/teachers from other countries. There were no academies such as existed in Russia and France, where students were trained through rigid curricula and became professionals in state-supported companies. Several European émigrés established studios at the turn of the century in New York. Los Angeles in 1910, when Gould was twelve, was a city of 319,198, and Hollywood a village of just over 3,000 residents. Thus, at an age when a girl would study dance, there were scattered offerings available in the city, and these consisted of a mixture of ballet and ballroom lessons, and possibly variations on vaudeville routines. Performances would have been few and far between.

New directions began inside and outside the ballet world both in Europe and in America at the turn of the century, and eventually also impacted Los Angeles. Some of the innovations, mainly through the work of Serge Diaghilev's *Ballets Russes* (Jane Pritchard, ed. *Diaghilev and the Golden Age of the Ballets Russe 1909-1929*), were related to various artistic movements within the first two decades of the twentieth century: Cubism, Dadaism, Surrealism, Constructivism, and Futurism. Two American iconoclastic rebels are harder to label. Various terms have been used to describe their work: interpretive and aesthetic dance; modern dance; pre-modern dance. Isadora Duncan (1878-1927), born in San Francisco, rebelled against restrictions of classical ballet (Peter Kurth, *Isadora, A Sensational Life).* She sought free-movement expression and with her Paris debut in 1900 created a sensation. Ruth St. Denis (1877-1968) premiered her new dance form in 1906, again rejecting ballet to explore in freedom of expression (Suzanne Shelton, *Divine Dancer, A Biography of Ruth St. Denis).* Both Duncan and St. Denis had mixed training similar to that of Gould, and any of the labels could apply to her innovations and experiments. The dance activities of these three women indicated they were outside established systems, working to create their own worlds.

In Los Angeles, Gould began teaching dance in her home at 1615 Georgia Avenue, after graduating in 1905 from Polytechnical High School. It is not clear what kind of dance she was teaching, but it was most likely a curious mix of ballroom, ballet, and freer, expressive movement explorations. Her scrapbooks and various notes do not give any information on her early teaching or training, although there is an indication that during high school she went at some point to New York for dance studies. In 1911, a young man named Ted Shawn arrived in Los Angeles (Walter Terry, *Ted Shawn, Father of American Dance).* He had studied ballet in his native Denver and became restless in search of new adventures and more dance. His search for studios and teachers in his new city led him to Norma Gould, and they formed a partnership. Both young artists were interested in developing ideas beyond classical ballet and decided that working as a ballroom team would finance other creative work. They danced together at late afternoon tango teas in the Angelus Hotel, and later in the evenings at the Alexandria Hotel for the after-theatre set. They also performed for various clubs, such as the Friday Morning Music Club, and numerous organizations.

Gould and Shawn made a movie in 1913 for the Thomas Alva Edison Company in their Long Beach Studio (available for viewing at http://digitalcollections.nypl.org/items/d08ab170-

f875-0130-dc17-3c075448cc4b#2:54). These two adventurous, eager artists, with limited background but large imaginations, made a short movie with their students in two weeks, "Dances of the Ages." The movie is available online through the New York Public Library's digital collection housed at the Jerome Robbins Dance Division at Lincoln Center. It is in eight sections, almost five minutes long, and shows the history of dance through the following short episodes: the Stone Age, Prehistoric dance of Primitive Man; Egypt 1200 B.C., Dance of the Priest of Ra; Greece 400 B.C., The Bacchanalia; Orient 200 A.D.; England 1760, The Minuet; France 1850, The Carnival; American 1898, The Cakewalk; America 1913, Ragtime. The movie was followed by an engagement at San Diego's Majestic Theatre, where the duet had a two-week engagement. They performed five shows daily, and publicity noted these were "dances of every nation, dances of every age, with a change of program Monday, Wednesday, Saturday." Pictures show Shawn and Gould in costumes and poses ranging from ballroom dances to Oriental interpretations to Greek numbers complete with loose tunics, flowers, and draperies across Gould's bosom, torso, and hips. Two of the dances were shown in Gould's scrapbook: *Oriental Love Dance* and *Marsovia, A Panier.*

In 1914, Gould and Shawn set out on a trip to New York on the Santa Fe Railroad. They were hired as entertainers to play employee recreation centers along the line. The commitment was to play nineteen performances for the Santa Fe in return for round-trip tickets, Los Angeles/New York. There was a company of six, with two other dancers (Adelaide Munn, Otis Williams); Blanche Ebert, pianist; Brahm Van Den Berg, soprano soloist and violinist. They billed themselves as the "Shawn-Gould Company of Interpretive Dancers . . . in the rendition of classical and historical works of the Masters." We have to keep in mind how radical such a trip would have been for a young woman in company of other men. In addition, at that time, many considered dance itself somewhat suspect and outside conventional norms. A dancer could be suspected of loose morals, and not acceptable to bourgeois society, given the costumes, duets, movements, and traveling life. In Shawn's biography, *One Thousand and One Night Stands,* written with Gary Poole, he quotes the announcement of their Santa Fe program: "Some people may object to an entertainment of this character because it is dancing; but please do not commit an error here. It is a portrayal of perfect development by the most exacting labor and much self-denial. It is the drama acted and illustrated by music and the graceful movement in artistic forms of the human body guided by pure hearts and active brains. It is an attempt to personify history. It is an effort to make a past age live in the present" (Shawn 1960:16). The dances performed were listed on the bottom of this announcement: *Dances of Henry VIII; Diana and Endymion; The Cycle – Winter, Spring, Summer, Autumn.*

Before coming to New York on their way from Los Angeles, Gould, Shawn, and Adelaide Munn spent one month at the Unitrinian School of Personal Harmonizing and Self-Development in New Canaan, Connecticut. For many Americans, dance was associated with low-brow commercial entertainment, and was often seen as crude. Isadora Duncan, Ruth St. Denis, Norma Gould, and Ted Shawn were seeking new meaning and validity in dance, and were emphasizing its spiritual nature as an art form. The Unitrinian School was run by Canadian poet Bliss Carman, and a woman named Mary Perry King, who had founded the school in 1911 at Moonshine, Twilight Park, in the Catskills. Their method of education consisted of free gymnastics and movements based on expressive use of voice and body. In addition, there were exercises developed by Francois Delsarte (1811-1870), who sought to free the body through numerous and specific structured movements. Gould saved a copy of the 1911 speech by Bliss Carman to the first graduating class, and utopian elements are strong and clear. This was a long speech, and only a small fragment is quoted here:

> But here in the establishing of a school for the education of personality, our feet are on the foundations of the world, partial aims are merged in those which are universal and we become co-workers with the Lord of Life. We are no longer merely students acquiring knowledge for our own gratification, no longer merely artists proud in the possible achievements of our skill, but seers and prophets of a new day.

A utopian spirit pervaded these early dance seekers of truth and freedom, and established norms were rejected and discarded. When Gould and Shawn came to New York, they performed in various recitals and clubs, and seemed to have done quite well. This did not last very long. Shawn met Ruth St. Denis, and they became not only husband and wife but also dancing partners.

Shawn's homosexuality and St. Denis' involvement with many lovers did not detract from their staying together in artistic ventures for quite some time. Gould returned to her studio in Los Angeles, and continued to establish her own career.

During 1915-32 Gould was very active as teacher, performer, and presenter at national conventions of the Music Teachers' Association and the Dance Masters of America. She gave performances by herself and with her students at many clubs, among them: Ebell Club, Gamut Club, Philanthropy and Civics Club, Hollywood Women's Club, Wa-Wan Club, Matinee Music Club, Los Angeles and Pasadena Chapters of the Drama League of America, McDowell Club, Friday Morning Music Club, Shriners, Elks, and others. These clubs played a major role in bringing arts to the community and in making possible a forum for presentation and discussion. It may be that in Los Angeles, clubs played an even more important role than in some eastern cities, because it lacked an established tradition in presenting the arts. These clubs, many led by women, helped the community come together to share ideas and build an interest in civic and community affairs. It could seem a bit paradoxical that women living lives within the mainstream would be interested in performers who were not, and whose dances were not in keeping with conventional expectations. Many of these women were well placed in the socio-economic order, and looking for activities that would be challenging and interesting outside of their homes, husbands, and children. It is also possible that the women and clubs they led were attempting to combat the scandal, commercialism, and false values they felt were emerging in the movie community.

Gould also performed with her students at various theatres that had emerged. In Los Angeles the Pantages and Orpheum Theatres were integral to the vaudeville circuit. The Philharmonic Auditorium, at Fifth and Olive Streets, was used by impresario L.E. Behymer for the occasional visiting ballet company or for stars considered really significant.

Another concert venue was the Egan Little Theatre, at Figueroa and Pico, usually referred to as just the Little Theatre. Trinity Auditorium (later called the Embassy Auditorium) and the Ambassador Hotel Ballroom were also considered professional performing spaces. Some time between 1919 and 1920 Gould studied in New York, according to an article dated 1920 in her scrapbook. The article indicates this was not her first trip, supporting evidence in the scrapbook that she studied in New York while still in high school.

In 1919 Gould began teaching at the University of California, South Branch (now UCLA), and in 1920 at University of Southern California. Probably one of the first professional dancers to become involved in higher education, she was also a pioneer in training her own students to become university teachers. During the years 1919-1924 she functioned in a dual capacity at these two institutions—as faculty member in the Physical Education Department and as director of pageantry. If financial success is any indication, Gould was doing well by 1923. It was then she moved into a studio built to her own specifications at 460 Western Avenue. The structure consisted of seven auxiliary studios and a main studio designed to be used as a theatre, with special lighting equipment. The building was low-lying in the style of old Spanish architecture and was approached through a patio and courtyard with a small pool and water plants.

Gould's classes were popular during this period; several articles report that there were waiting lists for her classes. She had some of her advanced students teaching in branch schools in Santa Monica, at the Beverly Hills Hotel, and at several girls schools such as Westlake. The summer courses for teachers were popular, and in the new studio she produced evenings of dance, pageantry, and dance pantomime. During this period she sold two pageant scripts: *Diandra* and *A Desert Nocturne.* She was also a popular lecturer for women's clubs on three major topics: dance as an educational factor, dance and pageantry, and the development of dance.

The years 1926-1929 signified widespread public acceptance of Norma Gould as a major choreographer in Los Angeles, and it was during this period she appeared in two major performance spaces—the Philharmonic Auditorium and the Hollywood Bowl. On June 11, 1926, Norma Gould appeared at the Philharmonic Auditorium in *The Pearl of Kashmir* accompanied by 75 dancers and Adolph Tandler's Little Symphony. On August 30, 1927, and September 4, 1928, she appeared on the Hollywood Bowl stage in two post-season evenings called "California Night of Music." In her 1928 Hollywood Bowl appearance she was accompanied by Adolph Tandler's Little Symphony in the premiere of her new ballet *The Shepherd of Shiraz.* The story was by Alice Pike Barney and the music by Sigurd Frederickson. On June 15, 1929, she presented a dance drama, *The Twilight of the Gods*, at the Windsor Theatre.

On August 30, 1929, Norma Gould and her group were asked to appear at the Hollywood Bowl as part of the regular summer concerts. She was the first California native to be given this honor. The Hollywood Bowl program notes relay the regard in which she was held. "Hailed as one of California's distinguished native daughters among the arts, Miss Gould has long occupied a position of esteem in the community. Her artistry as a dancer is matched by her skill as a teacher and many of her pupils have won acclaim in the artistic field of their choice. This Bowl engagement, therefore, comes as a fitting reward for her long endeavor in upholding the best traditions of her art in the West." The program consisted of two dances. The first was set to Schubert's Symphony No. 8 in B Minor (the "Unfinished") and the second to Tchaikovsky's *Nutcracker Suite.* The critic Bertha McCord Knisely in a *Los Angeles Saturday Night* article dated September 7, 1929, reported on this performance. "Color and rhythm, utilized with taste and skill by Norma Gould . . . delighted the largest audience of the season . . . For the symphony, a dignified, serious conception of humanity's vacillation between faith and doubt was carried out by two groups of dancers, and a solo dancer, Norma Gould, representing the human soul."

Between 1920 and 1930 Los Angeles grew rapidly, as the population increased from 576,673 to 1,238,048. Movies were booming. Young future stars were coming, anxious to become famous and make money. It was valuable to have some dance training for silent movies, as they were demanding in terms of bodily expression. Movement and gesture had to relay meanings that would normally be expressed in words. Dance was acquiring prestige and cachet as a respectable and interesting art. Ernest Belcher, trained in England as a ballet dancer, came to Los Angeles in 1915 and established a studio, eventually developing a large following. Theodore Kosloff, who had been an important member of Diaghilev's *Ballets Russes,* arrived in 1917, and became active as both movie star and ballet teacher. Research in the Los Angeles Public Library by this author in 1980-81 uncovered scrapbooks with newspaper clippings. Many of these were only dated by year, and did not list author, specific day, or month. One of the scrapbooks, dated 1929, had a *Los Angeles Times* headline: "L.A. Takes Lead as Dance Center," but no information regarding when specifically this was written and by whom. The first talking movie in 1927, *The Jazz Singer,* generated a large number of movie musicals requiring dancers and choreographers. The 1929 depression did not affect the movie industry to any large degree. Nowhere else could dancers be employed during those years with such large and steady salaries. This spilled over into the non-commercial world, as the Hollywood Bowl, with its huge audiences, began to feature large and important dance performances. As an example Adolph Bolm, a Russian émigré artist with an illustrious career as performer and choreographer, arrived in 1931, and both choreographed and taught.

Gould moved to a new studio in 1932, at 118 Larchmont Boulevard, which she designed herself, and it included stage and lighting facilities. She taught classes but went beyond being just a teacher to becoming an impresario and created what she called the Dance Theatre. Larchmont was the physical focus until 1935, when Gould moved her studio and Dance Theatre activities to 831 South La Brea. A scrapbook clipping dated 1938 had a brief announcement explaining what the Dance Theatre was:

> The Dance Theatre of Los Angeles is a movement rather than an organization. It is a non-profit and . . . its purpose is to form a nucleus for a large and appreciative audience for the concert dancers that they may eventually enjoy the support and following that attends symphony orchestras, art galleries and theatres of drama. It presents only professionals and has no connection with any school . . . Dancers interested in being presented by the Dance Theatre will be granted an interview with Miss Gould. Suggestions for interesting dancers and groups who might be invited to appear are welcome at all times.

The Dance Theatre, both on Larchmont and on La Brea, was a place for artistic exchange, where artists were encouraged to make their own statements. Gould encouraged dancers, musicians, composers, and critics to lecture, teach, and perform. The list of dance artists involved with the Dance Theatre is impressive and wide-ranging. among them: Carmelita Maracci, Tina Flade, Waldeen, Teru, Tom Youngplant and Hopi Indians, Angna Enters, Detru and Aztec-Mayan Dancers, Harald Kreutzberg, Grace Borroughs, Hans and De Negre, Jack Reinhart, Hasoutra, Charles Teske, Okajima, Lester Horton, Lux Garoes of Mexico, Sumita and Lilivati Devi, Prince Modupe and the Nigerian Ballet. Without going into extensive biographies, the names alone provide a broad range of performers: dancers from

Indian, Native American, African, and Spanish traditions. Not only were different, culturally specific, and non-western traditions presented, but there were also many different genres of western dance: tap; ballet; American modern dance; and German modern dance as performed by artists touring the U.S. in the 1930s.

There are two interesting examples of Gould's wide-ranging presentations. She showcased an African production, and collaborated with an African American composer to create an original dance work. Karin Gaynell Patterson, in her dissertation *Expressions of Africa in Los Angeles Public Performance, 1781-1994* (UCLA, 2007), writes about *Zungaroo,* presented first at the Dance Theatre in October, 1935, and soon thereafter at the Philharmonic Auditorium. It was a theatrical presentation that included dancers, musicians, and singers. The man who created this work was Prince Modupe. He was raised in West Africa and left in 1922, living in England and later in the U.S. He came to Los Angeles in 1935 and "worked as a composer, choreographer, theatrical producer, music consultant for film, and a lecturer . . ." (Patterson, p. 122). As noted above in the list of groups performing at the Dance Theatre, the program identified his appearance as "Prince Modupe and the Nigerian Ballet." The critic Isabel Morse Jones wrote on October 8, 1935, in *The Los Angeles Times:* "The Dance Theatre of Los Angeles timed its presentation of the Nigerian Ballet in the auditorium of the new Norma Gould Studios almost to the day of the outbreak of hostilities in Ethiopia. Sunday evening a capacity audience gathered to witness the astonishing performance of Prince Modupe and his company of twenty natives, with the assistance of the Etude Ethiopian Chorus led by the capable Frieta Shaw."

Gould collaborated with African American composer William Grant Still in 1938 and produced a dance work called *Lenox Hill.* Still (1895-1978) is now recognized as an important composer, but in the 1930s African American artists were not easily accepted in Los Angeles. It is unfortunate that we have almost no visual records of the work accomplished and presented by Gould, Still, and the Hall Johnson Choir, but we do know it was enormously successful. The first performances took place on May 1 and 2, 1938, and they were so popular the work was repeated on May 22 to serve those who were turned away. To coincide with the production an exhibit was mounted of African American cultural life: books by African American authors and those concerning African American life; manuscripts and printed scores by William

Grant Still; photographs of the sculpture of Sargent Johnson, a well-known African American artist; photographs of African American dancers; and handicrafts by Florence Russell Phillips, an African American craftswoman.

By 1938, Still had already accomplished a great deal. From 1919 to 1921 he was active in various orchestras and groups. He arranged scores for W.C. Handy's band; played for the orchestra assembled for Noble Sissle and Eubie Blake's musical *Shuffle Along*; and in 1929 was hired by Paul Whiteman. In the 1930s he worked as arranger for two popular NBC shows, those of Willard Robison and Paul Whiteman. In 1934 he received a Guggenheim Fellowship, and in 1936 conducted the Los Angeles Philharmonic. When he moved to Los Angeles, he met Verna Arvey, a white woman of Russian Jewish heritage. She was a musician and composer, and they married in 1939. Avery was involved with Gould and her studio, working as an accompanist, and it was probably through her that the collaboration developed. The information from Gould's scrapbooks tells us that the music and dance for *Lenox Hill* were based on a scenario by Verna Arvey. The story was about a man who came to Harlem from the South, and experienced many different things: the sidewalk characters, the rescue missions, night clubs, and rent parties— all shown in a choreographic montage. Preceding the ballet were five sections tracing the transition of African dance to its current character in Harlem: "Primitive Rhythms," "Cakewalk," "Salute to Damballa," and two rhythm and buck dances.

There were various kinds of special programs at the Dance Theatre, bringing together artists from many disciplines. Two pianists, Verna Arvey and Francisco Avellan, gave lecture demonstrations on music and dance, including "The Oriental Heritage of Spanish Dance Music." Gould's scrapbook listed a series of "lecture teas," and two participants are particularly interesting. One "lecture tea" was presented by Dane Rudhyar (1895-1985), a man of many parts: writer, composer, and astrologer. Born in Paris, he came to New York in 1916, and supervised performances of his contemporary polytonal music. In 1920 he came to California, and was active as a composer. He wrote mainly for piano, and among his compositions from the 1920s are: *Tetragram; Pentagram; Syntony;* and *Granites*. Other modernist composers from that period were influenced by him, including Ruth Crawford Seeger, Carl Ruggles, and those associated with Henry Cowell, who wrote a piece in his honor, *A Rudhyar* (1924). Rudhyar also wrote several books on music and astrology, and was an early student of Zen Buddhism. David Edstrom (1873-1938) was another artist Gould featured in her "lecture teas." He was a sculptor, born in Sweden, who also spent time in Paris and was part of Gertrude Stein's circle. He came to Los Angeles around 1920, and was involved in developing what would become the Los Angeles County Museum of Art.

One of the last programs at the Dance Theatre was a benefit for British War Relief on May 26-27, 1941. The evening was called *Present Pagan Primitive* and ranged far and wide in terms of style and content. Listed on the program were: Jose Cansino and Carmela (Spanish); Nico Charisse Group (ballet); Gene Cole and Partner (jitterbug); Leela Devi (Hindu); Jac and Laura Diegger (tap); Eliner Hague's Jarabe Dancers (Mexican); Martin Herrara (American Indian); Virginia Hall Johnson (modern American); Thurston Knudsen (jungle drums); Lani (Hawaiian); Joe Stevenson (African); Julia Taweel (Syrian); The Dancing Velascos (ballroom dance in the modern mood); Allan Cook, Sally Dick, Julia Ann Reynolds, Anastine Powell, Lester Shafer, John Stanley, Charles Teske (Western cowboy dancers); and a Scotch Highland dancer and piper.

Norma Gould's Dance Theatre proved to be a powerful and lasting force in the development of dance in Los Angeles and also had repercussions for the art form nationally and internationally. Several emerging artists during the 1930s were given special opportunities to teach, perform, choreograph, collaborate, and experience new ideas because of the existence of the Dance Theatre. Lester Horton, who was on the board of the Dance Theatre, and deeply involved as a teacher, student, and choreographer, went on to become one of America's leading choreographers. He was the prime mentor and teacher of Alvin Ailey, whose company tours internationally and nationally to great acclaim. Horton, Gould, and a group of Hopi Indians collaborated in 1935 on a work they called *Sun Cycle*, and program notes read as follows: "Sun worship, one of the earliest forms of emotion to inspire dance will be the motif of the program. Four groups will contribute compositions to this Cycle, so that a great diversity of choreographical tradition will be represented by the various groups."

Fig. 3: Sun Cycle, 1935, Norma Gould, choreographer
(Personal Collection, Naima Prevots)

Percussion was used by all except Gould, whose work was accompanied by piano and flute. It was not long after, in 1937, that Horton was invited to the Hollywood Bowl and choreographed the first West Coast interpretation of Igor Stravinsky's *Rite of Spring*. One of the major dance critics in Los Angeles during that time was Dorothi Bock Pierre, who wrote for a nationally circulated dance publication, *The American Dancer.* In the October, 1937, issue, she wrote: "One word describes the ballet Lester Horton created to the music of Stravinsky's *Le Sacre du Printemps*, and that word is: Exciting! It was one of the most exciting experiences I have had." Horton, who had already attracted attention with his work, was recognized more widely because of his choreography for the Hollywood Bowl. He was very active as teacher and choreographer, and in 1948 opened his own Dance Theatre, proceeding to train a new generation of artists.

Among other young artists who received important training and exposure at Gould's Dance Theatre were Bella Lewitzky and Carmelita Maracci. For Lewitzky, the first modern-dance classes with Lester Horton at the Dance Theatre proved to be eye-opening and profound experiences (Figure 7). She went on to be a member of his company, and then a choreographer, arts advocate, and education leader in her own right. She was instrumental in the development of summer arts programs at Idyllwild, and in the creation of the California Institute of the Arts, where she headed the dance program from the very beginning. Maracci was of Spanish and Italian descent and became a choreographer who merged Spanish and balletic techniques into a strong, personal artistic statement. As with many of the other young artists involved with the Dance Theatre, it would have been difficult for her to find places to teach and perform on her own. At an early and crucial point in her development, this environment provided her with opportunities for growth and understanding, and she went on to choreograph for her own company, the American Ballet Theatre, and other companies, as well as to influence other performers through her inspired teaching.

Norma Gould's free spirit, utopian vision, and strong belief in the spirituality of the arts were core to her life and work. Certainly the Dance Theatre would never have come into existence if she did not have the belief that conventional frameworks of artistic expression as exhibited by mainstream artists did not signify all aspects of dance and the arts. She herself had challenged conventions and sought her own expressive way of life. In her teaching and role as impresario, Gould was creating possibilities and exchanges for other artists, challenging them to find their own voice. She may not have thought of herself as a brave woman, but today we can see that in forging her own pathways, she gave others a chance to find their own expressive powers. She danced of the Sun and its bright inspiration, and she danced in the Sun, growing up as an artist and woman in Los Angeles.

<u>Norma Gould Archives and Collections:</u>
Norma Gould Papers, Music Division, Library of Congress
Los Angeles Philharmonic Archives, Los Angeles
Los Angeles Public Library, Main Branch, Music Collection, Yearly Scrapbooks, Los Angeles

Looking for Bohemia: The Los Angeles Art Scene of the Sixties and Seventies

Richard Hertz

One: Bohemia in the New York Art Scene During the Late Forties and Early Fifties

For Los Angeles artist Tony Berlant

> There is a great cultural fascination with the idea of the art world. It's always idealized and romanticized. When I think of the art world, I think of a small group of friends, people who came up together and still hang out in each other's studios. It's made up of people who have intertwined lives. (Hertz, 2009: 21)

Closely connected with the cultural fascination with the idea of the art world is the cultural fascination with the idea of bohemia—the small group of friends who hang out together and have intertwined lives. In the New York scene of the forties and fifties, groups of friends initially got together based on geography—they had studios close to one another and hung out at the same bar or club. In the Los Angeles scene of the sixties and seventies, groups of friends got together because they exhibited at the same gallery or went to the same art school or made similar art.

The cultural fascination with bohemia came out of American fascination with the chic bohemias of Europe. During the twenties and thirties, Berlin and Paris were the centers for La Vie Bohémienne, which became fashionable and stylish. With the rise of the Nazis, the beginning of World War II, and the arrival of European artists and intellectuals, New York became an increasingly important cauldron for artistic activity. As described by John Gruen in *The Party Is Over Now*:

> The New York School's stylistic impetus was established after World War II had seriously disrupted the energy and focus of European art movements. In fact, many of Europe's leading artists had come to America before and during the war, settling primarily

> in New York and working alongside the ranks of American painters and sculptors.
>
> Artists like Max Ernst, Mondrian, Léger, André Masson, Jacques Lipchitz, Chagall, André Breton, Dali, and Duchamp—all of them out of the European avant-garde—brought their personal esthetic and beliefs into a milieu that was, on the whole, friendly and receptive. It was as if Paris had been transplanted to New York, and this sudden influx of sensibilities encouraged more and more experimentation. (Gruen, 1972: 129)

John Gruen was a composer and critic married to the painter Jane Wilson. In the early fifties, John and Jane were considered "an attractive couple" constantly being taken up by older people who would invite them to their homes "to supply a whiff of Bohemia."

> Cash and security were the last things on our minds. All we wanted was to "live," and let the future take care of itself. We only needed money for rent and food, the rest was a question of using our "ingenuity" to make this "living" as interesting as possible . . . We wanted to look *outré* at any cost, and the cost was sublimely within our means. (Gruen, 1972: 127)

John and Jane began hanging out at the Cedar Bar (a.k.a. the Cedar Tavern) at 24 University Place.

> We did not go to the Cedar simply to be seen; we also wanted to belong. We had been going to the Cedar for a number of months meeting, say, Joan Mitchell or Barney Rosset, and as we sat talking we would watch the door to see who was coming in, or look around to see who was already there. (Gruen, 1972: 128)

Bill de Kooning, his wife Elaine de Kooning, Franz Kline, Jackson Pollock, John Cage, Helen Frankenthaler with critic Clement Greenberg, critic and poet Frank O'Hara were just a few of the people who hung out there.

> Because we appeared again and again at the Cedar Bar, we got to be on a more friendly footing with the habitués and, ultimately, their ritual of booth-hopping because our standard activity. (Gruen, 1972: 128)

In their biography of William de Kooning, Mark Stevens and Annalyn Swan describe the Cedar as smelling of spilled beer and tobacco smoke and shining a "bilious yellow-green light that made everyone look worse than they already looked." An important attraction of the Cedar Bar was that it was a working-class bar, with none of the "chic" that the Parisian bohémien scene became known for in the twenties and thirties.

> The Cedar—reminiscent of the "brown bars" of Rotterdam that de Kooning grew up with—was a working class bar without distinction. And that, in the New York of the 1950s, was precisely its distinction. It appealed to the downtown painters because it was *not* French, *not* tasteful, *not* smooth, *not* witty, not, that is, a Parisian café where artists chatted and sipped. These were important "nots" to painters determined to declare their independence from Paris. The Americans were hard drinkers at a dive whose existential aura owed more to Brando and the docks than to Sartre at Deux Magots. The Cedar represented a perfect blend of high and low, or proletarian circumstance and intellectual aspiration. (Stevens and Swan, 2004: 361)

In Gruen's book, Larry Rivers describes his circle of friends in the forties as outcasts:

> We were artistic outcasts, derelicts, who felt they weren't part of society—whereas in the fifties, this situation, our feeling about ourselves, was quite different. By the fifties we felt our power and our strength. We felt that New York was becoming the artistic center of the world. (Gruen, 1972: 256)

Gruen characterizes the "bohemia" of the New York art world in the forties and early fifties in a way that also applies to the "bohemias" of the Los Angeles art world in the mid-sixties to the mid-seventies:

> Artists came to the Cedar to relax, to drink, or to find a partner for the night. But it was also a place that typified the atmosphere of the creative fifties . . .
>
> America had not yet become infected by the culture bug and painters and sculptors of that generation were not the darlings of the public. For the most part, they

> were men and women working in shabby lofts, improvising a livelihood by teaching, or by taking on jobs that were mostly unrelated to their work as artists. Everybody was struggling and almost no one made money from the sale of work. (Gruen: 1972: 129)

Working in shabby lofts, improvising a livelihood, taking on jobs unrelated to their work as artists, creative drinking, and not making money from the sale of their work characterized the New York bohemia of the forties and fifties and of the Los Angeles bohemia from the mid-sixties to the mid-seventies.

By August, 1975, when artist Tom Lawson arrived in New York City from Glasgow, the scene had changed, but there was still some semblance of a bohemian milieu. The young upstart artists were rebelling against the New York School and creating their own scene:

> Within about eight months of having moved to New York, I was living the Bohemian life in a raw loft, attending classes, painting at night, and then going out to an artists' bar called Barnabus Rex, a tiny little place with a great jukebox and a pool table, which for a brief moment was the coolest bar downtown. The reigning, supreme figure at Barnabus Rex was Richard Serra .
>
> For a couple of years Barnabus Rex was the place where people gathered and where many of us met for the first time. This continued until the Mudd Club and the Odeon opened, two early signs that, after all, New York was going to be ruled by money. (Hertz, 2009: 250)

Two: Bohemia in the Los Angeles Art Scene of the Sixties and Seventies

The Los Angeles bohemia of the sixties and seventies was more diverse than those in the forties and fifties in New York. There were many bohemias, many circles of intimate groups of artists who made up the art scene. They shared creative exploration but had not yet been infected by the "culture bug" and were, for the most part, not making much money from their work. Not many of the artists spoke about living a "bohemian existence," which was part of European cultural mythology. They did speak about the groups of which they were a part, defined by the art schools they attended, the kind of work they did, the art dealers and galleries they shared, and the personal relationships that grew out of their group affiliations.

For artist Alexis Smith, the important differences between the art scene of today and the "bohemian" Los Angeles art scene in the mid- to late-sixties, when she attended the University of California, Irvine as an undergraduate, are how much larger the scene is today and the amount of money one might expect to make as a practicing artist.

> There is an old saying "You had to have been there." It isn't easy to understand how the art world used to be because today the context is so different. The big difference between then and now is that our world was small enough that everybody knew each other. It was very familial and wasn't about money because really there wasn't any money. It was like a fraternity in which everybody was interested in art, but since it wasn't worth anything there weren't the same kind of issues. It's a much bigger world than it used to be, and for better or worse, it's not so artist-centric. The art world used to be mostly about artists. (Hertz, 2009: 32)

Describing her art studies at Irvine, she says that art classes were offered, but there was no art major:

> I took classes with Vija Celmins and Bob Irwin and Ed Moses. I took classes with Bruce Nauman and Tony DeLap. Tony and I did some magic performances together; he was an amateur magician and I was interested in magic. It was one of those great moments. There wasn't any art program but there were great people teaching. Later these artists became my regular friends . . .
>
> In the sixties, before political correctness, there was a lot of fraternization between the students and the faculty, and I went out with Bob Irwin. As a young person in college, I was like a fly on the wall and learned a lot . . . (Hertz, 2009: 33)

According to Smith, the best thing about the art world was that everyone knew one another. "It was a very small interconnected world." Alexis broke up Chris Burden's marriage to Barbara Burden, and she moved in with Burden.

> I moved in with him and we lived together for as long as we could stand it, which was about three years. I left and for about thirty-four years he was mad at me. But his wife, Nancy Rubins, likes me so she kind of made it okay and now I see them—we run into each other. (Hertz, 2009: 34)

Talking about her life with Burden and the influential L.A. art dealer Nick Wilder, who "lived in a rough world and was always getting beat up," Smith says she was prepared because her father was a doctor at a mental hospital:

> There was all this craziness going on all the time. If I hadn't grown up on the grounds of a mental hospital, I probably wouldn't have felt as at home with Chris and Nick. But I had a high tolerance for eccentricity, so I was probably well suited for the seventies art world.
>
> It may have been strange, but it was certainly fun and exciting. In order to get that fun back, I would definitely be willing to go back to the days when art wasn't worth anything, when you had to be willing to be in it for nothing. It would definitely be worth it. (Hertz, 2009: 35)

Smith did not go to graduate school. "I had no patience for that."

> When I got out of school, I didn't have any debts and the world was very cheap. I didn't have to borrow a lot of money to go to school, and I didn't have to make a lot of money to pay off my debts. Today there is a lot of pressure on young people to get ahead. (Hertz, 2009: 39)

In 1974, Smith began showing with Riko Mizuno, then with Nick Wilder, Holly Solomon, and finally with Margo Leavin, who could actually sell some of her work.

> Very few people could be arm-twisted into buying stuff, that's the context for understanding the way those galleries worked. The galleries were more like social clubs. They showed the work and brought people together. The dealers were more like the artists than they are now, in the sense that everybody was a whole lot more eccentric. (Hertz, 2009: 36)

Since there was no money to be made from art, Smith got a job, first for an insurance company, then for about three years in Frank Gehry's small office.

> Nobody thought that of all the people we knew, Frank Gehry would be the big genius. (Hertz, 2009: 35)

In much the same way, Tony Berlant describes his experiences at UCLA in the mid-sixties, which was centered around fellow grad students. Unlike the New York art scene in the fifties, the L.A. art world of the mid-sixties came out of the art-school scene.

> The art scene usually starts in art school. Students recognize each other and become famous within that little circle of mutually adoring artists who support one another. (Hertz, 2009:21)

For Berlant, the difference between the New York and L.A. art scenes is that L.A. covers so much more space:

> In the art scene, the real power is in the reaction other artists have to your work . . . The art scene revolved around interpersonal relationships. The only time I ever felt I was there, on the scene, was in Max's Kansas City in New York. The scene in L.A. has always been more dispersed and hard to pin down . . . Multiple art scenes exist and dealers are busy traveling from one to the next. (Hertz, 2009: 21)

Multiple art scenes exist; multiple groups of artists congregate together to share ideas, to hook up, to gossip, to drink or to smoke.

In the mid-sixties in Los Angeles, there were two important groups of artists that long preceded the artists who showed in the Ferus Gallery, which began in 1957 and closed in 1966. During those nine years, the Ferus Gallery was the most visible hub of the "Bohemian" art scene.

John Altoon, Billy Al Bengston, Irving Blum, and Ed Moses (clockwise) in front of Ferus Gallery, 1959. Used with the permission of William Claxton photographer.

The first group included "older" artists who followed Rico Lebrun, born in 1900, and emphasized draughtsmanship and a "classical" tradition of old-master drawings of contorted human bodies. A 2012 exhibition called this group "Abject Expressionists" and presented them as precursors for much important art that came afterwards, including the work of Chris Burden, Judy Chicago, and Paul McCarthy. The title of the show—part of the Getty Museum-sponsored series of shows "Pacific Standard Time"—was *L.A. Raw: Abject Expressionism in Los Angeles 1945-1980, From Rico Lebrun to Paul McCarthy*. The catalogue for the exhibition stated:

> The exhibition includes commanding figurative works by Rico Lebrun, Howard Warshaw, Jack Zajac, and William Brice that provide a fascinating heritage for the darker side of the Ferus Gallery scene, exemplified with work by Edward Kienholz, Wallace Berman, Llyn Foulkes, and John Altoon.

The young artists of the mid-sixties regarded Lebrun and his followers with scorn, and the favor was returned. Curator Hal Glicksman relates the background story, which in retrospect is amusing:

> Rico Lebrun had a studio on San Vicente close to Syndell Gallery, which Walter Hopps started, but I didn't know him; he was one of the bad guys. There was an enemies list and I heard that Millard Sheets kept it—he was Director of Otis Art Institute from 1953 to 1960. Abstract Expressionists were on the top of the shit list. The L.A. art world was ruled by people like Lebrun and Howard Warshaw and their cronies. You had to choose who your friends were. (Hertz, 2009: 63)

A second group of "older" artists worked in hard-edge abstraction and were called "abstract classicists" by the critic Jules Langsner. The group included John McLaughlin, born in 1898, Lorser Feitelson, also born in 1898, his wife Helen Lundeberg, born in 1908, and Frederick Hammersley, who was born in 1919. In 1964, the Newport Harbor Art Museum organized a show bringing their work together titled "California Hard Edge Painting". They are sometimes referred to as "The Los Angeles School" because they were the pioneer group of artists in the Los Angeles scene, but they were more influential as teachers than as artists.

In the late sixties, Tony Berlant identified himself with the "UCLA crowd," including fellow students like Chas Garabedian and Vija Celmins, who "went on to have important careers, a real identity as an artist in the art world and the gallery world." It takes a long time to establish "a real identity" as an artist, based on your work. Before that happens, if it does, artists identify themselves with one art scene or another. Berlant never felt he was a part of the Ferus Gallery scene, which was started in 1957 by Walter Hopps and artist Ed Kienholz. A year later, Kienholz left, and Irving Blum took his place. For nine years, it was the most important gallery in Los Angeles and, arguably, as close to a "bohemian" center as Los Angeles would ever have.

> The UCLA scene was much more diversified than the one surrounding the artists at Ferus Gallery who, rather than plugging away as teachers, were a bunch of

> guys who for the most part rode motorcycles and did all sorts of weird hustles.
>
> Even though I had admired their work since I was a high school senior, I wasn't real close with the Ferus crowd, in part because they were eight to ten years older than I was, which seemed like a lot when I was in my twenties. But as the decades passed, I became very close with Larry Bell, Ed Moses, and Ken Price, all core Ferus artists. (Hertz, 2009: 28)

Ed Moses was part of the gallery from its beginning and had his first show at Ferus Gallery in 1957. He tells many amusing stories about the artists and how they competed with one another:

> For an artist, San Francisco was a horrible place to live because no one bought work. L.A. was bad enough, but in San Francisco it was impossible . . . In 1961, when we moved down to L.A. from San Francisco, Larry Bell was hanging out with Billy Al Bengston. Bengston invited Larry and Bob Irwin into Ferus. Larry had been a student at Chouinard under Bob Irwin . . . He became more successful than Bengston and that killed Bengston. All the other artists thought Bengston was the most talented guy but, like me, Bengston has a personality that didn't help promote his career . . . Ed Ruscha came into Ferus and Bengston wasn't pleased. Later on, he and Irwin sort of decided who was going to be in the gallery. They would boycott certain artists like Llyn Foulkes; they said that he had to be out . . . What's funny is that Richard Diebenkorn wanted to be in the gallery. Bengston and Irwin said that he was a cop-out—he couldn't be in the gallery because he'd gone back to figurative painting. They had enough influence over Irving to be able to say that they would walk if Diebenkorn got in . . . We almost got in a fistfight . . . But Diebenkorn was never part of the gallery. (Hertz, 2009: 159-60)

Bengston made some army belts with each artist's title or nickname. Ruscha's belt said "Water Boy." "He was the new young guy and that's how Bengston referred to him. Ed didn't care and Bengston had to eat those words."

Along with and then after Ferus Gallery, the "hip" and important galleries were run by Nick Wilder, Riko Mizuno, and Irving Blum. Ed Moses relates an amusing story about Riko

Mizuno that demonstrates her indifferent attitude to selling work. Someone walked in off the street and wanted to buy one of Ed's paintings. Ed happened to walk in at about the same time. For whatever reason, Riko wouldn't sell the painting to the gentleman.

> "No him", she said, "he asshole collector". I turned to him, "You heard what the lady said. You have any comment?" He said, "Find out what the price of it is and I'll give you a check for the amount." Riko refused to take his check . . . I got the check from the guy, walked over, handed it to Riko. Riko was nursing her little girl. She reached out as if she were going to take the check. Just as I was giving it to her, she pulled her hand back and it fell to the floor. I picked it up and put it on her desk. She said, "Shit collector. Fake check." He finally got the painting. (Hertz, 2009: 160)

Three: Choosing Your Friends

In the sixties and seventies, artists in the Los Angeles art world defined themselves, mostly, as being part of one group as opposed to being part of another group. After Ferus, multiple art scenes or "bohemias" arose, centering on which art school you went to and what kind of work you were making and where you lived. For Berlant, emphasis was on where you went to grad school.

Berlant went to UCLA. The other schools in the mid-sixties were Chouinard Art Institute and Otis Art Institute. All three programs emphasized craft. Beginning in 1970, CalArts and John Baldessari's Post-Studio program came on the scene, and there became an increasing bifurcation between those artists who worked in plastics and those whose work was based on ideas, information, and the "pictures" distributed by television. Depending on one's affiliation, artists congregated in downtown L.A. or at the beach: Venice and Pacific Ocean Park.

Those artists who worked in plastics—vinyl or resin—had a "fetish" about the sleek finished appearance of the work and became known as the "Finish Fetish" artists. In 2003, the Franklin Parrasch Gallery in New York City had a retrospective of some of the work of Peter Alexander, Billy Al Bengston, Larry Bell, John McCracken, Craig Kauffman, and Ken Price.

In its early experimental stages, the "L.A. Glass and Plastic" group and the "Cool School" referenced the movement that would eventually be known as Finish Fetish. The growing industrialization of the West Coast also influenced many of these artists to produce objects that were completely handcrafted, yet were so seamless and streamlined that they seemed to be machine-made, thus removing the focus from the artist's handling of the materials and placing it on other aspects of the viewing experience.

From "Finish Fetish," it was a skip and a jump to the creation of art that focused on perception within space, the "Light and Space" installations of Robert Irwin, James Turrell, and Doug Wheeler.

At some point, most everyone was influenced by the Finish Fetish group, even Jack Goldstein when he was at Chouinard. Wudl describes Jack's work:

> Jack would not make any work and then would come up with stuff. In the late sixties he was making extremely Minimalist, polished Plexiglas and resin objects . . . I remember being surprised that Jack's work had that extremely designed quality, which his work has had since. In his typical way, he rarely made the work himself; it was true even then that he had it made by someone else. (Hertz, 2003: 40)

In 1970, Chouinard was taken over by CalArts, and only three faculty members were invited by Paul Brach to join the CalArts faculty. Of those three, only one—Stephan von Huene—remained after the first year of CalArts.

Jack Goldstein and Hiro Kosaka, Los Angeles, 1969. Unknown photographer.

Chuck Arnoldi, Jack Goldstein, Laddie John Dill, Hiro Kosaka, and Tom Wudl attended Chouinard Art Institute before it closed in 1970. Tom Wudl describes the faculty:

> When I got there, I realized that Chouinard was the last place for anyone to have even the vaguest respectability; it was below being respectable, and everyone there was a n'er-do-well or had fallen short in life. All the instructors, all the administrators—it was a tattered place, but interestingly enough, all of the important artists came out of Chouinard rather than from Otis. (Hertz, 2003: 38-39)

Students gravitated into cliques: Arnoldi and Dill had a "one-stop shop."

All of the art ladies would come around to Chuck and Laddie's place to order Plexiglas frames, to get laid, and to buy their pictures. (Hertz, 2003: 44)

> To make some money, Goldstein and Kosaka formed GK Frames.
>
> When Chuck Arnoldi found out that we were making frames in competition with him, he called me up and told me very bluntly that he would ruin my career. The funny thing about that remark was that I didn't have a career yet, while he and Laddie John were already on their way locally. In my thirty years as an artist, he was to become the first among many enemies to come. I had to get used to having enemies. (Hertz, 2003: 21)

About Chuck Arnoldi and Jack Goldstein, Wudl says that:

> They seemed like sociopaths, people who had absolutely no conscience and were utterly untrustworthy. Chuck could on occasion be generous and gregarious and very giving; there would be an interchange. With Jack, I always felt threatened, perhaps because he knew he had the capacity to project a sinister aura and would exploit that ability. (Hertz, 2003, 39-40)

For Goldstein, during the late 1960s,

> Chouinard oriented itself to craft—learn materials, develop your methods, and then you are an artist. That was a very different sensibility from the one that CalArts was to offer me. (Hertz, 2003: 20)

Fellow student Hiro Kosaka, from Japan, introduced Jack to Conceptualism "at a time when the school itself was ignorant of anything outside of Billy Al Bengston, Bob Irwin, Craig Kaufmann, and Kenny Price"—all of whom were, at that time, making Plexiglas and resin-oriented work (Hertz, 2003: 20).

According to Goldstein, around 1970 the group that consisted of Laddie John and Guy Dill, Chuck Arnoldi, Ron Cooper, David Deutsch, and Michael Balog—all classmates at Chouinard—were making pretty interesting art.

> With the rise of Conceptualism—the rise of the Post-Studio program at CalArts led by John Baldessari—there developed a rupture between what was in and what was out. I dropped what I was doing, went to CalArts, and completely reinterpreted myself. (Hertz, 2003: 21)

Jack Goldstein was the only artist from Otis or Chouinard to enroll in the new graduate program at CalArts.

Early on, the Arnoldi-Dill group was ambitious, wanted to be important artists.

> A lot of the students I knew at Chouinard, like Laddie Dill and Chuck Arnoldi and people in their group, wanted to be important artists. They became more like decorators, but that was not their intention. They were striving to be famous artists. (Hertz, 2003: 20)

Writing about when he graduated from CalArts in 1979, Marc Pally remembers that most of his fellow students—including Mike Kelley and Jim Shaw—were less interested in success:

> It was an innocent time. People had lives in the arts but they didn't have art careers in the way we think of them today. It was more about signing up for the life; you didn't sign up for the career. The idea of success was to get by. Now the idea of success is to be rich and famous in the big world, not just the art world. (Hertz, 2009: 96)

Goldstein listed the other groups at Chouinard:

> There was the Arnoldi-Dill group. Another group included Bas Jan Ader, Bill Leavitt, Al Ruppersberg, Wolfgang Stoerchle, and Ger van Elk. This group felt like it was the most elite because they went to Europe a lot and were hooked up with Artt Projects, in Amsterdam, and with many European galleries.
>
> Artt Projects was a gallery in Amsterdam that put out a newsletter every other week discussing approaches to Conceptual Art. (Hertz, 2003: 23)

Goldstein mentions Bas Jan Ader's infamous journey around the world on his boat:

> He went everywhere in his boat, until he was lost at sea. He left on the boat trip but never arrived because the boat blew up. The difference between Bas Jan and me is that I wouldn't have to take that boat trip; a flyer would have been enough. He came out of a time when the artist had to be involved in making a piece; he physically had to make the journey, while I would have treated it as pure theater, so a publication would have been enough. (Hertz, 2003: 23)

Jack refers to Michael Asher, Mary Corse, and Doug Wheeler as a group who were involved in white-on-white paintings.
The primary split evolved out of those artists whom Helene Winer showed at the gallery at Pomona College and those artists involved in finish fetish and vinyl and resin who did not.

> Helene created a remarkable series of shows out in Claremont. She was the only curator interested in new work in L.A.; among others, she had shows for John Baldessari, as well as Bas Jan Ader, Chris Burden, Ger van Elk, Bill Leavitt, Al Ruppersberg, Wolfgang Stoerchle, and Bill Wegman. (Hertz, 2003: 26)

John Baldessari talks about the importance of Winer's exhibitions:

> In my VW bus, I would take students out to see Helene Winer's shows at Pomona College. In London she had worked for Whitechapel, and in L.A. she worked for the *Los Angeles Times* before taking over the Pomona

> College gallery. She would show work no one else was interested in. (Hertz, 2003: 62)

John Baldessari, Ojai, 2007. Photograph by Howard Preston.

Hiro Kosaka describes how Helene opened up the door for the kind of art that Hiro, Jack, and a number of their friends created:

> In 1971 one of the most important events was the exhibition of performance arts organized at Pomona College by Helene Winer. On the walls of the gallery were pieces by Bill Wegman; I think we all knew him. There were also pieces by Bas Jan Ader, John Baldessari, Jack Goldstein, Bill Leavitt, and Al Ruppersberg. Then came the performances by me, Chris Burden, Wolfgang Stoerchle—three of us did performances, some of the first in Los Angeles. Every week there was a different one.
>
> We were not known by anyone; we were separated from the Venice artists. There was a real bifurcation in our sensibilities towards life . . .
>
> There were maybe a dozen people, you could count them on your fingers, and we were outcasts, complete outcasts. That is why Jack and I could move into Ron Cooper's studio. Ron and his friends gave up their studios and moved down to Venice.
>
> This was the same split that took place at CalArts, between those students who worked with Allan Hacklin and those who worked with John Baldessari.
>
> There were the painterly beauty artists and there were the Post-Studio Conceptual artists. The two sides didn't cross over. Some people like Tom Wudl

> straddled both worlds, only to be dropped by both. It was like Viet Nam—there were the long hairs and the short hairs. It was a cultural and social dynamic that we may never see again. (Hertz, 2003: 34-35)

John Baldessari was the grandfather—or, perhaps, the Godfather—of the split between the "painterly beauty artists" and the Post-Studio Conceptual artists. Baldessari was hired by Paul Brach at the University of California, San Diego. When Brach left to become Dean of the School of Art at CalArts, Baldessari was the only one of the faculty members at UCSD whom he brought along.

> Paul asked, What do you want to teach? I said, I want to teach students who don't paint or do sculpture or any other activity done by hand. I didn't want to call it "Conceptual Art" so I called it "Post-Studio Art." I assembled a lot of equipment—Super-8 cameras, video cameras, photographic equipment—and supplied tapes and film.
>
> Essentially, my idea was that you can't teach art; there should be a lot of artists around rather than just a lot of people talking about art.
>
> I thought we needed as many artists from Europe and New York as possible because there seemed to be a stranglehold on the kind of art that was being supported in L.A. In order to lessen that stranglehold, Paul curated a show at CalArts called "The Last Plastics Show" because everyone was working in plastic. It included Peter Alexander, Ron Cooper, Ron Davis, DeWain Valentine. That was followed with a Roy Lichtenstein show.
>
> I would go into my class with catalogues from my travels; while I didn't think you could teach art, you could supply information. We were creating a lively community of artists. We were essentially getting information about European artists into our students' hands faster than students in other programs were getting this information, and that turned the students' heads around.
>
> I was constantly returning to New York, which I kept on urging students to do. I said, Nothing is going to happen in L.A! (Hertz, 2003: 60-61)

Four: Art as Religion

At the highest end of the art scene/art market, the "bohemian" life style died with the rise of ambitious art careers, mega-dealers, and multi-national auction houses and became, as in Paris, a Haute Bohémien or High Bohemian life style where the wealthy art investors hung out with artists and intellectuals. The big difference between "then" and "now" is that art has become a kind of religion.

Dealer Robert Berman describes the new leaders of the cult of art:

> Early on I understood that the art world is about the movers and shakers, about the people who have so much money that they don't need anything else. These people no longer need to be the head of a church or temple—art has become the new religion. With their money, the one thing they want is to be able to steer culture, and the one way they are able to do that, and wear the badge on their chest, is through the visual arts. With high performing arts . . . you'll always be a patron in the background . . .
>
> If you want power in the art world, you have to be connected to the bigger picture. Not only do you have your own collection, your own island, but you have to sit on the board of a museum, and like the elders of a temple, discuss what you should do . . . It's a very complicated three-dimensional chess game that they're playing. (Hertz, 2009: 233)

Collector Cliff Einstein also compares the contemporary art scene with a religion:

> I think of contemporary art like a religion. First, there is an artificial belief system that everyone signs up for. There is no literal divide between a good and a bad painting. Good paintings aren't the ones that look most like a photograph or indicate the best technique. Maybe that was a sixteenth-century Dutch idea, but today you can't write down what makes one painting good and the other great. This is determined by a reaction to what occurs in the collector and the issue is always, "Who gets to decide?"
>
> There's sort of a high priesthood made up of museum curators, dealers, key collectors, and critics. Art that enters society first enters as fashion; later the "priests" proclaim it good or bad. Only if that finally

> happens can a work of art become a permanent part of the art worlds' visual vocabulary.
>
> I don't know if this is fair, or right, or logical, but I think it's the way things work. (Hertz, 2009: 334)

Former L.A. art dealer Daniel Hug—now the Director of Art Cologne—explains his take on art and fashion and about how some art dealers like to show students right out of graduate school:

> I like to relate the art world to the fashion world. When art wasn't fashionable, Michael Hall and I saw fashion as being quite interesting, designer fashion as well as fashion in the sense of what's current, what's cool. Now I'm very opposed to the idea because the fashion world has caught on. I don't believe it's necessarily good that there's such a broad influx of opinions and voices and marketing strategies raising the profiles of young artists.
>
> In New York, there aren't many galleries that specialize in showing young artists from Columbia or Bard or Yale, whereas in Los Angeles there are galleries that specialize in showing new young talent out of the Southern California art schools. It's both good and bad. I finally realized that concentrating on young artists just out of school is not how I want to function. (Hertz, 2009: 183-184)

In most graduate programs today, students are pressured to promote their careers while still in school. Kathryn Andrews, now a successful young artist, discusses the pressure to exhibit during and after art school:

> For the first few years after school, there was a huge pressure to enter the marketplace. I rarely heard, "You should chill and figure out what you're doing. Don't worry about shows." Instead it was, "What do you have coming up? Who's visiting your studio?" The emphasis wasn't on developing a practice; it was about new opportunities. Sometimes I was asked to exhibit and would force myself to finish a sculpture or a drawing, but I'd feel very unsure about it . . . I was becoming increasingly uncomfortable exhibiting works under my name. (Hertz, 2009: 216)

Artist John O'Brien argues that if you don't begin to develop your career in graduate school, you are wasting your money and will never be successful:

> Graduate students pay thirty thousand dollars a year for their education. When they enroll in a graduate program they're mostly paying to develop a network in the art world. That network is the most significant thing they're going to take out of their studies.
>
> If they don't forge explicit connections with peers in their group and with professors with whom they want to have an ongoing professional relationship, they'll probably go nowhere. (Hertz, 2009: 319)

As a consequence of art production entering the realm of fashion, investment, and cultural elites, the role of the art dealer has changed. According to dealer Emi Fontana,

> If you look at the history of modernism, the dealers, the artists, and certain collectors who were inspirational for the artists, were all hanging out together, exchanging ideas. That has changed. Today the gallery figure is often a business figure. He or she is not an interface anymore. (Hertz, 2009: 137)

The truth is that, as in the rest of society, there is a top five percent of dealers, artists, and collectors, and then there is a vast "middle class" of artists who may not be making it "Big" but they are making art and they are showing their art and they are hanging out with groups of other artists, as defined by geography, dealers, or art schools.

John O'Brien was a pioneer in both alternate space and project spaces:

> The idea of alternative spaces, with an emphasis on performance and installation, first grew in New York. They were alternatives to exhibiting in a commercial gallery. In the seventies, Los Angeles Contemporary Exhibitions modeled itself on those New York spaces.
>
> When I was first writing about them and acting in them, I was saying we shouldn't call them alternative spaces, we should call them something else. Hence the work "project" came up, because a project is something you begin and then stop. Los Angeles is undergoing a project renaissance. It's so huge that unless you are

> tracking carefully, you're not going to know about all of them or even hear about all of them. (Hertz, 2009: 322)

It is in these less visible corners of the L.A. art world that the bohemia virus continues to thrive today.

SANTA BARBARA

Mountain Drive: Santa Barbara's Iconoclastic Experiment in Living

Katherine Stewart

The stretch of Mountain Drive in the hills of Montecito, centered around Coyote Road, is hypnotically scenic, winding through hills past eucalyptuses, oaks, and deep blue ocean vistas. Blink and you'll miss the 30-odd banged-up mailboxes clustered at the base of a dusty turnoff. Who would guess that this sleepy-looking corner of Santa Barbara was once the epicenter of one of California's most spirited utopian communities, where naked nymphs danced on grapes harvested from the Santa Ynez Valley, then rinsed off in the radical innovation we now know as the hot tub?

A bohemian enclave known for its handmade houses and larger-than-life personalities, Mountain Drive grew out of the utopian ideas of returning World War II veterans in the late 1940s, at a time when American optimism was at its apex and anything seemed possible. The community's founders balanced an insouciant critique of the conformist aspirations associated with the American Dream with an exuberant optimism about the American potential for rebirth. Theirs wasn't a commune or a planned development; in fact, some of its residents were barely on speaking terms. It was, if anything, an uncontrolled experiment in living, a combination of geography and state of mind. What the people of Mountain Drive had in common was a desire to be free of conventional society and lead fun, interesting, natural, and aesthetic lives.

Mountain Drive was what the 60s were like before the 1960s—before the Vietnam War made hope turn sour and young people turn against America. By the time the flower children came along, Mountain Drive was already well established. It gathered a reputation as a wayfaring station for hipsters traveling between Los Angeles and San Francisco, and was reportedly a destination for all the luminaries of the countercultural world: Dylan Thomas and Ken Kesey, Joan Baez and Lawrence Ferlinghetti, Timothy Leary and Baba Ram Dass. Their visits to various friends and acquaintances in the hills of Santa Barbara were something like pilgrimages to pay homage to one's forebears.

In Paramount Pictures' movie *Seconds* (Frankenheimer 1966), which starred Rock Hudson, the real Mountain Drivers performed cameos as symbols of a bacchanalian nature cult, exuding a frenzied hedonism no doubt intended to repel movie audiences nationwide. While the steamy hot tub was indeed invented up there, a proper archaeology of the counterculture would show that modern America owes more to Mountain Drive than celluloid depravity and communal baths. A passion for whole foods, green architecture, and a certain playfulness in personal style and literary expression were also practiced by Mountain Drivers. They were an artistic bunch, producing ceramics, paintings, and poetry. But Mountain Drivers tended to see their chief artistic work as their lives themselves: what they chose to eat, drink, and wear; the occasions they chose to celebrate; and, above all, how they chose to interact with one another. But like the road itself, the utopian enclave would not turn out to be quite as simple as it seemed at first glance.

On a fine summer day in 1948, Bobby Hyde, the unofficial founding father of Mountain Drive—which was a dirt road at the time—hiked up a trail to survey his fifty acres of chaparral. Bobby and his wife, Florence, or "Floppy" as she was widely known, had purchased the land after a hillside fire in 1940. Where other people may have seen a burned-down hillside, the Hydes saw much more, and what they did next is what made them different from typical land speculators. They offered the land to people they liked for token amounts of money—$50 dollars down, $50 a month. Deals were made as verbal agreements, often hollered into the wind as Bobby and his friends trampled through the wooded scrub.

Bobby was a wispy, light-hearted man who was fond of epigrams. One of his later favorites was "A good road is a bad road," by which he meant that Mountain Drive was better off somewhat inaccessible to outsiders. Born in 1900 to the painter Robert Wilson Hyde and Susan McKee, he was an artist, a writer, and an eccentric. He enjoyed classical music, gardening in the nude, and, before moving to Mountain Drive, lived with Floppy for a time in a cave on Arbolado Road in the Santa Barbara neighborhood known as "The Riviera" due to its resemblance of the slopes along the Mediterranean coasts. The Hydes had seven kids between them, six from prior marriages; later, in their fifties, they decided to foster six siblings, aged four to twelve. Bobby eventually wrote a book about the experience titled *Six More after Sixty* (Hyde 1960).

Bill Neely and Frank Robinson with statue of Baccus, circa 1964, photograph by Richard W. Johnston, © Richard W. Johnston

The dream was possible because, at least at the time, scorched land on the mountainside was relatively cheap. It didn't hurt that Floppy was an heiress, one of five daughters of Lilia McCauley Tuckerman and Wolcott Tuckerman. Floppy's great-grandfather was one of the founders of the Metropolitan Museum of Art in New York City. "Bobby didn't have a lot of money; Floppy did," recalls Hillary Dole Klein, a native Santa Barbaran, whose mother, Katherine Holcomb Dole, was a good friend of the Hydes. "The Tuckermans were from back East. One of Floppy's sisters married the painter Campbell Brown. It was that combination: the wealthy woman and the arty guy."

If the money behind Mountain Drive may have derived from one woman, the idea for it may have come, at least in part, from another. Prior to wedding Floppy, Bobby had been married to Lydia Tonetti, whose family lived on a communal artists' retreat on the family fruit farm in New York. Bobby's enchantment with the utopian idea of communal living evidently outlasted the marriage.

"Bobby Hyde was an iconoclast," says Andy Johnson, 49, a local sculptor and stonemason who moved with his family to the Drive when he was eight years old. "He lived ecological awareness 50 years before it became fashionable. His generosity and Floppy's were tremendous, and he had a strong moral code of ethics that set the tone for how life was lived up here."

As fate would have it, Bobby and Floppy were not the only iconoclasts in postwar Santa Barbara. Over at Santa Barbara College, then located on the Riviera, a remarkable group of war veterans were taking advantage of the G.I. Bill to pursue a college education. There was Frank Robinson, a gifted architect and builder, who lived on a boat in the harbor with his pregnant wife, Peggy, before moving to Mountain Drive. A theatrical spirit, Robinson was often said to embody the Drive's *joie de vivre*. There was Bill Neely, a forest ranger, avid naturalist, and potter. Known for his enthusiasm for wine and women, Neely acted as the Pied Piper for many of Mountain Drive's liveliest happenings, playing the accordion and presiding over rituals with pride and pomp. There was Vernon Johnson, a veteran pilot with an indomitable spirit, despite having lost a leg in the war. Prior to their move to Mountain Drive, Johnson, his wife, Ann, and their eight children, ranging in ages from two to seventeen, had traveled through five continents in a school bus to promote world peace. Ann later published a book about their experiences, *Home Is Where the Bus Is* (Johnson 2001).

These characters and a collection of others all moved with their broods to what was then affectionately called the "Chicken Yard of Montecito," where they could live freer and more creative lives than the "Flatlanders," as they referred to downtown Santa Barbarans. "Mountain Drivers seemed to radiate with a secret franchise: wealth without money," says Dick Johnston, who owned the classical music station KCRW in the 60s and moved to the area in 1963. "They were unbound. They were free. I was fascinated."

The first thing early Mountain Drivers did was help one another build their houses. Bobby Hyde, a great proponent of adobe bricks made from native soil, lent his cement mixer, and everyone would join together to collaborate on the latest homebuilding project, working with adobe, steel, reclaimed lumber, and other salvaged materials. "Frank Robinson was a brilliant architect," says Santa Barbara architect and graphic artist Jeff Shelton, who grew up near Mountain Drive. "He played a part in the design of 30 or 40 houses up there. Most architects have big egos; not Frank. He'd just design smart little buildings that fit people's budgets and allowed them to have lovely lives."

From building houses together, it was a short step to the talent that, more than any other, seemed to define the Mountain Drive community—the talent for throwing inspired parties. "Bobby and Floppy would invite everybody in the neighborhood up to their place for a great party once a week, usually on Saturdays," said Merv Lane in 2007, a (now deceased) professor emeritus and sometime writing teacher at Santa Barbara City College, who lived with his wife, Peggy, the former wife of Frank Robinson, in the adobe house he built more than 50 years ago.

"Bobby's and Floppy's house, which was little more than a living room and bedrooms, was about 200 feet above Mountain Drive," Dick Johnston says. "You could see from Point Laguna to Goleta. They had a picnic table, and there were always people sitting around drinking wine. You could put a foot on a very small cannon. They put regular gunpowder in it and ran a couple oranges in the thing and shot them out. It made a loud noise, but they only fired it on special occasions."

Many Mountain Drivers had an interest in winemaking, and the annual Wine Stomp, which first took place in 1952, soon became the community's signature party. A large wooden vat below Bill Neely's house was filled with grapes. The men sequestered themselves to choose a Wine Queen, while the women prepared an enormous feast. After the meal, the elected queen, wearing only her grape leaf crown, would step into the vat. Everybody, kids included, would strip down to their grape leaves to join her, and the group would stomp away the afternoon.

Mountain Drive wine stomp showing Paramount Pictures cameraman filming *Seconds*, 1965, photograph by Richard W. Johnston, © Richard W. Johnston

After a time, the men fostered a tradition called the Sunset Club. Every Saturday at sundown, they would climb the steep path to Jack Bogle's house and congregate on the tiled patio. With a view of the coast from Oxnard to Goleta, they'd share wine and gossip.

The Sunset Club led to several cultural offshoots. One night, the men renamed the gathering the Gentleman's Rifle and Wine Society. After sharing a variety of old vintages, they honed their shooting skills by aiming at corks balanced on the top of the bottles. Another time, in response to the growing Cold War hysteria and McCarthyism, they created a spoof of the John Birch Society by establishing the Jack Ash Society, whose members were encouraged to make "ashes" of themselves.

Before long, the women drummed up a gathering of their own, a knitting circle called Sip and Stitch. It was mainly held on alternating Wednesdays, usually down at Audrey and Gil Johnston's Frog Pond house. "You know, we used to talk about everything—art, kids, men, wine, who had gotten together with whom," recalled Sandy Hill, a regular participant. The women also formed Mu Ralpha Chi, a sort of female sorority.

Communal forms of living even extended to the children. Former Mountain Driver Susan Sisson, who was married to Frank Robinson, recalls:

> Children loved living at our house. They knew exactly what the rules were, and what was expected of them. We had most of our children's friends living with us at different times over the years, when they didn't get along with their own parents, or their families were going through difficult times, or when they just needed a break. Sometimes the kids would just be there for several weeks before we would call up their parents and ask them if they knew that their kids had been at our house for weeks, and sometimes we would get a call from the parents, asking us if we'd take their children for a month, or two or three months, or a summer, or a while, to be determined. It was definitely a fun way to grow up—for everyone, including me!

One day in 1962, Bill Neely and ceramist Ed Schertz, conspiring to wage a mock conflict, declared a Pot War. Dressed in Renais-sance garb—that is, Renaissance garb as imagined by a pair of mid-twentieth-century bohemians—they sold their pottery by the roadside, pouring wine into every purchased ceramic cup while musicians with guitars and recorders entertained the growing crowds, and a new tradition had taken root.

The Pot War became the inspiration for the Renaissance Pleasure Faire when Ron and Phyllis Patterson attended one on Mountain Drive and decided to host a similar event near Los Angeles as a fund-raiser for the alternative FM station KPFK. The tradition took hold, and today, Renaissance Faires are held all across the United States (see Rubin, this volume). Other celebrations, such as Bastille Day and an annual gathering on the birthday of Scotland's famed poet Robert Burns, fell into the "any convenient excuse for a party" category, and nobody wanted to miss the pageantry of Twelfth Night, the quasi-pagan ritual celebrating the coming of the Epiphany. Mountain Drivers used the occasion to don their version of medieval dress, consume a gigantic repast, propose numerous toasts, and elect a court, including Lords of Insanity and Misrule and a Bishop of Fools. The women baked a cake with a bean in it, and whoever got the bean was given the title Bean King or Bean Queen.

Unidentified woman and Bill Neely playing according at Mountain Drive Wine Stomp, circa 1964, photograph by Richard W. Johnston, © Richard W. Johnston

Many of Mountain Drive's ritual parties took place at The Castle, a rough-hewn structure made of heavy timbers salvaged from the old Ellwood pier and decorated with unfinished Mexican tiles. The largest house in the Drive community, the Castle was the family home for the Johnson clan for eight years; neighbors convinced Anne Johnson that whoever rented the castle was bound by honor to host community celebrations, and so the two-story living room, with its high rafters and large fireplace, was the setting for many an unforgettable night.

Visitors to the Drive were greeted with slyly subversive signage. Many homes were graced with inventive flags, such as the "NO" flag Bill Neely raised when he was not in the mood for visitors, or the Greyson family's Jolly Roger with skull and crossbones. The roads were marked with whimsical street signs, such as "Whoa," "Beware of Satyr," and "Tarantula Crossing."

"Mountain Drive was full of unwritten rules," says Dick Johnston. "You never went into anyone's house without being immediately offered a glass of wine, and if you failed to offer one, you were chastised for it. Another rule: nobody wore underwear. I don't know if it was a spoken rule, but it was certainly a fact."

As the parties gathered pace, of course, the clothing options grew wider, until clothing itself became optional, if not entirely unnecessary. Many Mountain Drivers, starting with Bobby Hyde, were committed nudists. Indeed, "Mountain Drive formal" was a term that came to mean bits and pieces of formalwear, but not the whole get-up. For instance, a man might attend a party wearing a top hat and tails, but nothing else.

"My sister and I went up there a lot when we were about six, seven years old, and we'd swim down a creek where just about everybody was naked," Hillary Dole Klein recalls, "or we'd go to this wonderful swimming pool that Bobby and Floppy had. It was concrete, with wine bottles embedded in the cement. The rule was nobody was allowed to wear clothes. But I remember that Floppy gave us a special dispensation and allowed us to wear swimsuits.

"I was so happy about that," Klein continues. "They were kind, kind people."

As the Drive's reputation grew, so did the number of visitors. Some, enchanted by the Drive's iconoclasm, found places for themselves within the community. Others wore out their welcome. In his 1994 book, Chiacos published a missive from Mountain Driver Jack Bogle, circa 1964:

> We learned long ago not to build up the Mountain Drive myth. And what is this peculiar fairytale? Quite simple. Mountain Drive is a magic land where nobody works, women wear few clothes if any, men spend their days making wine and wild bacchanals occur at every full moon . . . On this Scylla, or possibly Charybdis, is lured many a promising soul with artistic talent plus a permanent aversion to manual labor or any paid employment. They appear perennially, eat our beans and bread, drink from any open bottle, and depart gaily —lissomly leaving the sink full of dishes.
>
> So let us suppress the myth! Deny it ever. That worthy few we value will find their way to Mountain Drive Village without a siren song of fantasy and be most welcome. (1994:41-42)

An aspect of the myth that was most certainly accurate is that it was a community of oenophiles. Johnston recalls the night he arrived for a dinner party at Bill Neely's place. Neely took him down to the wine cellar, and there, amidst the "Stomp" product, was a dusty box lying on its side. Neely strode over and pulled out a bottle of 1937 Roman E Conti, which had been given to him years earlier by the celebrated California winemaker Walter Ficklin. "Roman E Conti is an incredible wine; it's still considered one of the best in the world," Johnston says with a smile. "It's certainly the best wine I ever had in my life.

"For awhile, Bill Neely was the absolute center of Mountain Drive, the unofficial emperor of the place," Johnston continues. "Things had to be done his way. He would always get into costume; he had all kinds of fancy clothes. He called himself, 'King Zog of Albania.' He was a real charmer and a real good friend of mine for many years. But one night, my girlfriend at the time, Brigitte, hit him over the head with a bottle of wine because he was messing around on his wife, and she didn't like that." Johnston sighs at the memory. "Ah, Mountain Drive!"

With so much nudity, naturally, the question of sex was never far from anybody's mind. There was certainly some kind of sexual freedom, but sexual liberation lagged. "Male chauvinism was at its height," says Dick Johnston. "The consciousness of the men had risen only to the level of the crotch."

Mary Sheldon, a native Santa Barbaran and owner of Tecolote Bookstore in Montecito, recalls her older sister Susan's brief marriage to Bill Neely following the death of his first wife. With six children to raise, Bill wanted to hire a housekeeper and au pair, so Susan took the job; they wedded shortly thereafter. Like a lot of men on Mountain Drive, Bill was ego-driven, intelligent, and clever, Sheldon asserts. But the interesting, inventive lives that he and some of his male friends were able to pursue depended, she says, on "a servant class of women."

"My sister was a good potter, and Bill knew it," Sheldon recalls. "But she wasn't allowed to throw anything over a certain weight, because she would have made something beautiful, not him, so instead, she did all the production. She'd get things to a certain point, and then he'd put his designs on it." Several years into the marriage, Sheldon says, her sister got fed up and left. "Bill was doing his thing and wanted his wife to handle all the hassles."

"It was a utopia if you were an 'alpha male'," observes Judy Young, 67, whose first husband, Noel Young, was the founder of Capra Press, publisher of the first book on hot tubs (Young 1973) and a Mountain Drive associate. "These men spawned dynasties, made their houses by hand, and worked whatever their art was. They wanted to have interesting, aesthetic lives, and they did.

They all drank heavily and smoked. They thought they could get away with it forever. But like all dreams, it didn't last."

Mountain Drive has always been more complicated than it seems. In the search for unconventionality, its free-thinking residents fell into certain conventions; in the quest for a natural life, they relied on a considerable amount of artifice. It was a place of sexual freedom and yet of sexual hierarchies; a place that celebrated defiance of authority but had its own share of authoritarian personalities; a place free from the moral strictures of conventional society but with deep moral codes of its own; a place dedicated to healthy living that developed its share of unhealthy habits.

For some, the dream was already starting to fade in the late 1960s. By the 70s, drugs had become intrinsic to California's counterculture, if not to the culture itself, and Mountain Drive was no exception. "There was an influx of people who thought that Mountain Drive was a grand place, and didn't understand the responsibilities that went along with that," says Sandy Hill. "Sometimes they'd just drop off their kids, expecting you to take care of them. You'd feel bad for the kids, so you'd do it." She shrugs. "Some of those kids made it, and some of them didn't."

At its low point, several Mountain Drivers were rousted for drugs, and one old-timer was prosecuted for child molestation. But by the turn of the millennium, the Drive was enjoying a renaissance of sorts. It pulsed with the desire of its residents to reconnect with and reclaim the creative heritage that was theirs by right. "The spirit waxes and wanes, but the collective spirit now is strong," Andy Johnson said in 2007.

The Wine Stomp had resumed in an informal albeit regular fashion in 2003. It had been resurrected in part by David Lafond, who lived for many years on the Neelys' old property. Lafond is the general manager of Lafond Winery, an offshoot of Santa Barbara Winery, which was founded in 1962 by his father, Pierre, with the help of Stan Hill, Sandy's husband. "Of course, one big difference with the Wine Stomp is that now, everyone attending is wearing clothes!" Johnson said. "Also, David Lafond makes good wine, as compared to the straight-to-vinegar stuff they used to make."

"Harvesting is a good way to bring the neighborhood together," said Lafond. "It also brings us back in connection with the food chain." Indeed, on the day of that year's wine stomp, Mountain Drivers and their friends gathered in the early morning at Lafond's vineyard in the Santa Ynez Valley to harvest grapes, cruising through the neat rows of planted vines on a flatbed truck. Later that evening, the designated (and fully clothed) Wine Queen gingerly stepped into the grape-filled vat, and was quickly joined by several dozen children who gleefully stomped on the ripe fruits.

The culture of the Drive had become distinctly child-friendly by then. Many events were held specifically with children in mind. During the annual May Fair, children turned out to dance around the maypole. At the yearly Cowboy Campout, young and old dressed up in western wear, sang cowboy songs, and told stories late into the evening. "Back in the 1960s, parents were off doing their own thing and weren't paying very close attention to us kids," said Johnson. "Today, however, the kids *are* the focus. There are 30 or 40 kids at every event, and they're well cared for."

New traditions had taken hold as well. Mountain Drive's street signs were often festooned with posters advertising upcoming events; the whimsical placards themselves were ample evidence that the absurdist spirit of Mountain Drive was alive and well. One poster advertised a party called Taco Stand, Mountain Drive's own bohemian take on "Fiesta," Santa Barbara's annual celebration of its Spanish heritage. Other posters announced the popular Bocce Ball tournament and the Croquet Match, not unlike the one in *Alice in Wonderland*, played with giant wickets made of odd pieces of sculpture and steel.

"Mountain Drive was always a very literary community, and today there is still poetry at every event," added Jeff Shelton, who designs and illustrates most of the event posters. The Pot War had also returned as an annual winter artisan fair, in which Mountain Drivers and others came together to sell their wares, from knitting to baked goods to books.

The Mountain Drive community was both conceived of and destroyed by fire. It was the Fire on the Hills in the 1940s that had allowed Floppy and Bobby Hyde to buy the large parcel of charred former estate lands that eventually comprised the community. The area survived two fires, the Coyote Fire in 64 and the Sycamore Fire in 77, before the infamous Tea Fire, which dealt the community a devastating blow.

At approximately 5:50 PST on November 13, 2008, a fire started at a historic structure called the "Tea House" above Mountain Drive. Investigators linked the inferno to a group of ten college-aged partiers. Spreading rapidly, the blaze was fanned by offshore winds, or "Sundowners," which blow down the Santa

Ynez mountains. The flames roared across the hills and down through the canyons, destroying over 200 homes.

"The Tea Fire was devastating," says Jeff Shelton, who now spends much of his time volunteering his services to rebuild in the spirit of the land and its independent people. "So many of us probably lost years of our lives dealing with the aftermath. Some people moved on; others are rebuilding. Now, a lot of new people have moved in. Some of them have paid a lot for their homes, and they're really great people, but they want to live a certain way. Not that I blame them," he adds.

Even before the fire, the spirit of Mountain Drive was bound to change. Montecito's housing market had reached surreal highs, and land in the area was fetching nearly $2 million an acre. In 2007, Stan Hill said that nearly every day's mail brought fresh missives from hungry real-estate agents. "They go straight in the trash pile," he said, firmly. "We have three and a half acres here, and I'd hate to think what they'd go for in today's climate." He spread his hands in a gesture designed to encompass the house and the hillside beyond. "But what could I get that means more than this?" He shook his head. "We're not selling. Not for any price."

Today, while faint echoes of the old animus can be felt—many residents are uniquely community-minded and help one another with home building and other projects—the times have moved on. Once the vanguard of ideas, the Drive has evolved into what is fundamentally a very nice neighborhood, albeit one that retains markers and reminders of its glory of yore.

Inevitably, Mountain Drive fell short of its utopian aspirations but was remarkable nonetheless. "It wasn't always sweetness and light up here," said Stan Hill, before his death in 2008. "But we wouldn't have traded it for anything. We are fortunate to have had *interesting* lives."

Endnotes

[1] All the quotes I obtained were from in-person interviews, either in 2007 or in 2014 and 2015, after Jay Ruby asked me to expand the article for inclusion in this book. I utilized local resources including the Santa Barbara Historical Society, and obtained assistance from its Director of Research, Michael Redmon. In addition, I consulted other published and unpublished works, including *Mountain Drive*, compiled and edited by Elias Chiacos (1994), and Dick Johnston's as-of-yet unpublished book, *Mountain Drive: A Novel of Sentiment*

MALIBU/TOPANGA BEACH

Idlers of the Bamboo Grove

Pablo Capra

The dirt road to my neighborhood was easy to miss, an opening in the trees. It dipped off the highway at a steep crooked angle like it was meant to impede the attackers of a medieval fortress. Wary visitors then had to cross a moat-like creek, bounce over oil-pan-breaking bumps, and decide if they wanted to continue into a dense bamboo casbah whose only sign of habitation was the baleful sound of barking dogs. Even from the air, the neighborhood was basically hidden.

The AmeriGas truck got stuck in the creek every winter. Pizza places wouldn't deliver there. Police never came to the neighborhood unless called. Firefighters battling the big blazes common to the area took their stand just beyond it. Left to their own devices during the 1993 Malibu fire, residents boldly set their own backfires.

Figure 1: "The Snake Pit and Rodeo Grounds (left), the city limit of Los Angeles (right)." © 2002-2015 Kenneth & Gabrielle Adelman, California Coastal Records Project, www.Californiacoastline.org

> Shortly after 5 a.m., as flames shot over the ridge above their homes and there was nary a firefighter in sight, they decided to go for broke. At the last possible moment, [Shane] McMahon and his friends lighted three backfires that with the wind's help zoomed up the ridge and met the oncoming inferno like a first baseman outracing a runner to the bag. In the aftermath of the devastating Malibu fire, "Shane's backfire" was the buzz of the canyon this week, as die-hard residents credited the volunteers with saving up to 40 houses in one of Topanga's oldest and most bohemian neighborhoods.
>
> McMahon, 38, a surfer and construction worker who has lived in the canyon 20 years, was philosophical. "We like to think of ourselves as rugged individuals up here," *he said.* "If there's no one to help us, we'll fend for ourselves." (Russell 1993)

Even the landlord was rarely seen. Residents were expected to handle home repairs themselves, including grading the dirt road and building an impressive suspension footbridge across the creek. Presumably this, and the fact that the old rustic houses were often damaged by heavy rains and flooding, is why rents were kept extremely low.

Figure 2: "Wary visitors then had to cross a moat-like creek..."
Photo by Baretta, early 2000s

Yet the natural beauty of the neighborhood was an inspiring compensation, bestowing a feeling of riches greater than living in luxury homes. Part-time resident and poet Robert Campbell perceived it as

> a lush green mansion
> just east of Malibu
> that abbreviates those palaces there . . .
> (Campbell 2000a)

We lived just outside the city limit of Los Angeles and across the street from the first beach in Malibu, but really it felt like we were in our own isolated village, perhaps in another country. At night, there were no streetlights. I loved taking night walks! I'd step outside and disappear. The darkness felt so sheltering, yet in walking distance we had our own market, motel, gas station, hair salon, feed store, bait shop, restaurants, and bus stop to downtown Los Angeles.

I think it was that feeling of frontier-town independence, combined with opportunities for idleness and the proximity to big-city culture, that turned this into a bohemian neighborhood. In the words of Campbell again, it was

> a perfect place just to get away
> from the annoying crossroads
> and noisy street signs
> from the hustle and bustle struggle
> just to stay alive
> a move back to the big sky
> with the flowers and trees
> to let his mind shimmer
> in the summer breeze. (Campbell 2000a)

When you're confronted with that kind of freedom, you really get to develop your individuality. Growing up, I rarely felt pressured to look a certain way or get a job. I never drove a car, partly because I never felt the joy in leaving. I lived in a greenhouse. I wrote a lot, and started my own poetry press called Brass Tacks Press, which also released a series of books about the neighborhood (quoted in this essay), and collaborated on two documentary films, *Malibu Song* by Natalie Lettner and Werner Hanak (2006) and *Last Bastion* by Anastasia Fite (2009).

The neighborhood attracted a diverse group of people, including artists, surfers, families, outlaws, and anyone looking for something different. People came because it was cheap, because it was a place to escape from society's expectations, and to be closer to nature. Most stayed for decades. They built outdoor bathtubs, totem poles, parade floats, and skateboard ramps (on the roof!). They painted their houses in Caribbean colors and lived in unusual structures like tree houses and water tanks. They grew pot, planted fruit trees, went nude, had campfires, fired guns at rattlesnakes, kept horses, and let their dogs and cats roam free.

Figure 3: The author in his greenhouse.
Photo by David Blattel, 2002

The neighborhood had a few different areas, but the main ones were The Rodeo Grounds (where I lived) and The Snake Pit (which was a little wilder). Some people kept to themselves; some fostered community. Either way the shared experience of living in this unique place became something of a group identity. The neighborhood's self-image was only strengthened by its individuals and eccentrics, like in John Steinbeck's *Cannery Row* (1945). In some ways, it resembled the nearby artists' colony The Property, which the founders had planned as a "Commune of Autocrats" (see Ruby, this volume). It took its lead from the hippie stronghold in the Topanga mountains, and the Hollywood coolness of Malibu. But the neighborhood was such its own animal that it almost had its own lingo, although Malibu as a whole has a tribal vocabulary, and words that seem normal there like "bitchin" are met with quizzical looks in more inland parts of Los Angeles.

As in many bohemian communities, there were plenty of opportunities for hedonism and abuse as well. The privacy was so seductive, and the low cost of living was such a relief, that it was easy to overindulge. As Campbell commented in his poem:

> Rodeo Grounds Eden
> a perfect setting for sin. (Campbell 2000a)

Pushing that freedom was addictive. There was almost a sense of torch-bearing, like we should do this because we can . . . before the end, which always seemed to be looming. One reason the neighborhood had remained in a kind of adolescent state was the rumors that the land would eventually be sold off for development or a park. As these rumors turned into reality around 2000, the hedonism of the neighborhood increased, and every year was celebrated as the last.

> Like a beautiful woman dying of cancer
> Our village counts the days,
> Each a gift of infinite pleasure.
> Is anything sweeter than another empty day? (Mathers 2002)

> What will we do with the cats
> When the bulldozers come?
> We don't like to think of it
> But we have to some.
> Do what you want while we have the canyon,
> Each day is a dreamy memory one. (McCrackin 2002)

I had just reached adulthood when I learned that it would all be taken away from me soon. This spurred me on to begin archiving the history of the neighborhood. I cherished the pictures and stories I collected, knowing that most would vanish if I didn't preserve them now. By 2007 not only were all the houses gone, but my whole street had been bulldozed into oblivion.

Figure 4: My street winds through the bamboo grove.
Photo by Pablo Capra, early 2000s

I felt like Ishi (Kroeber 1964). I was the last young adult left in the neighborhood, and my connection to it seemed like an almost mythical pedigree. I knew growing up here had made me different, but what were the values I had learned? How would they serve me in life? What had others done with this lifestyle?

It turns out they had done a lot!

Even though the neighborhood felt so far away from the outside world, it was nevertheless a hotbed of surprising contributions. Naturally, the neighborhood began as a place of recreation. An early tourist guidebook advertises:

> Swimming is the leading diversion at Topanga Beach, though dancing claims its share of the popularity. Cabin accommodations are to be had at Topanga Beach Tent City . . . Far enough inland to be among the oaks and sycamores yet near enough for an easy hike to the beach and swim, Elkhorn Camp is a pleasant spot for a week-end stopover. There is a store and café in connection with the cabins at Elkhorn, as well as a good dancing pavilion. (Brunner 1925:8)

Cowboy actor Tom Mix and his friends are said to have used my circular street as a rodeo ring: hence its name, Rodeo

Grounds. Mix "was Hollywood's first Western megastar and is noted as having helped define the genre for all cowboy actors who followed" (http://en.wikipedia.org/wiki/Tom_Mix). Rumors of an earlier Japanese fishing village have been harder to substantiate.

According to film historian Dan Price (Capra 2002), William Randolph Hearst bought the neighborhood and much of the surrounding coastline in the teens or 1920s. In the late 1920s, Hearst built several cottages where he and his mistress, actress Marion Davies, could throw parties and put up their guests. In 1938, Hearst sold the property to the Los Angeles Athletic Club, who leased the cottages out to a motel. Today these cottages are some of the last remaining structures in the neighborhood, intended to be preserved for their history, but no longer in use and falling apart. Famous actors reported to have stayed at the motel include Marilyn Monroe, Errol Flynn, and Peter Lawford. Other actors who lived in the neighborhood include Greta Garbo, Shirley Temple, Humphrey Bogart, Peter Lorre, Carole Lombard, Ida Lupino, Buster Keaton, Sally Field, Doug McClure, Jan Michael Vincent, and Sara Lane (Capra 2002).

But the discovery that fascinated me most was that my neighborhood had been twice as big. Right on the beach, there'd been a rambunctious community that had met the same fate as my area when it was bulldozed for public access in 1978.

Los Angeles was founded inland, and it wasn't until the early twentieth century that people started migrating to the beaches. Malibu was a private ranch owned by the Rindge family until 1929. Writer Reyner Banham coined the term "Surfurbia" to describe communities like Topanga Beach that began to alter the urban landscape.

> Sun, sand, and surf are held to be ultimate and transcendental values, beyond mere physical goods: "Give me a beach, something to eat, and a couple of broads, and I can get along without material things," said a Santa Monica bus-driver to me, summing up a very widespread attitude in which the pleasures of physical well-being are not "material" in the sense of the pleasures of possessing goods and chattels. The culture of the beach is in many ways a symbolic rejection of the values of the consumer society, a place where a man needs to own only what he stands up in—usually a pair of frayed shorts and sun-glasses.

> There is a sense in which the beach is the only place in Los Angeles where all men are equal and on common ground . . . It is roughly speaking possible for a man in beach trunks and a girl in a bikini to go to almost any beach unmolested—even private ones if they can muster the nerve to walk in. (Banham 1971:20-21)

Even though Angelenos had finally learned to appreciate the beaches, surfing didn't really catch on in California until the movie *Gidget* came out in 1959 (See Lawler, this volume). Topanga Beach resident Paul Lovas saw the film when he was 11, and describes the lasting impression it left on his generation:

> It was about this girl learning to surf all summer and hanging out at the beach. In the movie, the guys surfed because it was the greatest thing to do, and partied all the time, and met girls on the beach. That's what they lived for: having a good time. When you saw the movie, you wanted to do the exact same thing.
>
> Before Gidget, there were maybe 500 surfers in California. Afterwards, there were 25,000. It really changed everything. The whole culture came in: surf music (the Beach Boys, Jan and Dean, Dick Dale), surf shops, surf movies, skateboarding. Everyone wanted to be a surfer, or look like a surfer. (Lovas and Capra 2011:1)

For Lovas, Topanga Beach was a place where he and his pals could live that surfers' dream.

> Topanga was the surf hangout, groovy place to be away from LA. That's why we were there. It was a lifestyle, and getting used to it was a lot of fun. (Lovas and Capra 2011:43)

Another surfer nicknamed Baretta was equally impressed when he chanced upon Topanga Beach. He had moved from San Diego to Los Angeles, and was getting burned out on the city.

> But everything changed that day when I first saw how idyllic Topanga Beach was. It was a very shanty kind of village of makeshift places that had a lot of add-ons. None of the houses down there were spanking nice. They were rugged beach houses that were bootlegged, but they all seemed to have righteous decks in front where people would kick back, shoot the shit, and

> drink in the afternoon. And down towards the Charthouse [restaurant] all these groovy people were playing volleyball. There were several nets down there. It just looked like a totally bitchin' scene! (Baretta 2006:1)

High-school teacher Carole Winter found a personal meaning in the date that she first came to Topanga Beach, the Fourth of July, since she felt it marked the beginning of her own liberation:

> A friend of mine said he was staying down at Topanga Beach, and gave me the address, and I drove there and never left. And that was in '69, July 4th . . . (smiling) Independence Day. (Lettner and Hanak 2006)

Topanga Beach was so free-spirited that part of it became a nude beach. But what Reyner Banham saw as the ideal of "Surfurbia"—that anyone could walk onto a private beach and be accepted—was ironically no longer true once surfing took over. Topanga Beach gained a nasty reputation for keeping people out.

> I used to drive by Topanga Beach, and passing over the bridge by the creek, all this bamboo was growing out, and the leaves were blowing in an offshore wind. It looked so inviting and mysterious . . . but I didn't think about stopping because it was very, very private. There was a chain-link fence, barbed wire, and "No Trespassing" signs . . . The Topanga Bombers were the enforcers on the beach . . . They didn't like sneak-ins. The Topanga Bombers would break glass Sparkletts bottles in the creek because that was the only way to get to the beach. The glass would be in about a foot of water. Outsiders would be walking down with longboards on their heads and start falling down.
>
> Chicks would want to come down too, so the surfers would give them their own little trail, but no guys could get in. If you saw three guys coming down the creek with boards, the Topanga Bombers would get out of the water and go, "Get the heck out of here!" and start throwing rocks. Or they'd let them come out, then hit their car. Broken windshields. Flat tires. (Lovas and Capra 2011:4)

The surf culture that everyone knew through *Gidget* was born a few miles north of Topanga Beach at Surfrider Beach (which was public). But Topanga Beach had a lot to do with the evolution of that culture.

Figure 5: Topanga Beach
Photo by John Puklus, July 1973

Probably the three top surfers in '70s Malibu were Topanga Beach locals— George Trafton, Dave Hilton, and J. Riddle. Miki Dora, the top *Gidget*-era surfer, who also appeared in the movie, later started surfing at Topanga Beach when Surfrider Beach became overrun.

> The whole Topanga Beach scene in the early 1960s was this seething, artistic, alternative locale, and [Miki Dora] was a mentor in many ways. Topanga was sort of a retreat for him . . . (Rensin 2009:88)

The winner of the first International Skateboard Championships in 1965, Woody Woodward, grew up on Topanga Beach. Two well-known surfboard shapers lived in the neighborhood: Robbie Dick ("Natural Progression") and Mike Perry. Three well-known surf filmmakers lived there: Scott Dittrich (*Fluid Drive*), Hal Jepsen (*Cosmic Children*), and Grant Rohloff (*Men Who Ride Mountains*). Artist Jim Ganzer started the popular surf clothing company Jimmy'Z there.

Topanga Beach produced two important surfing publications: the *Surfing Guide to Southern California* by David H. Stern and Bill Cleary (1963), and *Surf Guide* magazine (1963-65, *Surfer's* early competitor). Among other things, *Surf Guide* is remembered for "Feigel Fables," a satirical column written by resident Bob Feigel. Feigel explains how Topanga Beach inspired his sense of humor:

> Back in the early-'60s a whole group of legendary comedy writers rented a beach house down by the traffic lights, Bob Schiller (*I Love Lucy, The Flip Wilson Show, M*A*S*H, All in the Family* and father of *Saturday Night Live* writer Tom Schiller), Bob Weiskopf, and others. There were some amazing, totally off-the-wall, impromptu sessions on the beach that pre-dated shows like *Whose Line Is It Anyway?* by many, many years. Those sessions were also what got me interested in writing, improvisation and general insanity. (Feigel 2014)

The beach had its own surf band called Blue Juice (occasional members included Bernie Leadon from The Eagles and Jan Michael Vincent). Their songs, penned by bandleader J. Murf, captured the joy of being a young surfer at Topanga Beach.

> Well you should have been there
> in them offshore winds.
> Corduroy, I swear!
> Sets were rolling in.
> The boys were out in force.
> Time to take command.
> Hurricane was the source.
> Getting tubed was the plan.
> . . . you're coming down the line.
> Nothing in the outside world can make you feel so fine.
> (Blue Juice 1979)

The greater music scene was enriched by resident Herb Bermann, who wrote lyrics for Captain Beefheart & His Magic Band. This surreal sample reflects the free expression Bermann sought in his life and art:

> bearded cowboy stains in black
> reads dark roads without a map
> free-eeeee

> seeking electricity.
> (*Captain Beefheart & His Magic Band* 1967)

A number of other well-known musicians lived in the neighborhood for shorter periods, including The Bear (Canned Heat), Mama Cass (The Mamas & The Papas), and Buddy Miles (Jimi Hendrix's Band of Gypsys). Rambling Jack Eliot was a frequent visitor. The punk rock band The Bags rehearsed there with early member and resident Johnny Nation. Ariel Pink's Haunted Graffiti shot the music video for their first single "For Kate I Wait" there.

One reason so many creative people came to the neighborhood was because of a few residents' communal approach to making art. Norton Wisdom was known to have parties where anyone could paint on his canvases. He also developed his painting into a nightclub act with a pioneering punk band called Panic. Michael Greene's (and later James Mathers's) art studio in The Rodeo Grounds was a major hangout spot for artists. In my era, most people who visited the neighborhood were going there.

Because the residents were so resourceful, it seems fitting that there were several inventors. One, whose name I've forgotten, but whom I obviously liked a lot as a kid, invented toys. More often, though, people were coming up with new ways to get away with stuff. A guy on the beach, Tim Harvey, built a remote-controlled lighthouse on his roof so the surfers could surf at night. Another guy in The Snake Pit, nicknamed Tool, made a career of building secret compartments to smuggle contraband. His description of a hiding place he built in his backyard sounds like something out of a Cheech and Chong movie.

> We ended up growing 300 damn plants! . . . all of a sudden my house was just full. There wasn't a flat space. My shower, every inch of floor, every tabletop was covered. There was barely a path to walk in, sit down on the couch, watch TV, and get to your bed. Everything was half-gallon milk containers with three-foot plants. And my house had too many windows by now for this kind of behavior. We had the curtains semi-pulled all the time, but I wanted the plants out in the sun.
>
> So my next secret panel was a deck I built in my backyard to hide the plants from the helicopters. I went to House of Plastic, bought brown, quarter-inch, smoked (but transparent) Plexiglas, had them cut it in

> 3.5-inch strips to look like planks of wood, and made a fake deck. I even sanded the strips so they weren't shiny, so they looked more brown and flat. And I had sun chairs and tables on top of it. (Tool 2007:22)

The neighborhood's most popular "inventor" was Craig Halley.

> Craigy was like a jack-of-all-trades, master of none. I mean, I always liked him. Craigy was classic. But he was always into some crazy stuff. Like, "Yeah, I'll fix your fridge," and he would MacGyver two pieces of tinfoil together with some gum, and it would work for a day, and then crumble down. Or, "Yeah, I know roofing!" and he'd throw some tar up there. Whatever the case might have been, he didn't really have a master in any of it, but he would do everything. (Rohloff and Capra 2009:47-48)
>
> When he was 15, he'd hook up your cable TV for a free pack of beer. He had 20 houses hooked up to one house. And he had access to everybody's house because they needed Craigy to fix their shit (because he would never fix things right the first time). All of a sudden, Craigy would be in your room going, "Hup, hup, hup, hup." And then he'd be gone.
>
> Craigy built a Jacuzzi in the hallway of his house. On Friday night, he would fill it for the girls who came down by draining the hot water heaters of the houses on either side. This is before there really were Jacuzzis. He just dammed up the doors in his hallway, made a cement tub, and put a floating motor in the water. (Lovas and Capra 2011:23)

Halley was like the mascot for the neighborhood's zany creative spirit. He was a rebel against consumer culture, and an aristocrat who had no intention of living like a "normal citizen."

> Sometimes at George's, you'd look over and see Craigy with tons of people in his car, people on the hood, and people on the top of the car, hanging on, wasted, just trying to make the stretch on PCH up Topanga Canyon to The Pit without getting caught by the cops.
> It was like, "Let's just go for it! Let's not be normal citizens and ride inside the car. Let's ride all over the car, on the roof, on the hood." (Rohloff and Capra 2009:48)

The neighborhood was so independent that it often resisted authority. There are numerous accounts of people outrunning cops by disappearing into the neighborhood. If you knew the roads and trails, you were as good as invisible. Even on the beach, residents could travel incognito from one end to the other on the roofs of the houses. People were allowed to live by their own rules, even if they were hardcore drug addicts and non-conformists. The following are three outrageous examples:

> George's Market was very close to some of the lanes, and the people who were really addicted to 'ludes, the sad cases, would crawl to it on a daily basis. Somebody would usually intervene on the way though and say, "Hey . . . I'll go to the store for you, bro. Just give me the money," so they wouldn't have to crawl the whole way. The village was so friendly, and everybody knew what biscuits did to you . . .
>
> I remember seeing some crawlers in the market that had made it all the way. They would just look up at the clerk and go, "Heyahsomemilk." And the market was so friendly too that they would help them. They knew what was going on. The addicts were accepted in the neighborhood. (Baretta 2006:16)

* * *

> . . . there was this PCP guy who was living naked on the roof below me. He didn't live in a room. The guy would eat only fruits and vegetables and be naked. And he wouldn't remove any of the peels, so it was like this bizarre debris of dried orange peels, and watermelon skins, and him naked doing PCP on the roof. (Tool 2007:41)

* * *

> And I remember once we got really deep in this bamboo forest, and all of a sudden we noticed there was a couch and a makeshift mini-house! That was my first time meeting Frank.
>
> Frank actually turned out to be one of the nicest guys to the kids. Our parents knew we were with him, and they knew he was basically harmless—which sounds trippy today. You'd be considered a molester or some weird freak for hanging out with kids like that now, but he never did anything. He just needed friends.

> My dad told me that Frank had been a scientist, a philosopher, and a professor at Ivy League schools . . . and then all of sudden Timothy Leary, acid, and the '60s happened. According to my dad, Frank had taken 100 hits at once, dropped out of the whole teaching profession, and ended up in The Snake Pit (where a lot of these people who had lost their minds would end up). He chose to stop living the "Big Brother" government way of life. He had no address, and was totally reclusive. I think he'd saved some money from his teaching days, and he had a rich family back east, so he had money coming in, but he still lived very meagerly on canned goods. (Rohloff and Capra 2009:13)

When the first lifeguards were brought to the beach at the transition to its going public, their rules were scorned—especially the ban on dogs. Tim Harvey built an alarm system that warned the whole beach to bring their dogs in whenever the dogcatcher was around. Eventually the dogs learned to run inside when the alarm rang, and the dogcatcher was stymied.

If surfers were fighting on the beach, they might prevent authorities from breaking up the fight.

> Ambulances showed up sometimes and then got scared off the beach, so they wouldn't pick anybody up. (Rohloff and Capra 2009:8).

There are actually reports of Wild West showdowns in The Snake Pit between gun-toting neighbors.

> They were more or less idle threats, but the guns were real, and they would shoot them off in the air sometimes, and I questioned my safety in this neighborhood that I had chosen. (Baretta 2006:23)

No wonder a few real outlaws liked this place. On the beach there lived a wild group nicknamed The Pirates. They were serious drug dealers, who were also wanted for armored robbery and killing a security guard.

> Their place was amazing. All the windows were blacked out, and the inside was lit purple with black lights like a nightclub. All the closets in the house had been turned into little orgy rooms. You opened the door, and there'd be a bed and a skylight in the roof . . . In the middle of the living room, on a table, there was a big

> bowl with every drug you could possibly imagine. They called them Monday through Friday specials. And on the weekends, they'd mix them up. Like, "Today I'm going to try a Thursday and a Friday special," or "a Monday/Wednesday combo." (Lovas & Capra 2011:26)

The neighborhood was also a hangout for a murderous biker gang called The Heathens, a rival of the Hell's Angels.

> The Heathens used to love to operate down in The Snake Pit around one or two in the morning. They rode gnarly Harleys—not nice, pristine, shiny ones but old Heathen ones put together with shoestring and tin cans—and they'd come in and ride, hooting and hollering, at night, scaring the locals out of their sleep. They'd be swooping around, pulling 360s, and the dust would be coming up like the Indians were going to attack. They had their adrenaline going, and who knows who they had fucked over, or killed, or beaten up earlier that evening. (Baretta 2006:31)

But the vilest outlaws (although no one knew it at the time) were Charles Manson's gang. They lived in a black bus in The Snake Pit, where Manson recruited a young girl named Diane "Snake" Lake and listened to The Beatles' *White Album* for the first time. Manson's son "Pooh Bear" was born there. Later, after a murder, the gang again took refuge in the neighborhood.

Fig. 6: Artist James Mathers scowls as the market is bulldozed.
Photo by Baretta, June 2003.

After all my research, here's what I think I learned from living in this neighborhood. I have a deep appreciation for art, and a communal approach to making it. I have a strong DIY ethic (although I'm not "rugged" enough to set a backfire or build a bridge). I think nonconformity is cool. Possessions don't carry status for me. I love surfing. I'm environmentally conscious. I'm suspicious of wolves in bohemians' clothing. I don't smoke, drink, or do drugs because I saw too many people struggle with addiction.

How have these values served me in life? I think mostly they've kept me healthy, honest, and positive. Finding my place in the outside world was a struggle and took me as far away as Germany, but I'm proud to have finally reached some stability in my 30s. However, I still long for those idle days that enticed me to explore my creativity, and hope to find a place that feels so much like home again.

The park that was meant to replace the neighborhood in 2006 never opened (some outlaws make the laws!). Several businesses still operate along the Pacific Coast Highway, but the rest of the land remains in an untended demolished-looking state. The beach is still a popular surfing spot, but only a fiery bougainvillea and a few pilings that protrude "Ozymandias"-like from the sand hint at the "wild life" that was once there.

> I'm glad it became a public beach instead of something else. They put in a nice parking lot. They have a lifeguard there to save you. There are no more cocktails on the beach. No smoking, dogs, nudity, or horses. No houses, no nothing. All those new rules, you get used to them . . . but, boy, we had a great time breaking them when we could! (Lovas and Capra 2011:43)

Southern California's Bohemian Surfers: Roots of American Counterculture

Kristin Lawler

When people think of the history of American bohemian communities, they tend to imagine midcentury beats in Greenwich Village or San Francisco, and trace the origin of American bohemia to iconic figures like Walt Whitman, Edna St. Vincent Millay, John Reed, Emma Goldman, and other artists, writers, and Communists hanging out at Village haunts in the late nineteenth and early twentieth centuries. Although all iterations of contemporaneous cultural uprisings are to some extent of a piece, there is, I argue, an independent history of American bohemia that deserves scholarly attention. Tracing its origin to early twentieth-century Waikiki, taking root in Southern California during the 1920s and the Depression, this subculture arguably became America's most enduring, compelling, and widely broadcast archetype of what bohemia represents—freedom from the repressions of everyday life in capitalist society. This essay will trace this highly influential and totally seminal piece of the history of bohemia in the United States. Although it is severely understudied by cultural historians, I argue that the southern California beach subculture deserves to be understood as a central iteration of American beat-hip bohemianism, and a powerful root of the liberatory strain of cultural politics in the United States.

An examination of these early surf communities, as represented in the popular press of the day as well as in the oral and especially photographic accounts of participants, shows that they mounted a form of collective lived resistance to the same kinds of restrictions that other, more widely acknowledged, bohemian communities did—the imperative to make paid work the center of everyday life and the manufactured material scarcity on which this imperative depends, the restrictions of traditional gender roles, and the techno-scientific logic that says that only the domination of nature by man will allow humans to thrive materially. The bohemian beach communities of the early (and later, mid-) twentieth century in California represent a powerful, countercultural resistance to that logic, and an affirmation of freedom, from work and from rigid masculine and feminine roles, of abundance, of collective leisure, and of ecological connection—all themes that became central to the explosion of countercultural sensibility in American society.

From the perspective of what is arguably most repressive about capitalist society—the cold logic of profit-making according to Marx; the Protestant work ethic and instrumental attitude to the lifeworld, including nature, that Weber lays out; and the regime of traditional gender roles criticized by feminist authors as profoundly limiting but functional for the reproduction of the class —the California surfer is countercultural through and through.

E.P. Thompson writes eloquently of the transformation in time sense and morality that was forced on the new working class with the advent of capitalist work discipline:

> Puritanism, in its marriage of convenience with industrial capitalism, was the agent which converted people to new valuations of time; which taught children even in their infancy to improve each shining hour; and which saturated people's minds with the equation, time is money. One recurrent form of revolt within Western industrial capitalism, whether bohemian or beatnik, has often taken the form of flouting the urgency of respectable time-values. (Thompson 1967:95)

For theorist Jock Young, countercultural lifeways oppose what he calls the "formal, official values of the workaday world" in contrast to the "subterranean values" that oppose them. In his 1971 study of *The Drugtakers*, Young deploys the psychoanalytic distinction between pleasure and reality principles elaborated in Marcuse's *Eros and Civilization* to bring the difference into sharp relief. The formal work values, or what he calls the "ethos of productivity," consist of: deferred gratification; planning future action; conformity to rules; routine and predictability; instrumental attitudes; and the moral valuation of hard, productive work. On the other hand, the subterranean values are: short-term hedonism; spontaneity; ego-expressivity; novelty and excitement; activities performed as ends in themselves; and disdain for work (Young 1971).

As described by Thompson, Young, and others, these bohemian sensibilities—broadly speaking, living for the moment, not by the clock—have been central to what California surf culture is all about. They run through the culture of the Hawaiian beach-boys culture who explicitly inspired it—a group of fun-loving, easy-living ukulele-playing surf instructors to the rich and famous who defined Waikiki beach in the early years of the twentieth century—to the first "beach bum" community in San Onofre during the 1920s and 1930s, to the 1950s Malibu surfers who explicitly emulated the world of "San O" and who were depicted in the 1959 film *Gidget*. *Gidget* broadcast the 1950s surf-shack Malibu subculture of tanned, shirtless, surf-and-party beat-hip bohemians on the beach to America at large; in its wake came scores of beach movies, television shows, advertisements, as well as an explosion of surf music, during the 1960s. The ethos of this subculture—pleasure rather than work as the center of life, libidinal freedom from repressive social mores, ecological connection, and an anti-authoritarian bent—is a generally unacknowledged but totally central piece of the countercultural explosion that defined 1960s America. Although the image of late 1950s Malibu is widely resonant, what most don't know is that the outlines of this subculture were formed far earlier, on the beaches of southern California during the twenties and thirties.

Unlike the early twentieth-century bohemian radicals of New York City, the surfer bohemians of California, with a few exceptions, didn't write about their lives. Instead, the documents of the subculture are mostly photographic, and in addition to the activity of surfing and the long periods hanging out on the beach between waves, looking at pictures of themselves and others (especially from Hawaii) was one of the big activities that cemented the solidarity of the group. In fact, surfing continues to be one of the most-photographed and filmed leisure pursuits in America. It has always been so; we can read the surviving sepia-toned photographs as a visual ethnography of one of the key subcultural roots of the American bohemian sensibility.

Although surfers were generally not writers themselves, the popular press of their day couldn't stop writing *about* them, and these press accounts provide more evidence of the southern California beach culture as a bohemian subculture foundational to the post-WWII countercultural explosion (and in many ways, outliving it). The fact that the early seed culture of surfing was written about in the popular press in the U.S. so frequently and with such breathless fascination speaks to the enduring appeal of surf culture in particular and of bohemian, countercultural lifestyles more generally. This press coverage also provides the cultural researcher more data on what the southern California surf bohemia was all about.

Several key elements of a bohemian ethos emerge from an examination of the surf photos and popular press of the early twentieth century: a certain primitivism that rejects modern efficiency, rationality, and alienation in favor of a mythical pre-capitalist culture seen as more free, less repressed, and more elementally connected to the abundance of the natural world and to other people (here the yielding, sharing, relaxed Hawaiian "aloha"); [1] the accompanying sexual freedom that has been central to all bohemian, countercultural challenges to conventional lifestyles; and, clearly related to the first two, the truly defining feature of all bohemias—literary, artistic, or otherwise—the countercultural refusal to make paid labor the center of life and relegate collective pleasures to the margins.

Surf culture in earnest began on the Hawaiian beach of Waikiki during the first years of the twentieth century. Beach developers and tourism promoters used the few Hawaiian surfers who remained after American Puritan missionaries (and the sugar planters whose economic interests were served by the pastors' rigid work morality) had basically extinguished Hawaii's vibrant and democratic surf culture, to sell Hawaii as a pleasure destination. Hawaiian male surf instructors called "beach boys" hung out on the beach, played ukulele, served as gigolos for wealthy women, performed a fantasy "ancient Polynesia" for tourists, and, most of all, surfed. The beach boys were deployed incessantly, and successfully, to promote the islands to wealthy mainlanders, so their image was spread far and wide in the U.S. during this time. Their image sold Hawaii, but it also inspired a generation of California surfers to emulate their lifestyle on the then-wild and relatively inaccessible beaches between San Diego and Malibu.

Also, Hawaiians like beach boy and Olympic swimming champion Duke Kahanamoku, and surfer life-saving hero George Freeth, came to southern California themselves and brought their subcultural ethos of freedom and pleasure in the moment with them. Tom Blake was a kid from Wisconsin who'd been inspired by an early 1920s news reel about, and then a chance meeting with, Kahanamoku, and in short order moved to Hawaii, photographed, and wrote about the native culture and the beach, and migrated back and forth between Hawaii and southern California for most of his adulthood. He took photos and wrote stories for *National Geographic, Life, Sunset,* and others, and wrote the seminal surf classic, 1935's *Hawaiian Surfboard*. Through his work, which included reproducing ancient Hawaiian surfboards, innovating new board designs, and inventing most of the life-saving devices still in use on beaches today, Blake was a key figure in the development of southern California surf culture and its explicit references to the relaxed and purportedly environmentally connected lifestyle of beachfront Hawaii. In addition, his personal style—rumpled blond hair, deep tan, loose bleached-out clothing—became the prototypical beachcomber look, still in effect today.

Fig. 1: Tom Blake at Diamond Head, Honolulu. Photo by Tom Blake, 1932.

Blake became a celebrity, known as "Ye Olde Beachcomber," and his relaxed, in-tune-with-nature lifestyle became forever linked with surf culture. This easygoing surfer lifestyle is broadcast in all Blake's work. In *Hawaiian Surfboard*, he writes that

> someone expresses my sentiments very well in these simple lines:

along the shore I wander, free,
a beach comber at Waikiki,
where time worn souls who seek in vain,
hearts ease, in vagrant, wondering train.

A beach comber from choice, am I,
Content to let the world drift by,
Its strife and envy, pomp and pride,
I've tasted, and am satisfied. (Blake 1935:40)

Blake's book, articles, and activities are largely credited with providing the inspiration for the California beach subculture that took hold on the coast during the 1920s, 1930s, and early 1940s. Although the first printing of Blake's 1935 *Hawaiian Surfboard* was very limited, the book was extremely influential because of who read it. It's been said of the Velvet Underground that only a few thousand people bought their first album, but each one of them started a band. The impact of *Hawaiian Surfboard* is similar. It wasn't exactly a best-seller, but many who did read it moved to the beach and gave birth to the surfing counterculture in California.

These young (mostly) men were hugely inspired by Tom Blake, in whom the Polynesian fantasy and counterculture came together and were broadcast for all to see.[1] In the words of Blake biographer Gary Lynch: "Tom Blake is the obvious link between the ancient South Pacific watermen and the twentieth-century Anglo watermen . . . he understood and adopted the aloha frame of mind . . . at the same time Albert Einstein was finishing his accepted e=mc2 theory, Tom Blake was carving 'Nature=God' into the sandy bluffs of what is now Malibu . . ."(Lynch, quoted in Kampion, 2003a:45), and long-time *Surfer* magazine writer and editor Drew Kampion says of Blake: "vegetarian and pantheistic, he was the prototype for an emerging lifestyle" (Kampion 2003b:45).

Blake was the organic intellectual of the early surfer, making explicit and circulating their reverence for ancient Hawaii, and for nature, and their disdain for "normal" ways of life. According to Tommy Zahn, a protégé of Blake's and a famous fifties surfer in his own right,

> Tom has seen it all. He was the most significant link between Hawaii and U.S. mainland surfing—much more than George Freeth or Duke . . . in his lifetime, Blake has emerged as a bona fide cult figure . . . one aspect of his lifestyle was . . . giving yourself more time, more *freedom*—and freedom is a big part of what Blake is all about. His life was not . . . cluttered up with all the garbage of the basic nine to five trap . . . (Zahn, in Lynch and Gault-Williams 2001:184)

Along with Blake's many, widely broadcast photos, the most important archives from this early era are the photographs taken by two other surfers: Don James and John Heath "Doc" Ball. Together, the work of these men provides a rich portrait of the seed that was planted by the Hawaiian beachboys and that eventually— after the interruption of WWII, which closed off much of the beach and drafted many of the men, but also exposed legions of young men to beach culture in the Pacific as well as to new, lightweight materials that could be used for surfboards—flowered into a full-on California surf counterculture during the 1950s.

Both James and Ball credit Blake as their inspiration for beginning to surf, and to document the surf life that they were living. According to Don James, "When I saw Tom Blake's surfing photos in *National Geographic* that was it. We'd go to the library and pore over Blake's stuff . . ." (James 1996:11). Doc Ball, in a recent interview, said that

> Tom Blake was one of my idols—he was a hero to me—the reason for all this was that he had a set of pictures, he photographed surfers surfing there at Waikiki Beach, printed in the *Los Angeles Times*—I just about flipped my lid—I put them under a glass tabletop and looked at them every day and thought—I gotta get some of this. Thomas, he was an inspiration to me, the way he lived and the way he took those pictures and everything . . . (Ackerman 1999)

James and Ball influenced the growth of the culture with their photos, just as Blake had. According to surf historian Craig Stecyk, "A claim can be made that [Don James] is the best known surfing photographer of all time . . ." He shot covers for *Vogue* and *Der Spiegel*, and contributed to *Time, The Saturday Evening*

Post, Honolulu, and *Sports Illustrated,* as well as "national television, billboards, and advertising campaigns" (James 1996:18).

Ball's photos were similarly world-renowned: they were published in *Life, Parade, Panorama, Encyclopedia Brittanica, National Geographic,* and the *London Daily Mirror*. According to Doc, he published his seminal 1946 collection, *California Surfrider,* because "the kids started demanding the photos that I took of them—so I figured I'd get all the negatives together and make a book" (Ackerman 1999). Like the beach boys who came before them, surfers have always loved posing for the camera and watching themselves on film, which is why a major part of surf culture involves watching footage of other surfers, and always has. For instance, Doc describes the founding of the legendary Palos Verdes Surfing Club in the late 1920s as being primarily for the purpose of watching the moving films of surfing that Doc himself was taking. His 16mm film, also titled *California Surfrider*, contains some of the most compelling early moving footage of surfing's halcyon days.

Like the Hawaiian beach boys revered by these surfers, the men in the photographs are not constricted by a dominating or austere masculinity. They are strong, powerful, and secure enough to frequently act downright feminine. In fact, several of the pictures are nothing if not homoerotic. Although most just represent a more often than not homosocial world of men enjoying the company of other men, drinking beer, playing music, eating, laughing, and, above all, surfing, several take the gender-bending of surf culture a bit further. One especially striking photo from the 1930s looks onto three naked surfers posing like pinups, lying next to one another on the sand. Looking back on the photo, Don James commented in 1996 that "this . . . bathing beauties parody has caused three decades of surfing magazine editors to recoil in disgust . . ." (James 1996, 110) and goes on to identify one of the "beauties" as Bill Bridgeman, who later appeared on the cover of *Time* magazine in his role as a well-known American fighter pilot.

Fig. 2. The "bathing beauties" photo, Point Dume, California. Don James, 1942.

Another photo shows two surfers dancing gracefully atop a beached surfboard; they both face the camera, and the man in the rear has his hands on the hips of the foregrounded man. Both have their legs and feet in a graceful sort of curtsy (James 1996:92). Yet another shows three smiling boys lying on the beach, two of whose half-naked bodies are entangled in a languid pose (James 1996:34). In Doc Ball's film, we see two surfers, each on his own board, maneuver the boards close to one another and then ride the wave in together, holding hands (Ackerman 1999). Other examples of an utter lack of the insecure, defensive machismo that anchors the capitalist reproductive apparatus of the twentieth century nuclear family are ubiquitous, especially in the surfers' decidedly un-masculine habit of constantly posing for the camera. Waikiki beach-boy culture is echoed in the feminized posing, the comfort and pleasure that the surfers take in being the one beheld, the object rather than the originator of the admiring gaze at the half-naked body. The surfers are frequently seen posing on their boards, self-consciously enjoying surfing *and* being watched surfing. All of these feminine images are surrounded by more typically masculine images of giant "bone-crushing monster" waves being ridden by fearless, strong, powerful men. In the early photos, just as in the images of the Hawaiian beach boys, powerful watermen *and* paid sex objects, the masculine and the feminine flow into one another.

Fig. 3. Masculinity and femininity in balance, with beer. Laguna Beach, California. Don James, exact year unknown, between 1936-1942.

As was the case in Hawaii, this is true for the women in the photos as much as it is for the men. Women, although not nearly as heavily represented in the photos (or among the "beachcombers"), are represented according to both typically feminine and more masculine signifiers. One particularly telling photo depicts three ukelele players on the sand, two men and one woman. In the foreground of the photo, facing the musicians, another woman, this one in a bikini, dances a hula-like dance in front of them. Here the woman is free to play both the masculine—generator, beholder, subject—and feminine—dancing, beheld, objectified—roles (James 1996: 50), and everybody looks like they're having a pretty good time with the relative freedom from compulsory gender identities that seems to flow on the beach.

Fig. 4. Performing and gender play on the beach, San Onofre. Don James, 1939.

Another photo, this one taken by Doc Ball, is a perfectly lit glamour shot of a young woman in a bikini. Her hair is done, and she's posing like a Hollywood pinup. According to Doc, "she could have gotten a job in the movies with that picture" (Ball, 1946:47). It seems a typical depiction of the period's conventional femininity, until we realize that this woman is Mary Ann Hawkins, widely acknowledged to have been the best female surfer on the coast during those years, and just as strong and talented a surfer as the boys. The other photos of Hawkins show her in what was clearly her more usual stance—strong and joyful, riding a 100-pound surfboard at 30 or 40 miles per hour, the men looking on admiringly. Other photos of men and women tandem surfing show the male and female as equals on the board. The women are free to play with the pleasure of the masculine and the feminine, just as the men are.

Clearly, the sexual freedom associated with American bohemia was alive and well on the early twentieth-century California beach: overtly sexual pleasures rule as well as all the other libidinal freedoms in effect. Many of the photos and the footage in Doc's film depict men and women in positions that would have been considered quite scandalous for the time, when, according to Cliff Tucker, the 1940 state surfing champion, "a *man* could still be arrested at Santa Monica Beach for not wearing a top" (Lueras 1984:109). Everyone is half naked, and several photos show men and women lying on the beach together, kissing. There are also several shots—similar to ones from Waikiki beach, and quite racy for the era—of a man and woman together on a board, paddling out on their stomachs together with the woman in front and the man's smiling face right between her spread legs (Ackerman 1999).

The documentary evidence is clear that the lifestyle these few hundred pre-WWII surfers embraced went counter to the spirit of hard work and competitive individualism that defines bourgeois values. They made the beach, not the factory or the office, the center of their lives. They surfed all day, every day, and lived off the fat of the land, gleaning ripe fruit from picked-over orchards and pulling abalone and lobster from the sea for nightly campfire dinners. They sold their time for money—on Hollywood films, running rum during Prohibition, and fishing for the local fancy restaurants—only when they needed cash for gasoline or beer.

Fig. 5. Collective leisure. Don James, exact year and location unknown, Southern California between 1936-1942.

In fact, in addition to the ubiquitous Polynesian references—the thatched hut shacks, the straw hats, the ukuleles—and the quite radical gender-bending, what's most apparent from even a casual perusal of these photos is the simple abundance that surrounded the subculture. This theme is related to the others, in that part of the embrace of the image of primitive freedom from repression is an acceptance of the idea of natural abundance. This contrast— to the artificial scarcity that capital needs to perpetuate in order to keep people working, striving, stressed, doing what they're told—is particularly striking given that so many of these photographs were taken during the Great Depression. Scarcity was the order of the day. As far as most Americans were given to understand, the *entire world* had been plunged into *massive crisis*. There simply *was not enough* for everyone. But for the surfers, things were different. According to Stecyk, "Don [James] recounted tales of catching reef fish and pulling huge abalone and twenty-pound lobsters from the sea that were then boiled over beach fires. He and his friends would raid orange groves for all the fruit they could eat" (Stecyk, in James, 1996:11). The Great Depression was supposed to have quashed the irresponsible exuberance that characterized the Roaring Twenties. Americans, who'd spent the twenties living on credit and embracing the spectacular new consumer culture, were now to weather the crisis times of high unemployment with a newfound austerity. It seems that news, though, didn't make it out to the beach.

The surfers' "bohemianism of enough" was countercultural during the roaring capitalism of the twenties; it was positively radical during the Depression. When material scarcity was the order of the day, the surfers enjoyed a primitive affluence in the sense in which Marshall Sahlins discusses in "The Original Affluent Society." Debunking commonly-held notions about the life of scarcity lived by hunting and gathering societies, Sahlins argues that these simple societies had more abundance than our own, since people had everything that they needed. They didn't collect surplus items, food or otherwise, because "things" weighed them down, but even more important, they consumed everything in the moment because they assumed abundance rather than scarcity. That is, the hunter-gatherers knew that there would always be more, so they just enjoyed whatever they had. In contrast, in our society—purportedly with so "much"— insecurity and economic anxiety are the norm for most people. Capitalism's manufactured scarcity fuels the imperative to work; refusing it is key to challenging the regime of endless work and eternally deferred gratification central to capitalist culture (Sahlins 1972).

Fig. 6. Self-portrait of primitive affluence, Point Dume. Don James, 1942.

When the surfers did need money, generally for gasoline to drive up or down the coast to another remote beach in search of waves, the "locals who knew both the lay of the land and the nuances of the sea always found lucrative employment functioning as guides, facilitators, and transporters in the underground economy" of the illegal import trade. During the 20s, this had meant running booze from Canadian boats to movie stars hanging out at the coast, and from that time forward "enterprising surf fishermen filled orders for copious amounts of lobster, crab, and fish for top restaurants, studio parties, and society dinners." Also, many of the guys were lifeguards during the summer, when, according to Stecyk, "there was no lifeguarding profession to speak of . . ." (Stecyk, in James, 1996:11).

Of course, there were always the movies. Surfing actors like Kahanamoku, Buster Crabbe, Peter Lawford, and Johnny Weismuller hooked up their buddies with day jobs on films, with which, according to Don James, "you could pocket a hundred bucks a day" (Stecyk, in James 1996:14). Here was continued the revered surfer tradition, begun by Hawaii beach boys and continued today by pro surfers, of making money for being what you are primarily, a surfer. "The life" always comes before the work world, to which it makes no concessions. (Here is where the term "surf bum" originated. According to Doc Ball, "we sort of developed a whole new language—that was why people called us 'surf bums' and everything—they couldn't understand our language, I guess . . .").

The most prized entity among these surfers couldn't be bought anyway. Waves were in abundance on the southern California coast, and the energy to ride them came easy, from peaches and avocados plucked out of roadside orchards, and from the abundant fruit of the sea. Several of the photos show smiling surfers holding giant lobsters fully half their size, or depict scores of young people, women and men, gathered happily around a campfire, feasting on seafood as boys play ukeleles and the group sings. These photos are, it goes without saying, in stark contrast to the more familiar Depression-era images of dirty, haggard faces and breadlines.

Doc Ball had this to say about how surfers were affected by the Depression: "well, as far as surf was concerned, not really. Of course, we had a little trouble getting gasoline, but then it was 7-cents a gallon in those days . . . it [the Depression] kept us kinda limited in certain ways, but we had surfin' to take care of everything. Long as there's waves, why, you didn't have to pay for those. All we had to do was buy the gas to get there" (Ackerman 1999).

Above all, the refusal of work is the central theme present in the image of the surfer. More than anything, it's made up of a privileging of play over work, the image of a life constructed in the countercultural manner of centering on a leisure pursuit and relegating paid employment to the margins of one's existence. From Hawaii to California, the most prominent characteristic of the surfer is the fact that paid employment never wins against good waves: "round Honolulu run the words 'big surf' and early in the afternoon young men desert the offices." A 1942 *Christian Science Monitor* article entitled "Humper!" highlights the employment habits of the surfers. "They work, those who are not yet in military service, in the post offices, the stores, theatres, the fishing tackle and bait shops, and anywhere there are jobs not more than a half mile, by preference, from the surf. Such a [rough] sea becomes an automatic holiday for experts such as these"(Arms 1942).

The setting of all these images on the beach is key to the sense of plenty that they evoke. Besides representing an abundance that feeds the refusal of alienated labor, the image of the beach and its natural abundance has an ecological component as well. Since the construction of "the beach" in American culture as a meaningful and desirable space, just before the turn of the last century, it's been defined as totally "other" to the routine alienation of the civilized world. It's where we all indulge our inner primitive—the sand in our bare feet, the sun and salt water on our bare skin. If America's newly industrial cities were the spaces of work, the beach was explicitly coded as a space of play, and specifically of play with a benevolent natural world. Days on the beach are long and langorous, and what makes the hours on the beach so pleasurable—the sun, the sand, and the waves—is endlessly renewed, without human toil or industry. The images that we see coming from early twentieth-century California evoke this free, joyful, relaxed connection with nature.

Another theme that greets the peruser of the early surfing photographs is also a profoundly countercultural one: surfing life as a collective, connected life, in contrast to the competitive individualism and alienation that were increasingly coming to define the industrialized, modern spaces of American life. Even the many shots of surfers riding waves more often than not depict several surfers riding a wave together. Men and women surf together, sing together, eat together, road-trip in beat-up, surfboard-laden cars together, camp on the beach together, and, more than anything else, are seen laughing together. Just as we saw in the representations of that time, the surfer life is depicted as one of collective frolic, play, and pleasure.

For instance, a photo spread in the *Los Angeles Times Sunday Supplement* during 1931 entitled "Riders of Sunset Seas" features a Tom Blake photo of four male surfers about to catch a wave. This is certainly similar to the earlier images of the Hawaii beach boys, much of whose pleasure in life was depicted as coming from their tightly-knit group, singing and drinking together, hanging out at the beach together, and so on (*L.A. Times*, 1931). Surfers were reflected to the public as a collective basically as soon as they became one on the California coast. Much of the earliest press coverage of the California surfers had covered them in their capacity as lifeguards, the only profession that allowed them to basically live on the beach and surf whenever the waves were good. They were usually described as dashing heroes, and in many of the photos that accompanied the brief stories, the early surfer look comes through: men, on the beach, standing in front of their surfboards, tan, strong, frequently laughing, and nearly always photographed as a group (Lynch and Gault-Williams 2001:120, 121, 115, 116, 117). What's reflected is what Roy Rosenzweig calls a working-class ethos of collectivity made up of countercultural values of mutuality, solidarity, and rowdy fun, which are in stark contrast to the Puritan work ethic and competitive individualism encouraged by the bosses.

Fig. 7. All together on the wave, Palos Verdes. Don James, 1937.

In an early nod to the power of the moving image of surfing to inspire new surfers to join the tribe, Doc Ball said of the Palos Verdes Surfing Club that "when we got that club going, it began to attract college kids, and high school kids, and they'd come down to see what was going on, and pretty soon they were stoked . . ." (Ackerman 1999). The images of these early surfers had commercial beach developers and tourism advertisers to disseminate them, as well as surfers themselves. The upshot was that, with the interruption of the war years (when all surfers were either drafted into the service or dodged the draft, and the beaches themselves were locked down and militarized, but also when the new technologies that would revolutionize board design and make possible the mass production and mass use of surfboards were developed), a massive beach subculture grew that would take American popular culture by storm once postwar affluence, the baby boom, and the rise of a youth market were added to the mix.

By the 1950s, the center of gravity had moved definitively from San Onofre to the beach shack at Malibu, where its denizens, Terry "Tubesteak" Tracey, Miki Dora, Dale Velzy, and several hundred other surfers, male and female, were immortalized in the 1957 novel and 1959 film, *Gidget*. Gidget, a.k.a. Kathy Kohner, was a young Angeleno from the Valley whose surf-stoked coming of age among the beat-hip bohemians of Malibu was documented by her father, Frederick, a Hollywood writer. The subculture described in the novel and broadcast in the film was of a piece with the primitive abundance, Polynesian references, focus on collective play and leisure, and culture of libidinal freedom that Depression-era surfers had forged, and which became a key building block of American counterculture. It's largely ignored, though, in descriptions of the counterculture, although the historical record indicates that the prewar California surf scene was an independent source of the beat-hip bohemian counterculture that, it can be argued, transformed American culture in the second half of the twentieth century.

Fig. 8. The original California beach party, San Onofre. Don James, 1937.

Still, acknowledging the early California surfers as seminal to the bohemian thread of American culture is not only about getting the record straight. As I show in my book *The American Surfer* (Lawler 2011), from Hawaii to San Onofre to Malibu to *Gidget* and onward, every amplification of the countercultural image of an imagined primitive past, of play, and of freedom represented by the archetype of the surfer resulted in more and more people becoming inspired to take up the liberated lifestyle themselves. Our imagination, our historical memory, even our fantasies of the past, can have material import.

This is because there is an intimate relationship between memory and desire, one that produces action aimed at recouping the pleasure that's been lost with "reality" but the memory of which is never erased. The more this memory is pumped up, the more chance that it will burst through civilized repression and push for real pleasure and freedom *now*. Herbert Marcuse is eloquent on this point:

> [Memory's] truth value lies in the specific function of memory to preserve promises and potentialities which are betrayed and even outlawed by the mature, civilized individual, but which had once been fulfilled in his dim past and which are never entirely forgotten. The reality principle restrains the cognitive function of memory—its commitment to the past experience of happiness which spurns the desire for its conscious re-creation. The . . . liberation of memory explodes the rationality of the repressed individual. As cognition gives way to re-cognition, the forbidden images and impulses of childhood begin to tell the truth that reason denies. Regression assumes a progressive function. The rediscovered past yields critical standards which are tabooed by the present . . . The liberation of the past does not end in its reconciliation with the present. Against the self-imposed restraint of the discoverer, the orientation on the past tends toward an orientation on the future. The *recherché du temps perdu* becomes the vehicle of future liberation. (Marcuse 1955:19)

For those of us who see the bohemian cultural politics of freedom in everyday life as an enduring challenge to the most exploitative and alienating aspects of capitalist society, let's hope so. In any case, the accepted narrative of the roots of beat-hip bohemianism in American society has been missing what I see as one of its keystones, and it's high time to correct the story.

Endnotes

[1] "Acquaintances in the States have asked me why I bury myself in the Hawaiian islands. The reason is because I like it. It fits my nature, it is life's compensation for a nature such as mine. I like it because I can live simple and quietly here . . . I can dress as I please, for comfort . . . I can keep one hundred per cent sun tan here the year around, rest and sleep for hours in the wonderful sunshine each day . . . I like it because of the natural beauty of everything here, the very blue sky, very white clouds, very green mountains, clothed in foliage to their ridges. My greatest pleasure in life is through my eyes so why should I stay around Main Street or Broadway? The coco palms waving in the clean trade winds, the colors of the water on the coral reef, greet my eyes each day as I near the beach and when the giant waves of the Kalahuewehe surf are breaking white, far from shore, it means royal sport is waiting and I actually break into a run to get to the Outrigger Club, don trunks and get out my favorite surfboard of teak wood . . . " (Blake 1935: 40-41).

Photography credits

Fig 1: Photo from the Tom Blake Collection courtesy of the Surfing Heritage and Culture Center. Fig. 2-7: Photo courtesy of T. Adler Books and the estate of Don James

Bohemia in Malibu: A Hidden Treasure

Jay Ruby [1]

INTRODUCTION

When people hear the word Malibu, images of surfers and wealthy people living in mega-mansion beach houses emerge. Those living in the same locale who have chosen to live outside the mainstream are frequently overlooked. Southern California's beaches and canyons make it easy to maintain an informal lifestyle (see "Introduction" for details). It is often hard to see the difference between the sun-tanned, long-haired man in shorts and a tee shirt, who happens to be a high-priced corporate lawyer and lives in an expensive condo, from an artist in the same community living in a rambling, weather-beaten rental. Both enjoy the benefits of the climate and geography of southern California even if they literally live in different worlds.

Like other essays in this book, this discussion is designed to demonstrate that southern California has had a long and interesting history of bohemians and bohemian communities. It will discuss *Coffee House Positano, 1957-1962*—one manifestation of bohemian Malibu (Ruby 2012) that until quite recently was known only to those who had lived there or who happened to visit.

In 1957, Mike Dutton, a radio/television pioneer, and his wife, Lorees Yerby Dutton, an aspiring writer, opened a coffee house on the southern border of Malibu. They had moved from New York when Mike became a producer for Lux Video Theater. They rented a ramshackle house on 130+ acres of undeveloped chaparral on a cliff above the Pacific Coast highway. As there was no equivalent in Los Angeles to the compact urban neighborhood of the Village, Lorees had to create an approximation in "rural" Malibu by finding creative people who resided all over Los Angeles county and inviting them to her new "home/coffee house" as customers and participants. There were transplanted theater people residing in Malibu, such as John Houseman, actor/director, who became Lorees' writing mentor. Gloria Sokol and her husband, David Stone-Martin, art director, were Malibu neighbors and friends of Mike and Lorees in New York. An actress who appeared in the

1954 New York revival of *The Threepenny Opera,* Gloria Stone-Martin was a close, supportive friend of Lorees in the early formation of Positano. David, who created the famous image of "Mack The Knife" used in *The Threepenny Opera,* generously gave the drawing to the Duttons to use as their logo. Positano was formed, in part, to recreate the semblance of an arts community and creative lifestyle Lorees had left behind.

Fig. 1: Sunday on the veranda at Coffee House Positano. Jay Ruby

They bought an Italian espresso machine, collected an assortment of second-hand tables and chairs, added a second room, and on July 12, 1957, Coffee House Positano opened. For the next five years, the Duttons shared their living space with a coffee house.

Fig. 2: Meals for the Duttons were held at one of Positano's chess tables

The Duttons sent out an invitation to a few people Mike knew from work and people Lorees met in Malibu. It was all that was needed to attract a public. Positano became a success even with no highway sign to indicate where it was located. The Duttons only advertised once when they opened Playhouse Positano in 1960. In the very strict sense of the word, Positano was an underground establishment. People learned of its existence by word of mouth. For some, knowing about Positano became a sign that one was hip and informed.

Oh, do ye but meet
with a friend to your Mind,
A joyous Companion
the right sort of Kind,
Then together steal out
and range up the hill,
Drink the black Coffee
and Eat to your fill
Oh there you will see
all the Gentlemen Rakes

And hear the Sweet Cry
of Sandwiches and Cakes
while the Maids in their way
in their bright summer Gowns
Do allure the fine sparks
from the flirts of the Town

There's Chess and there's Darts
and Pastries and Cheese
the Coffee is Hot
and soft is the Breeze
There's art and there's Music
There's most every Warm Sight
So take up your Pleasure
and join us this Night

FOR HEATING THE STOMACK

Espresso	30c
Roman Espresso	50c
Russian Coffee	50c
Cappuccino	50c
Darjeeling Tea	35c
Quenching Waters	35c

TO WAKETH THE PALATE

Positano Pastries

Mushroom Sandwiches & Others

Fair Fruits with Pungent Cheeses

Ices Creams

FOR THE
BETTER ACCOMODATION
and
EASE of the PEOPLE
and the
UNIVERSAL BENEFIT
of the
COMMONWEALTH
in point of

PUBLIC INTERCOURSE

At the sign of the Rancho Budwood, in old Malibu, ** 19453 Pacific Coast Highway ... the drink called COFFEE IS TO BE SERVED at eight of the clock in the evening until most late from Friday through Sunday, which is very wholesom and Physical drink, having many excellent vertues, closes the Orifice of the Stomack, fortifies the heat within, helpeth Digestion, Quickneth the Spirits, and maketh the heart lightsom.

Fig. 3: Invitation

To reach the coffee house you parked along the highway. The only sign you were there was the sight of other parked cars. You waited at the bottom of the driveway for the VW microbus to take you up to a parking lot.

Fig. 4: The driveway to Coffee House Positano

Next you traversed a gravel path, climbed a few stairs, and opened a door to a dimly lit room with mismatched old tables and chairs. You had arrived at Positano where there was a host of possibilities: one could order an espresso or cappuccino, choose a sandwich or dessert, and people-watch for hours or participate in a large variety of artistic and intellectual activities.

While the orientation of the coffee house was fundamentally urban, that is, focused on what was happening in the world of art, politics, and ideas (see below for details), the setting was pastoral. Once you were up the cliff, the rest of the world disappeared. One could not see the electric poles or wires or hear the highway and the cars below. On one side, there was Santa Monica Bay and, on a clear day, the Channel Islands. Turn your back and you saw the underbrush, trees, and then the foothills. The building itself was poorly constructed with peeling paint and sagging doors. Inside was an ménage of junk-shop tables and chairs. The staff was attired in basic California causal: sandals, shorts, no suits, and no ties.

Fig. 5: Menu cover

Depending on the night, someone might be playing jazz piano or folk guitar, never any rock and roll. If you were a chess player, several tables were available. There might be a performance of a play or an author reading from a new publication or someone giving an informal lecture. If you wandered into Bookstore Positano, titles associated with Beat and bohemian literature and others were available.

Fig. 6: Mike talking to a customer in front of bookstore

Positano differed from other Los Angeles coffee houses. They were located in an urban neighborhood, an easy-to-find place with parking close by. No one could accidently discover Positano while walking. It was a dangerous and foolish activity at night. Other establishments tended to appeal mainly to a young crowd and were often focused on folk music.

MEMBERSHIP, MEMBERS, AND BULLETINS

The almost immediate popularity of Positano prompted the Duttons to create a membership structure. People could visit only three times before joining. The fee was modest, at first only $5 per year. By 1962, there were over 2,500 members. One of the rewards of membership was a monthly bulletin detailing scheduled activities.

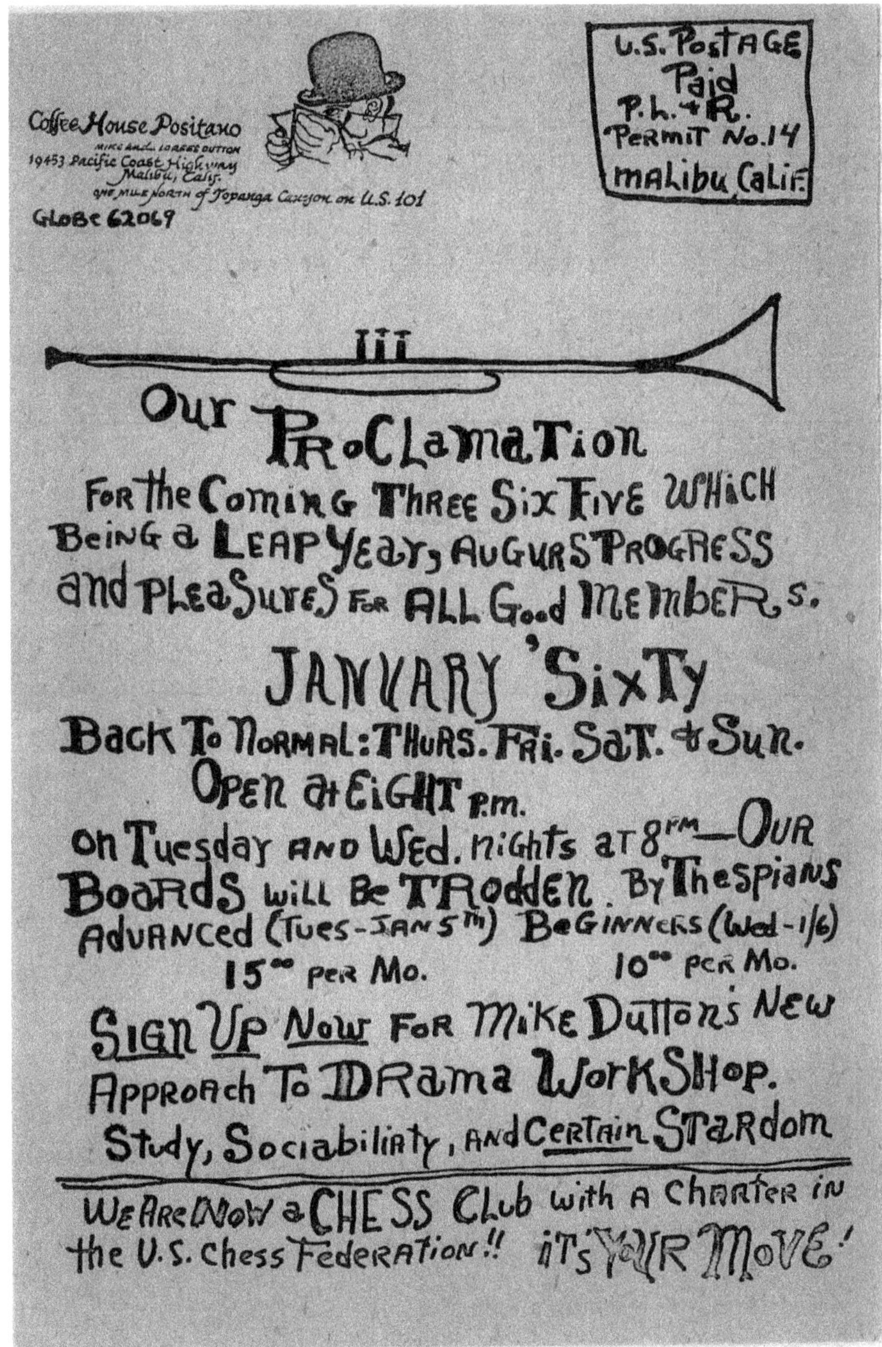

Fig. 7: Positano Bulletin, January-February, 1960

People in the entertainment business, particularly those living in the Malibu area, frequented the place: David and Gloria Stone Martin, Dudley Murphy, John Howard Larson, Barbara Bel

Geddes, and John Houseman, to name a few. Some people from the European exile community, including Aldous Huxley and Christopher Isherwood, also visited. Allen Ginsberg, Gregory Corso, and other Beat poets came down from San Francisco when they appeared at the trial of Big Daddy Eric Nord and The Gashouse (Maynard 1991), and stopped by. Hollywood actors and actresses such as Jane Fonda, Jane Russell, Lee Marvin, comedian Mort Saul, and even Rock Hudson were also sighted. The policy of the Duttons was to ignore celebrities so that they could enjoy themselves without being hassled. As a result, listing all of the "famous" people is impossible.

THINGS TO DO WHILE VISITING POSITANO

Positano offered some of the same things other coffee houses did: exotic coffees, desserts, sandwiches, chess games, art works on display, a bookstore, poetry readings, and a place to hang out where the wait staff would not hassle you to buy more or get out. However, the Duttons offered an amazing array of activities not commonly found: avant garde theater performances, evenings of political debate, writers reading from their work, and university professors and others speaking on a vast array of topics. On days when Positano was closed, classes in voice, drawing, and language were offered. This was made possible partially because Mike had been in radio, television, and the theater since the 1920s and knew a great number of people whom he could ask to direct a play or in other ways perform. Lorees had been politically active in New York and continued to be so in Malibu. She was also an aspiring writer and interested in the theater. She sought out people she thought to be interesting. With their combined interests and knowledge, the Duttons were able to entice people to come to Positano as performers or speakers. None was ever paid.

Fig. 8: Mike and Lorees waiting tables

The following is a summary of those activities that made Positano unique among the coffee houses in Los Angeles and perhaps all such establishments in the U.S.:

> CHESS was very popular. Positano was a member of the U.S. Chess Foundation. Sometimes formal competitions were available, but more often one simply found a partner and started a game. At times, the players didn't even bother to introduce themselves or speak.
>
> MUSIC – Jazz and folk music was unannounced, spontaneous, and free. People simply appeared, played, and left. On Sunday mornings, musicians from bars in Malibu would come to Positano after the bars closed. While the place was technically not open, the Duttons allowed the musicians to stay and jam. Peter Evans, the son of Frank Evans, the M.C. of "Frankly Jazz" FM program and an old friend of Mike's, was brought to Positano when he was a teenager and a novice flamenco guitarist. Over time, Peter became quite accomplished, even visiting and learning from some of the masters in Spain. Peter's performances were the only ones announced in the bulletin.

Fig. 9: Jazz at Positano

ART – The Duttons offered the walls of the coffee house as space where artists could informally display their work and offer it for sale. While Keith Finch, an accomplished Abstract Expressionist painter, exhibited several times, most were at the start of their careers: Dale Harrison, John S. Farrow, Ed Pagac, Barbara Talman, Tom Ryan, and Leon Levy.

POETRY READINGS - While less common than other performances, there were some readings. Neal Oxenhandler, a UCLA French professor, offered some Rimbaud. Painter Ed Pagac and Jay Ruby performed some obscure and not very good poetry with the Wanderberg Jazz Quartet. In 1959, Allan Raitt, a coffee-house employee, read some of his early poetry that was published by the Duttons. With Raitt's work, the Duttons started a small journal, *Public Intercourse*. It folded after a single issue, the beginning and end of Positano Press.

POLITICAL TALKS AND DISCUSSIONS - Positano offered a wide array of topics and speakers, from Murray Chotiner, Nixon's campaign manager, to Al Lewis, Executive Secretary of the Fair Play for Cuba Committee debating Manuel Gonzales, UCLA, about the Cuban revolution. Israel was often a topic: Yaacov Nash, Israel's Consulate General, Fereidoun

Esfandiary, a transhumanist philosopher, and Rabbi Jacob Ott all presented, at different times, their ideas. The Duttons organized a panel discussion, "How To Combat the Communist Menace," with Paul Talbert, the John Birch Society, Herbert Dinerstein, Rand Corporation's Russian expert, and Jerry Pacht, an attorney. Talbert never showed up, apparently too afraid of the audience. Edward Kneifel, former German soldier who fought the Russians, offered a conservative idea about "How To Combat Communism." Bob Baker, secretary of the Socialist Labor Party, talked about "What is Socialism?" Philip Wright of SSM and Dr. William F. Quinn, A.M.A., debated "Should America Have Socialized Medicine?"

GENERAL INTEREST TALKS ranged from the profound to pop. Authors such as Ray Bradbury (*October Country*) and Lawrence Lipton (*The Holy Barbarians*) read from their new works. Academics/intellectuals presented their ideas about a variety of things, for example, philosopher Byron Pumphrey on "A Summary View of General Semantics"; Gerald Heard, historian and philosopher, on "The Intellectuals' Last Chance?"; Hans Myerhoff, UCLA philosopher, on "The Philosophy of History in our Time;" , Theater Arts, UCLA, on "The Living Theater: Yesterday, Today and Tomorrow"; and Council Taylor, UCLA anthropologist, on "Sub-Culture – Genuine or Spurious or Is the American Beatnik an Imitation Negro," and "Negritude: Is Black Supremacy Coming or Is It Here?" On the lighter side, Jacob Zeitlin, Los Angeles antiquarian dealer, presented his "Reminiscences of the Book Trade"; Adela Rogers St. John spoke about her career in journalism; Dobyns Zipporah, astrologer, offered her views on "Is Astrology a Science?"; Valentine Davies, President of the Academy of Motion Picture Arts and Sciences, answered questions about the awards and Hollywood in general; and finally, John Guedel, producer of Groucho Marx's television show, *You Bet Your Life*, discussed the state of American television.

THEATRICAL PRODUCTIONS - Prior to the advent of Playhouse Positano, performances of one-act or excerpts from three-act plays were a regular occurrence. Here is a partial list: George Bernard Shaw's *St. Joan*, Cocteau's *Human Voice*, Arrabal's *The*

Two Executioners, Horton Foote's *Young Lady of Property,* Edward Albee's *The Zoo Story,* Samuel Beckett's *Krapp's Last Tape,* Christopher Fry's *A Phoenix Too Frequent*. Elizabethe did a concert reading of a Frank Stockton short story, "The Tiger and the Lady," Auguste performed as the Surrealist Pantomimist, and there was a staged reading of "A Non-Musical Feiffer" with Susan Barnes, Dave DePaul, and Frank Mahony. Perhaps the most esoteric theatrical venture was a production of Pablo Picasso's 1941 one-act play, *Desire Trapped by the Tail.*

Fig. 10: Desire Trapped by The Tail

INSTRUCTION/WORKSHOPS – On Wednesdays when Positano was closed, classes/workshops were offered at a modest fee. Saul Bernstein taught a life drawing class, and Keith Finch presented life drawing, water color, and design courses; Bryon Pumphrey offered a ten-session course in general semantics, and Mike Dutton held a New Approach to Drama workshop.

> PLAYHOUSE POSITANO - The Duttons opened Playhouse Positano on July 12, 1959, with George Bernard Shaw's *The Shewing Up of Blanco Posnet.* For a time, admission was either one sofa or one chair. Later an actual admission in dollars was established. Among the Playhouse's offerings were: George Bernard Shaw's *Catherine the Great*, *All She Wanted*, a musical revue, and *Everyman Revisited*: *A Modern Adaptation* of the old morality play, directed by John Houlton. Even though the plays were well attended and reviewed, Playhouse Positano closed after two seasons, partially because of a conflict with the actors' union and a harassing neighbor who called various county agencies to complain.

SOMETHING ENDS AND SOMETHING NEW BEGINS

The end of one thing is sometimes the beginning of something else. What caused Positano to close is complicated. There was the pressure brought to bear from their neighbor, who wanted Positano to go away. She frequently called government agencies like the health department to complain. When the health department found out that Positano had only one bathroom, they, at first, restricted what "entertainment" could happen there and eventually threatened to close the place if a second bathroom was not built. Unfortunately, like many small businesses, Positano was underfinanced. In addition, the Duttons were suffering from marital strife and eventually divorced. It all proved too much. After six years, Positano closed forever.

While Positano was closing, Jerry Ziegman, a television script writer, rented one of the cottages on the coffee-house property. He then convinced the owners to allow him to become the new property manager of the entire 130 acres, including the closed coffee house. His goal was to rent out spaces to young and struggling artists. The owner agreed, and for the next thirty-one years over fifty people lived and worked in what become known simply as "The Property." [2]

THE WIDER CONTEXT

Positano was established, in part, because Lorees, an aspiring writer and young mother, needed something to relieve her isolation and boredom. While her husband, Mike, had access to Los Angeles' entertainment industry, this world did not interest Lorees. She felt disconnected from the people and was not attracted to their opulent lifestyles. Lorees had been a habitué of bohemian Greenwich Village, where she led a life "of the mind" where stimulating ideas circulated among painters, authors, and theater people. Because she had thrived in this environment, she attempted to recreate the atmosphere of a Village coffee house/café where creative and like-minded people could congregate to drink coffee and discuss matters of artistic, cultural,and political importance. She was also used to having easy access to the cultural offerings of New York University and the New School: authors reading from their new works, professors lecturing on a vast range of topics, and off-Broadway theater productions.

Given the success of the place with a membership of several thousand, the absence of any mention of Positano among various publications about bohemian/Beat culture in Los Angeles is mystifying. Lisa Phillips (1996), in her definitive exhibition catalogue, *Beat Culture and the New American, 1950-1965,* makes no mention of the coffee house, but then it may simply reflect her East Coast bias in that Lawrence Lipton and other Venice West writers and artists are also omitted. This exclusion extends to Maynard's study *Venice West* (1991).

Positano was physically and culturally isolated. Unlike other coffee houses, it was not part of any community. It sat on the cliff away from other people and places, but in a more profound way it was not like other Los Angeles coffee houses. Positano undoubtedly catered to a left-of-center group of educated adults, some college students, and even a few surfers. Legendary surfer Miki Dora rented a cabin there in the early 1960s. It may be that the place was too far out for some, physically and intellectually.

By pure happenstance, Positano opened when there was an explosion of coffee houses, at least partially the result of the popularity of the Beats, which in turn was part of a cultural and artistic transformation of Los Angeles. *On The Road* was published in 1957, the same year that Lawrence Ferlinghetti was arrested for selling Allen Ginsberg's *Howl*. The Beats received a lot of media attention in *Life*, *Newsweek,* and so on and on television (remember *Dobie Gillis*). The movement took alternative culture out of the underground and transformed it into a commodity that could be sold to the masses. This emergence can be seen with the July, 1959, "Beat issue" of *Playboy* that featured work by Ginsberg and Kerouac. Yvette Vickers was the Beat playmate photographed by soft-core porn filmmaker Russ Myers in Cosmo Alley, a Hollywood coffee house owned by Lennie Bruce and Theo Bikel. Jim Morad's article on "The Coffee Houses of America" in this issue strangely enough ignores Positano. Grey Line tours were available for tourists to gawk at the Beatniks in Venice West. If you could "rent a Beatnik" for your parties or buy a Beatnik costume (beret, shades, and a beard), then these people were hardly a threat to the status quo. The Beats made being a bohemian safe and salable and thus meaningless, at least, in a traditional sense of the notion that being a bohemian meant being in rebellion against the mainstream. It became nothing more than a style or evidence of being chic.

The media presented coffee houses as places where Beats hung out. Robert Courtney (ND) estimated that from the late 1950s into the 1960s there were over forty southern California coffee houses. It seems logical if not self-evident that like all of these establishments, Coffee House Positano was a Beat establishment. However, it is not that simple. Some Beat writers did present their work at Positano; for example, Lawrence Lipton read from the *Holy Barbarians*, the definitive work about Venice West, and some leaders of the movement, such as Allen Ginsberg, visited the place. However, a closer examination of the taste world represented by Positano, that is, the music played, the plays performed, the variety of speakers, and the art displayed, suggests that at least some of what Positano offered was more a reflection of an earlier form of bohemia than what is normally associated with the Beat movement. In other words, Positano can be seen as a place where the transition from a classic form of bohemia (think Paris in the 1920s and Greenwich Village in the 1950s) to a Beat variation of bohemia occurred. In a very complicated way, the Beat movement enabled Positano to be successful in that people went there assuming they would experience what the media was calling "a beat experience," while at the same time, what was offered at Positano was more traditional/old-fashioned bohemian fare.

The core values that define Positano reflect those of late-period bohemia when such establishments were part of the underground (see "Introduction" for details). The food and drinks reflected a taste-public outside. The existence of this place was implicitly a criticism of white middle-American cuisine. Chess was a recreation of an educated minority. Jazz, folk, and classical guitar dominated this musical world while popular music was ignored. The theater offered could be favorably compared with Off-Broadway fare. The condition of the building and the quality of the furniture were at best funky and undoubtedly in violation of a number of building codes. The dress of the staff and many patrons was often shabby and clearly outside the notions of middle-class good taste, even though some of the patrons were more formally dressed. Perhaps the only thing missing was screenings of avant garde/experimental films.

Some of these Beat coffee houses featured musicians involved with folk revival (Bonnie Raitt and Linda Ronstadt), "roots music" (Muddy Waters, Brownie McGee, and Sonny Terry), and protest songs (Joan Baez and Phil Ochs). Among the most prominent establishments were The Troubadour and the Ash Grove, both opened in 1957. In time The Troubadour evolved into a venue that resembled Whiskey A Go Go more than a bohemian coffee house. It was during this time that the transition from acoustic to electrified folk music was evolving. Groups like the Byrds and Buffalo Springfield and other Laurel Canyon musicians were leaving their folk music beginnings. By 1965 when an electrified Dylan shocked the folks at the Newport Folk Festival, folk rock was born. As Simon Warner (2013) and others have pointed out, rock and roll has been greatly influenced by Beat writers like Ginsberg, Burroughs, and Kerouac. In stark contrast, no amplified music was ever heard at Positano. Only folk revival and flamenco guitar music were played by unannounced anonymous musicians. No one at Positano saw any artistic merit in rock and roll. The jazz musicians who played there stylistically resembled the West Coast Cool jazz played by Bud Shank and Chet Baker.

The late 1950s and early 1960s, the time when the coffee house was open, was the period when Los Angeles emerged as a major art center. By the 1970s, Los Angeles had transformed itself from "a cultural backwater" to a center for avant -garde art where critics looked to see the future. A mélange of artistic styles emerged that are sometimes referred to as California Pop and included works labeled Cool, Assemblage, Finish Fetish, and Light and Space. The painters associated with these works are considered to be part of the Beat movement (Whiting 2006, Drohojowska-Philp 2001, Grenier 2006, and Peabody, et al. 2011).

From 1958 to 1966 exhibits at the Ferus Gallery by artists such as Wallace Berman, John Altoon, Ed Ruscha, Dennis Hopper, and Edward Kienholz created a sensation, attracting even the notice of the New York critics (see Hertz and Polkinhorn, this volume). As a demonstration of Positano's contrarian position, it appears that none of the Ferus gallery artists exhibited there. Since exhibition space was extremely limited, and the Duttons were open to showing young artists, it is strange that people like Ed Kienholz or Billy Al Bengston did not see Positano as a place where potential buyers or patrons would see their work. There is no way to know if any of these artists even knew about the coffee house. There is no mention of Positano in what these artists have written about themselves and what others have had to say. It could be that Positano's location was a factor. Most of these painters lived in Venice and hung out in places like Barney's Beanery in West Hollywood. Malibu was miles away from them.

Walter Hopps, one of the founders of Ferus, felt that there was a clear prejudice against the kind of art he exhibited. "Although a quasi-official Los Angeles avant-garde, centered around the post-Cubist painter, Rico Lebrun, was visible enough throughout the city, alternative modern art could be seen only in a few experimental movies houses or on the walls of Bohemian cafes"(1996:27). Hopps is probably referring to the Coronet Theatre on La Cienega Boulevard, where Raymond Rohauer formed a film society and screened avant-garde and foreign films (James 2005). Which "Bohemian cafes" he is referring to is a mystery, apparently not Positano.

It is also possible that the Duttons did not like the work of the Cool School painters. How the Duttons decided which painters they would exhibit is unknown, but two painters seemed to dominate the art world of Positano, Keith Finch and his protégé, Ed Pagac, both California Abstract Expressionists, a style in some conflict with the Ferus artists. If Finch was the Duttons' primary artistic advisor, then it is no wonder that none of the Ferus painters was shown. They occupied different art worlds (Becker 1982). The art revolution that was critical to the development of Los Angeles was absent from Positano.

In the catalogue for the Whitney Museum exhibition *Beat Culture and the New America: 1950–1965* (Phillips 1996), Allen Ginsberg attempted his definition of the basic values of the Beats. They included the need for liberation—sexual, spiritual, and political—the acceptance of drug use for spiritual and artistic purposes, the importance of rock and roll, a development of an ecological awareness, opposition to the military-industrial complex, and a respect for indigenous peoples and the land.

Several of the concerns Ginsberg mentioned were not to be found at Positano. While the Beats advocated serious changes in just about all aspects of life, the general tenor of Positano was more liberal than revolutionary. People seemed content to lead unconventional lives but in the underground. The environment, the military-industrial complex, and the rights of indigenous peoples were never discussed. Spirituality was also not a topic of conversation. The notion of serious political liberation was likewise something of no real interest. Among the speakers, regular customers, and staff one could find "old lefties," socialists, even Communists, who had watched the demise of any serious challenge to a capitalist world fade away. The notion that there was hope for some sort of liberation was simply not there. This was a time when the old left was dying and the new left was being born. Attitudes toward sex among people at Positano were classically bohemian and not dissimilar to those of the Beats. While "sleeping around" was common enough, the idea that this was a sign of a sexual revolution did not exist. While gay people frequented Positano, they were silently accepted like Blacks and other outsiders, as a normal part of the outsider status of all bohemians. Mike Dutton was strongly opposed to the use of any drugs, nor was it ever a topic of any of the talks. Alcohol was overwhelmingly the drug of preference. A few staff and customers experimented with peyote and magic mushrooms and smoked marijuana. If Ginsberg's list of Beat values is representative, then Positano was an odd mixture of these values with some of the characteristics of an older bohemian world. While it may sound strange to say, Positano was, at the same time, avant garde and *retardataire*.

Positano is and will continue to be a conundrum never to be resolved. If thousands of people were patrons of the coffee house, why did none feel motivated to create a similar establishment when Positano closed, and why did none of the patrons, many who were writers and scholars, fail to write something about this unique experiment in recreating Greenwich Village on the cliffs of Malibu?

ENDNOTES

[1] A Methodological Note. This essay is based upon the personal experiences of the author living and working at Positano from 1957 to 1959 and to an ethno-historical study that resulted in the publication of an enhanced ebook, *Coffee House Positano: A Bohemian Oasis in Malibu, 1957-1962* (2012).
[2] The Property is the subject of another study (see www.jayrubyworld.com).

Photographs courtesy of Lorees Yerby papers (Collection 2242). UCLA Library Special Collections, Charles E. Young Research Library, UCLA.

VENICE

Space/Time and the Radical Image: Wallace Berman's Semina.

Harry Polkinhorn

Introduction: Being "Cool

Even though those who have written about Wallace Berman's contributions to the avant-garde culture of his time have emphasized his importance in various ways, the exact nature of that contribution has remained somewhat vague. One explanation may be his premature demise (died at 50 in a vehicle accident). However, a more important explanation lies in the nature of Berman's work itself in the context of when it was produced. Those around him went on to distinguish themselves for the most part as poets, painters, actors, filmmakers, and so on, carving out more distinct identities for themselves within the received structure of social roles, whereas Berman was variously active as a photographer, filmmaker, writer, assemblage artist, and editor; apparently consciously rejecting the pursuit of an artistic identity in any given single area. Also, as Solnit (1990) indicates, those with whom he was associated (Herms, Jess [Collins], Hedrick, DeFeo, Conner) did not form an identifiable group. Furthermore, those visual artists with whom he was early associated in Los Angeles through the Ferus Gallery (Bengston, Altoon, Kienholz, Alexander, Kaufmann, Bell, Ruscha, Moses) went on to establish themselves through the usual channels. As has been frequently noted, Berman shunned the pursuit of fame and wealth, instead cultivating a posture of indifference towards those core values and practices of the L.A. cultural milieu in which he moved for most of his life. Even when his close artistic colleagues began to build an audience through the breakthrough of the Beats into mass-media celebrity and the inception of an L.A. style in the visual arts, Berman stood off on the sidelines, a position that perhaps many of those around him misunderstood and characterized as a quality of 50s "cool," an indefinable *je ne sais quoi* that was the then equivalent of "taste" or "personal style;" it couldn't be specified, but either one had it or didn't, and those with it were to be envied, as though they were celebrities with an aura, etc., etc.

Wallace Berman. Courtesy, The Estate of Wallace Berman and Kohn Gallery, Los Angeles.

How can we penetrate through these mystifications at a distance of half a century in order to arrive at a better appreciation of Berman's work? Who was this so-called "kingpin of the Los Angeles underground artists' culture" (Solnit 1990:5), this "casual connoisseur of art and personalities . . . [this] discriminating esthete" (Duncan andMcKenna 2005: 14), this "devotee of the Jewish mystical tradition of Kabbalah . . . [this] progenitor of assemblage art" (Fox, in Grenier 2006: 34), who supposedly was so central in the mid-century revitalization of the arts in Los Angeles and later in San Francisco?

Berman's work crystallizes a conflict between a kind of radical individuality, on the one hand, and a flight from it, on the other. According to Joan Brown, "'He just stood, for me, for the whole idea of the individual'" (in Solnit 1990:6). What does Brown mean by "individual"? We can guess something like someone who doesn't care much about the current trends but is content to go his own way. Berman dropped out of two art schools, worked for a while in a furniture factory, and developed his early sense of culture through frequenting blues and jazz clubs and reading the surrealist poets, identifying with artists who expressed themselves in an idiosyncratic fashion, who worked outside of the main conventions of their time. As arguably many of his generation did, "He studied surrealism, art history, western mystical and esoteric traditions" (Solnit 1990: 7). With regard to the latter, however, let's not forget, as Baigell points out, that Berman's relationship to the Kabbalah remained superficial: "Berman explained that they [the Hebrew letters he incorporated in his work] made 'no specific, translatable sense,' that because he could not read Hebrew, he 'liked [instead] the decorative form of the lettering and the moods that the shapes evoked' " (2006: 116-17). Furthermore, ". . . Berman used Kabbala (*sic*) on an intuitive level . . . his use belonged more to the 'mystical' dodginess of the hipster than it does to any thiophay [*sic*] or Zionist propaganda," that his Hebrew letters "make more sense visually than verbally" (117). Baigell dismisses Berman's use of these letters with the blunt assertion "it is not Kabbalah" (117). Did Berman's relationship to art history and surrealism, as he understood them, also remain superficial, merely a matter of intuitive or decorative mood? As I will discuss, *Semina*, Berman's underground magazine, will help us resolve some of these questions.

"Pulling It All Together"

During the late 1940s and 1950s Berman began gathering objects and putting them together into artworks, such as "Homage to Herman Hesse (1949) and "Cross" (1957). Such work came to be called assemblage. Solnit says,

> Assemblage—sculpture made of found objects—challenged conventional ideas of workmanship, originality, value, and purity . . . assemblage artists rejected its conventions for an art that brought the dump into the gallery and the manufactured and accidental into the realm of handicraft . . . Assemblage emerged in the fifties as a medium uniquely capable of addressing those disparities; it dealt with abandonment, redefinition, juxtaposition, fragmentation, and ideas of order. It proposed an order that was neither absolute nor eternal, but conditional and personal. (1990: ix)

These latter qualities appear in Berman's conception of *Semina*. However, clearly neither Berman nor his colleagues were the first to adapt popular-culture elements. What about the example of

Schwitters and Merz from earlier in the century, not to mention those documented by Dubuffet reaching back into the nineteenth century? In fact, the pre-history to the very surrealism that Berman studied contains these important seeds of *Semina*.

Considered as a "book" or book-like anthology, *Semina* can perhaps best trace its roots to the nineteenth-century examination of the function of that cultural form by Baudelaire, Mallarmé, and others. According to Arnar, and somewhat ironically as it turned out,

> The mixed assemblage of writers and the scrapbook-like structure of accumulated fragments are precisely the qualities that many writers, including Baudelaire and later Mallarmé, determined to be antithetical to a true book. The function of the terms *album, almanac,* and *recueil* in their critical vocabulary serve thus as shorthand references to facile and formulaic publications that lack internal structure . . . Similarly, the inclusion of multiple authors in *Scènes de la vie publique et privée des animaux* represented an implicit rejection of any single authorial vision. Indeed, this publication's segmented structure and multiple voices was part of its appeal—it legitimized discontinuous and nonsequential reading experiences based on individual desire or whim. (2011: 33-34)

I am not arguing that Berman was specifically aware of these aspects of the French literary tradition in which he supposedly immersed himself but that its preoccupations nevertheless may have shaped his view of the possibilities of the book form. After all, Berman's focus on this form was carried forth with *Semina* for a number of years, as Duncan and McKenna illustrate. The magazine appeared in nine issues between 1955 and 1964.

> Seven of its issues were printed on loose-leaf pages inserted in a sleeve; five of those issues had no prescribed order or sequence. Photographs, drawings, and collages by Berman and others were juxtaposed with texts, often on the same page. Attributions were at times enigmatic, with some texts ascribed to authors by initials and some artworks completely unattributed. Reproductions of several of Berman's mailers to friends were included and treated as discrete works of art. Disseminated without any regular or predictable publication dates, *Semina* was sent out like a surprise

> communication from an erratic correspondent . . . He abdicated his role as a sequencing editor, presenting an array to be experienced as a reader saw fit. (2005: 22)

The surprise element, perhaps the most important aspect of *Semina,* of course falls away altogether in Duncan and McKenna's exhibition catalogue, so we must imagine what it would have been like to open an issue of *Semina* and to examine its contents as the recipient wished. The rejection of the role of sequencing editor aligns Berman with Mallarmé's impersonality, curiously at odds with the heightened individuality Brown and others have commented on. Indeed, the ties between Berman and Mallarmé are multiple. Note Sontag's observations: "That most logical of nineteenth-century aesthetes, Mallarmé, said that everything in the world exists in order to end in a book. Today everything exists to end in a photograph (1973: 24)." (Berman became an accomplished photographer; one could argue photography was his chief means of artistic expression, aside from *Semina.*) Later, she extends the historical context into Surrealism, the way Berman himself seems to have done, when she says, "Bleak factory buildings and billboard-cluttered avenues look as beautiful, through the camera's eye, as churches and pastoral landscapes. . . . it was Breton and other Surrealists who invented the secondhand store as a temple of vanguard taste and upgraded visits to flea markets into a mode of aesthetic pilgrimage" (1973:78-79), recalling Berman's appropriation of "junk" into his assemblages and collages.

Although we don't have direct evidence of Berman's conception of what he was up to with *Semina,* we can see multiple developmental lines leading back to the nineteenth and early twentieth centuries. Berman had a small letterpress on which he printed the pages of his "magazine." The temporal element of my title is seen both in the structural nature of each issue of *Semina,* with multiple units to be viewed in varying sequences, and in the nature of a periodical, which appears at regular (in this case irregular) intervals over time. Berman loosens time in both of these aspects. Arnar says,

> For Mallarmé, then, the term *Book* ("Le Livre") appears in his writing as an unrealized project, the planning of which preoccupied him throughout his entire career. The ambitiousness of this project can be glimpsed from a bundle of over two hundred manuscript notes published posthumously in 1957 by Jacques Scherer

> under the title *Le "Livre" de Mallarmé.* Although Scherer has numbered the unbound sheets, there is no coherent beginning, middle, or end. Moreover, many portions of the manuscript are nearly incomprehensible, containing obscure diagrams or mathematical formulas. . . . The first theme to emerge is Mallarmé's preoccupation with numbers and measures. . . a preoccupation with structure and symmetry. (2011: 43)

Similarly, Berman was arguably more concerned with structure than the content of individual pieces, as this concern appears later in his Verifax series of an image of a handheld transistor radio with different images collaged onto it.

Courtesy galerie frank elbaz, Paris".

What seems to have mattered to Berman for the recipients of *Semina* was a kind of validation of the role of the viewer; it would not be the editor (or artist) dictating to the viewer what a work meant, but rather he or she was being offered a means whereby individual interpretations would be made possible, indeed necessary. This, too, was foretold in the example of Mallarmé, since ". . . he envisioned the Book as a theatrical performance . . . it demonstrates his efforts to transform the typically private medium of the book to a collective one" (Arnar 2011: 44). Of course, such a transformation happens within a particular historical moment and, in Mallarmé's case, coincided with and was propelled by the efflorescence of a new middle-class culture made possible by the Industrial Revolution's creation of mass-market commodities that had to be advertised, through newspapers, in order to be sold. In Berman's case, there was a similar reaction to the explosion of mass-media effects in the post-war boom economy of the U.S. Arnar, speaking of Mallarmé's time, says,

> What I identify in Mallarmé's critical essays from the 1880s and '90s, and especially in his comments on the newspaper, is a pointed critique of contemporary cultural practices that had fundamentally neglected the creative role of the public. . . As a collective and popular site, the newspaper represents a unique kind of public space that seems to be inclusive and participatory. Thus, despite its fragmentary structure, the newspaper provides viable alternatives to more autocratic forms of art because it has the capacity to reach a wide audience but can also "yield intelligently" to the potentials of this audience. (2011: 50-51)

In Berman's time, however, although the newspaper was beginning to be replaced by network television, there was no opportunity for the kind of validation of the viewer (to sequence his or her own viewing) as there had been for Mallarmé's audience of newspaper readers. Nevertheless, the two artists shared a similar concern for the leveling impact of societal massification on the individual as a creative center of his or her own life.

The most oft-cited example of a reader-oriented text may be Mallarmé's *Un coup de dés jamais n'abolira le hasard,* suggesting as it does a dimension of game-playing.

> The game concept and the implied participation of its players are most forcefully proposed in *Un coup de dés jamais n'abolira le hasard*. The dice metaphor simultaneously evokes chance and certainty, because no clear outcome of the game can be predicted yet given the conventionalized format of dice, a fixed number of possibilities exist. Like Mallarmé's conception of language, these defined parameters regulate the game yet allow for a rich array of maneuvers. But Mallarmé has introduced a new set of rules to the game of reading by abandoning the columnar structure of the page as well as narrative sequence. (Arnar 2011: 168)

Likewise, Berman invents new rules that engage his readers' expectations in various ways. A journal issue can contain visual as well as verbal materials in any combination. It can feature the work of a single artist or writer, or that of a collection of artists, whether living or dead. Duncan and McKenna point to Berman's interest in Hesse's *Magister Ludi,* which features the game metaphor as a central organizing figure. Although *Semina*'s efforts can be easily misinterpreted as random gatherings of whatever struck Berman's fancy at the time he was putting a particular number together, such conclusions would forfeit Berman's much more ambitious purposes, which, as we have seen, so much resembled those of his French predecessor.

> But how does this powerful vision for an inclusive and flexible reader-oriented text measure against *Un coup de dés*? This work has been hailed as a singularly important prototype of the *livre d'avant-garde* since it focuses not only on the materiality of reading but on self-generated change and transformation. The work's self-conscious acknowledgment of mass-cultural forms and structures reveals Mallarmé's commitment to reinstating poetry's—and the book's—social mission since these forms and structures provided means to address a diverse and fractured society. (Arnar 2011: 238)

There can be little doubt that Berman felt he was living in a "fractured society." His reaction to his arrest on obscenity charges is perhaps the best illustration; he moved his family from Los Angeles to the Bay Area for several years as a response to the trauma of finding his artwork so radically misunderstood as to result in prosecution by legal authorities.

> Such open-endedness was central to Mallarmé's articulation of an impersonal aesthetic. . . Mallarmé defined the primary task of the poet as revealing fundamental patterns. One need not create these patterns from scratch, he explains, but simply arrange preexisting parts: "things exist, we do not need to create them; we have only to seize their relationships; and it is the threads of these relationships that form verses and orchestras." Mallarmé's focus on arrangement and composition is significant to my present analysis because it relocates the emphasis from the maker to the work of art itself. Indeed, the ideal

> work, Mallarmé explained, is impersonal; it is an anonymous text that "speaks for itself." (Arnar 2011: 254)

Can one not make a similar argument for *Semina,* as well as Berman's so-called assemblages? Impersonality understood in this way becomes a central critical concept in any attempt to understand what Berman was up to with his work. The importance of impersonality, whether or not created by Mallarmé (arguments exist on both sides, of course), was also of obvious interest to another French artist, but one whom Berman had met: Duchamp.

Duncan and McKenna point out the obvious parallel. First, there is that between Duchamp's "readymades" and Berman's assemblages. Then with regard to Duchamp's *The Box in a Valise* (1935-41), "Berman conceived of *Semina* as a kind of traveling group show in an envelope. . . ." (2005: 27). Like Berman, Duchamp "repeatedly made new works by assembling his previous ones. *Boite-en-valise* (1938-41) and *The Green Box* (1934) are carefully executed facsimile collections of his notes. . ." (Kuenzli 1990:4). Again, as with the Mallarmé example, it is not the surface-level innovation that matters but what it implies about Berman's attitude toward the role of the artist in a "fractured society." Duchamp is perhaps best known for his life-long interrogation of the artist's role. Like Berman, "His chief strategy consists in multiplying identities in order to undo any kind of fixity" (Kuenzli 1990: 5), and "Through the indeterminacy of his works, [he] hoped to activate the viewers" because "Works that conform to the viewers' expectations do not activate them" (8). Ultimately, Duchamp gave up making "art" (in the received sense of the term) and spent years playing chess, one of Berman's favorite pastimes as well. But earlier, Duchamp (again like Berman) had learned printing; he did ". . . an apprenticeship at the Vicomté Press. He learned the crafts of typesetting and presswork and also practiced the separate art of printing graphics" (Marquis 1981: 36). Rather than rely on the judgments of others as to the aesthetic value of his work (Duchamp's early application to art school had been rejected), Duchamp attacked the very structure of expectation and assumption that underlay such judgments. For his part, Berman was apparently hesitant to exhibit his work, and when he did the response, as indicated above, was less than enthusiastic, reinforcing his belief in the necessity of controlling the production and distribution of his own work through letterpress printing (later Verifax) and *Semina* distribution to people he knew. As Catherine Grenier put it,

> For artists like George Herms and Wallace Berman, for instance, the actual making of the work took precedence over its conservation . . . Berman worked for several years on a "magazine" made up of elements that were entirely handmade and destined to random scattering. (2006: 19)

As with Duchamp, Berman reveals an ambivalence through turning inside out a seemingly nonchalant attitude towards the conservation of works of art as well as over their ultimate reception by the art establishment, accompanied as this must always be by the powerful forces of commercialization.

Is there a contradiction between critiquing the commodity culture of mid-century America, on the one hand, and refusing to work for a wage, on the other? Marquis comments on Duchamp's ". . . dandified, aristocratic attitude toward any kind of steady work, an attitude he was to maintain successfully for the rest of his life" (1981: 92), even though he did work as a kind of advisor to the wealthy Arensbergs, his patrons, as to the art he thought they should buy, in addition to his own. After his job at the furniture factory, Berman, however, chose to stay home to raise their son, and since he rejected pursuing the sale of his work, his wife Shirley took paid work as a secretary.

At the same time they were variously confronting the depredations of a rampant consumer culture, both Duchamp and Berman found meaning in the nonphysical dimensions of human experience. As Marquis says, Duchamp's attitude was that ". . . if a machine could turn out millions of exact replicas of the visible world, then the artist's role was to unearth and depict the invisible world" (1981: 101). As is well known, Duchamp made a study of the fourth dimension, which he incorporated in his works. Berman, for his part, as mentioned above, had some interest in Jewish and other mystical traditions. According to Fox, "Berman's art was both a response to consumer culture of mass produced objects and the American obsession with newness as well as his personal animistic reverie of divinity in all things" (in Grenier 2006: 34). Whatever the exact nature of this supposed "animistic reverie," not to mention Duchamp's depictions of "the invisible world," clearly central to Berman's concerns as an artist during his most productive years was *Semina,* a project that can be seen as conflating the themes outlined above. As Smith summarizes,

> During his five-year sojourn in northern California, Berman focused almost entirely on the production of his underground journal *Semina.* Already at work on the second issue at the time of his fateful Ferus exhibition, he completed it in December 1957 after his relocation. The nine issues documented Berman's concerns over an eight-year period. The first four issues focused on the relationship of drugs, madness, and the salvific function of art. The fifth issue was dedicated exclusively to representations of Mexico. The last four issues increasingly commented on the relation of art and poetry to social turmoil in the United States . . . He printed from 150 to 300 copies of each issue on his own five-by-eight hand press. Of the nine editions, only the second was bound. The third, sixth, and ninth issues consisted of a single poem with a cover photograph. In the other five issues, the journal assumed the form that distinguished it from the dozens of other small literary magazines of its day. Berman placed approximately twenty loose-leaf pages of poems, photographs, and drawings into a pocket glued to the inside of a folded cover. (1995: 232)

Berman knew that *Semina* would be his response to the multiple conflicts he was experiencing, both personally and in terms of his understanding of the role of the artist in a fractured society, which may be why he concentrated his efforts on this work for the years specifically following the Ferus debacle. With the decline of representation in the arts that was initiated by the historical avant-gardes, of which Duchamp was a central figure, how could the artist retain a social function without withdrawing into pure abstraction or dandyism, which in any event was instantly absorbed by commodity culture, or, like Duchamp, abandoning the field and working in secret? How can an artist make a serious contribution to his or her time without being radically misinterpreted or outright crushed by the ignorance of a public so completely colonized by the utterly hypnotizing affects of the mass media?

Semina was Berman's answer to these questions. Through it he could offer a structural examination of the relationship of space to time, since the imaginary audience the magazine projected would understand the work as a periodical publication, although one of irregular and unpredictable appearance. At the same time, Berman was free to posit an editorial subjectivity (stand-in for the reader's individuality) liberated from conventional expectations and constraints in terms of choice and sequencing of works to appear, thereby validating the reader/viewer's unique individuality itself. These organizing concepts, I would argue, made it possible for Berman to establish a more functional division between inside and outside, closing off the erosion of this boundary which had taken its most disastrous, externalized form in his arrest; that is, when the outside came in. The main result of this newfound clarity and focus was the social critique that began to appear in the last numbers of *Semina*. These contributions, then, are what make Berman stand out from those around him, reversing the naïve critique that he exemplified the Bohemian as "outsider."

When a Coterie Meets the Carnival: The Poets of Venice West as the Neo-Anarchists of a Mid-Century Bohemia

William Mohr

The scattershot development of bohemian communities in any culturally significant city, such as Los Angeles, reflects the economic contingencies impinging on its various neighborhoods. Malcolm Miles's "Cities of the Avant-Garde" in *The Cambridge Companion to the City in Literature* (2014) conflates the avant-garde and bohemian impetus in urban configurations in a manner typical of commentary on these subjects.

For artists and writers, the larger cities of Europe from the 1850s onward and of North America from the early 1900s, afforded a critical mass of support systems such as café society, the presence of critics and dealers, small magazines, and the anonymity and proximity of difference that was the defining quality of the metropolis . . . (Cities) became the centers for transnational avant-gardes whose members could validate their work outside the restrictions of the academies of fine arts, using culture to reveal society's contradictions. But here ambivalence begins. Artists and writers who were all strangers found common cause as migrants in a solidarity of outsider status. The term bohemian denoted this in the mid-nineteenth century . . ." (Miles 2014:158)

In a similar vein, one barely begins to dig into Richard Candida-Smith's 500-page examination of California bohemian scenes when one finds a footnote-reinforced commentary on the relationship between avant-garde culture and bohemian community formation on the fourth page of his introduction (Miles 2014: xx). The explicit connection between risk-taking art and the alienation devices of bohemian life is too prominent a factor not to receive immediate attention in any study of these subjects.

Described by Lawrence Lipton as a "slum by the sea" (Lipton 1959), Venice was perhaps an inevitable site of a bohemian or avant-garde renaissance. The once independent city had been annexed into City of Los Angeles proper in the 1920s and then largely left on its own to deal with the withering fantasy of its initial incarnation. The subsequent combination of the Great Depression and the riptides of global conflict between 1936 and 1945 ensnared Venice in a dead-end stage of development. In the late 1940s, Venice's most prominent features were oil derricks and the on-going grotesquerie of its impoverished amusement park. By the mid-point of the 1950s, Venice had been relegated to an urban sideshow that held little interest for the real-estate agents and bankers in southern California who were intent on converting the San Fernando Valley's orchards and pastures into suburban housing.

For those seeking an outlet from the pressure-cooker of what Alan Nadel labeled "containment culture," however, Venice was made to order: cheap rent allowed those on the artistic margins of Los Angeles to free themselves from having to play it safe. Although other clusters of poets in Los Angeles at the same time were also engaged in their own programs of social resistance, the poets who assembled in Venice between 1955 and 1960 provided the basis for a legendary incarnation of a bohemian community. So successful were these poets in adhering to their ideals of non-success that the literature about their writing is relatively limited. Such an outcome is hardly surprising, given that American society is organized primarily to reward those who vigorously pursue individual acclaim and awards. Despite the disappearing act of Venice West's poets, their sincerity and idealism continue to allure the archaeologists of social resistance.

As the most famous of the bohemian communities in Los Angeles, however, Venice West was more of an enclave of artists and poets embedded in a neighborhood than a locale permeated with like-minded individuals committed to listening closely to one another's aesthetic proposals or manifestos. Certainly that is the presupposition of John Arthur Maynard in his path-breaking study, *Venice West* (1991). Maynard pointedly denies in the opening pages of his book that Venice West was a community. Rather, his account of Venice West ends up portraying the aspirations, antics, and tribulations of a representative subculture that was closer in spirit in many ways to anarchism than to the Beat movement with which it is usually associated. Regardless of its stature as a community or a provocative subculture, the *image* of Venice West as "bohemian" is so firmly established at this point that perhaps this conflation is the one point that can be agreed upon by any inquiry into its history or significance.

Its provisional sociological rubric notwithstanding, it should be noted that Venice West in the late 1950s became as well known nationally as an "alternative" community as Haight-Ashbury was a decade later. Donald Allen's brief preface to his famous anthology, *The New American Poetry* (1960), cited Venice West as one of the crucial locations at which the poets in his book found welcoming comrades. It is telling that Allen felt no more need to inform his readers that Venice West was in Los Angeles than someone might feel to offer an apposition of locale to the Grand Canyon or Niagara Falls. Short of scandalous tragedy, though, places or personalities rarely become nationally famous without some serious publicity, and Venice West benefited from a potboiler, entitled *The Holy Barbarians,* by its publicist-in-residence, Lawrence Lipton (1959). Featuring thinly disguised sketches of the denizens of Venice West, *The Holy Barbarians* oscillates between middle-brow social commentary, modestly objective reporting, and lavish caricatures of young poets who had accepted Lipton's invitation to a bohemian version of a skid-row mission. Lipton's well-stocked refrigerator was the larder, but first his true believers in "voluntary poverty" and "social disaffiliation" had to listen to his sermons.

Intrigued by the Beat phenomenon and Lipton's polemical depiction of an artistic underground, *Life* magazine devoted an entire article to Venice West, which opened with a photograph of Lipton reading his poetry in his living room; the household audience, however, was not the poets featured in *The Holy Barbarians* (*Life* magazine, September 21, 1959. "Kansas Squares Vs. Coast Beats"). In fact, none of the poets I will discuss in this article were even mentioned, let alone photographed for the article. *Life*'s article is almost weirdly anonymous in its documentation of Venice West, the central gathering point for a scene in Los Angeles that counted over 2,000 people in its affiliated membership. The scale of these artistic scenes, which included painters as well as poets, is especially pertinent, for what makes a scene *bohemian* is first and foremost a sense of multiplicity. Individual genius, flourishing briefly or for a lifetime, can never be categorized as emanating out of a bohemian scene unless she or he is actively engaged with the development of like-minded people with whom she or he is in continual, daily contact. If American culture, writhing within its death-wish fascination with the chimerical great American novel, is obsessed with conjuring up a *representative man*, bohemia implicitly deconstructs that project with its emphasis on the ensemble. To that extent, the preference in the Venice West community for jazz's emphasis on collective expression is yet one more piece of evidence for its bohemian status.

It should also be noted that if Venice was the site of a bohemian lifestyle so contumacious as to align with a variety of neo-anarchism, its affiliated residents were doing so within an unusual context, for no other major city was as identified with a culture industry as Los Angeles with its massive industrial production of movies. To be a poet in Los Angeles in 1955 was to challenge the very premises of imagination that served as the superstructure of what David James has called "industrial writing." The dichotomy between poets and Hollywood should not be given the aura of a strictly demarcated binary. Many poets who might not seem to have had any association with Hollywood did in fact seek out careers here. Shortly before Perkoff and Boyd moved to Venice, for instance, Charles Olson, "Mr. Postmodern Poet" himself, spent several weeks in Hollywood trying to get a career in the "industry" kick-started (see Tom Clark's 1991 account of Olson in Hollywood). This bohemianism, therefore, was not merely the aesthetic attitude of marginal figures looking for a way to challenge the conventional premises of middle-class society, whether it be Paris, Berlin, or New York City. This is to say that the "Beats" in Venice West were more than a subculture of truculent *flaneurs* who had given themselves a license to dawdle in a public pose of counter-cultural opposition. There was simply too much pressure from the valorization of industrial writing in Los Angeles for someone to pretend that he or she could be left alone to focus on his or her writing. It should also be noted, however, that in choosing to write in a genre that blatantly rejected the commodified language of cinema fantasy, the poets in Venice West were not necessarily any more oppositional to hegemonic culture than the non-academic poets in Los Angeles at that time (such as Mel Weisburd, Gene Frumkin, Alvaro Cardona-Hine), who were associated with *Coastlines* magazine. On the whole, though, the poets in Venice West chose to underline their contumacious poetics in bold italics through a bohemian lifestyle.

At the same time, the poets and artists in Venice West could be said to serve as the prime example of Richard Candida-Smith's (1995) observation that this was a period during which there was a thinning of the line between bohemia and popular culture. It was not just Lawrence Lipton's best-seller that made the Venice West one of the best-known places for artists indifferent to commercial success to gather and collaborate. Popular television shows included depictions of Beat characters and Venice West's best known poet, Stuart Z. Perkoff, made a remunerative appearance on Groucho Marx's "You Bet Your Life." Perkoff was also invited to read his poetry at the home of filmmaker Paul Mazursky, though he showed up too "out of it" due to drug use to give a proper reading. On one hand, therefore, Venice West's emphasis on poetry was both in immediate conflict with the hegemony of Hollywood's commercial emphasis and at the same time an alluring instance of what bohemia does best: serving as dialectical force that enables the ruling class to reconcile its internal aesthetic, ethical, and social conundrums.

Given the slightly mythical status of Venice West, the actual scope of Venice West cannot be delimited often enough. Rather like the exaggeration of the number of people who protested the Vietnam War in the mid-1960s, the scale of active residents in the Venice West can easily be transfigured into a more substantial cadre than actually was at work. As Sophie Rachmuhl's chapter on Venice West in her recent study, *A Higher Form of Politics*, illustrates, "What came to be known as the third American Beat community was, in reality, composed of a few dozen often penniless people who had been attracted to Venice at different times through the 1950s. They included the writers and poets Lawrence Lipton, Stuart Z. Perkoff, Alexander Trocchi and Charles Foster; painters like Tony Scibella (who was also a poet), John Altoon, Ben Talbert and Mike Angeleno; the folk singer Julie Meredith, impresario Jimmy Alonzi, sculptor Tati, and boxer Joe Greb, as well as various wives and girfriends who hovered around them, in this rather masculine world" (Rachmuhl 2015:40-41).

The first two writers cited by Rachmuhl are in fact the prime figures who have received the bulk of the attention in narratives and commentary about Venice West. Lawrence Lipton served as its scriptwriter, director, and producer, while Stuart Z. Perkoff played the role of rebel with a neoanarchist cause. Lipton did in fact yearn to be recognized as a poet, and even published a book with "Venice West" in the title. Lipton's poetry, however, is not of a quality that will ever overtake his chief claim to fame as the prime publicist for Venice West. In truth, Lipton's career in Los Angeles is the equivalent of a musician who wants to be in a rock and roll band, but whose real use is as a manager and roadie. Let it not go unsaid that he was assiduous in this role and continued to support the people he regarded as protégés far longer than most people would have found the strength to give freely of their own relatively meager resources. Nevertheless, as we approach the half-century mark of the death of Venice West, it is imperative that some of the more substantial poets be given some much overdue consideration. In particular, what is most striking about this list is the absence of five figures who contributed significantly to Venice West. To provide some sense of the heterogeneity of this bohemian community, therefore, I am going to concentrate on these neglected figures. Lipton's focus on Venice as a community sustains interest in his poetry. One of his poems is included in the first book to provide extended exegesis of poems concerned with Los Angeles as subject matter, *Poetry Los Angeles* (Goldstein 2014).

The first is the most obscure, though also one of the most essential to be named in any account of Venice West. Without Charles ("Charley") Newman, Venice West would not have had that particular name bestowed on the nascent gatherings in the living rooms of its poets. Although Lipton's house may have become a cynosure of the scene in 1957 and 1958, the poets were meeting with one another and sharing poems (and drugs) well before then, and it was during that period of coterie conversation that Newman began to refer to their communal status as Venice West. The name caught on with the group and started to circulate within the larger community, after which Lipton picked up on it, too (see Mohr 2011). The letter by Stuart Z. Perkoff to Donald Allen in which Perkoff credits Newman with naming this bohemian community can be found in the Archive for New Poetry, University of California, San Diego Geisel Library.

Newman was both a poet and a painter, and a photograph of him at work as a painter appears in a portfolio at the back of Lipton's *The Holy Barbarians*. His struggles with self-doubt about his place within the scene are vividly recorded in Stuart Perkoff's one-act jazz verse play, "Round Bout Midnite." In his journals, Perkoff noted that the role of "The Poet" was based on Newman. According to Perkoff, Newman retreated from the scene by the late 1950s, apparently unable to reconcile the demands of an overbearing mother with his own artistic aspirations. [1]

John Thomas is perhaps the most astonishing omission from Rachmuhl's list and Maynard's book-length study. While it is true that Thomas was a late arrival to the scene (in the summer of 1959, just after the publication of *The Holy Barbarians*), nevertheless his place of honor in this community was earned three times over by being the only one of the community to have lived in Venice for at least some portion of five different decades:

the very late 50s, the very early 60s, and the 80s, 90s, and first few months of the new millennium. When he co-wrote a book of poems with Philomene Long entitled *The Ghosts of Venice West,* he was not remembering some distant place: he was living in Venice. Appropriately enough, a selection of his memoirs from his years at living at the Elliston Apartments in Venice in the 1990s is entitled "Destitute Bohemian Royalty."

In less than a year after Thomas (birth name: John Idlet) arrived, Venice West had crumpled under the dual pressures of middle-class tourism and the shift in the choice of drugs from marijuana to heroin. Perkoff's addiction, in particular, made him a target for police surveillance. It would seem from a journal entry by John Thomas that the police put pressure on the Gas House communal arrangement set up by the owner of the building, Al Matthews, to make his building a drug-free zone. This in turn drove away the very people who gave the scene its most credible literary underpinnings. Without Perkoff and Rios and company, the bottom-feeders of bohemian dabblers and dilettantes moved in and struck a pose as poets in hopes of gaining attention. In the following journal entry, John Thomas records the dissolution of the community under the pressures of police surveillance and amateur beatniks.

> Friday, March 25, 1960
> The Gas House has become a sort of mausoleum. Al [Matthews] had a good chance to create something meaningful, something organic, something even (oh cynical I!) could have felt was sort of value. But he flubbed it. Fear, mostly, as with all of us. As soon as he felt that his professional reputation was threatened, as soon as he got the sound "narcotics" he copped out. He has destroyed the thing he tried to build. He has chased all the real people away. Late August, September, October, something was happening. Now nothing is happening.
>
> The place is a meaningless museum where a few tourists wander, gaping at collages and riffling through the books and listening to "poetry" readings—Clare Horner and David Topoulos and Art Diamond—"poets." A hollow mockery, to coin a phrase. And I am a little bitter, feel a little betrayed. Because there was a time when poets and artists lived here, worked here. Here I partook in the sacrament of breakfast with Stuart Perkoff, Tony Scibella, Frank Rios, Maurice Lacy, and other men of stature. I felt honored to feed

> them. Well, all gone. All gone. The only salvaged thing is the poetry workshop, which I created and which I have saved from the wreck . . .
>
> And so? Well, I won't read here any more and I won't hang my collages here anymore. I just don't feel right about it. I'll take down the collages right now and it will have been done.
>
> Did it. Feel better. Won't read here any more either. Feel good about that too. Just sell books. Read, write. Brooding? Pique? Vindictiveness? Posturing? Yes, yes, all right, but something else too. If one must psychoanalyse each positive action, each decision, and boil it down to a motive that can fit within the doctrinaire limits of some school of psychoanalytic theory, then nothing is left and there are no longer any meaningful acts. It can't be that way. One must act "as if"—always "as if" but with perfect seriousness and good humor. There is joy in action. There is joy in thinking, if one can assume that thought can bear fruit and expand into new life.
>
> Think / act/ Feel / think / act. Act; think. Feel / act / think. As in Zen. Except that I must reject the non-rational mystique of Zen. I am a Western man. I have great respect for my forebrain. There is no salvation for me without it. (Thomas 1972)

Thomas moved up north to San Francisco and lived there for several years before returning to Los Angeles, where he died in 2002.

The third person is Frank T. Rios, who arrived in Venice before John Thomas and had become a prominent part of an improvised troupe of poets engaged in a kind of guerrilla warfare with the tourists who came to gawk in the summer of 1959. Their counter-attack approached a dadaesque celebration of the absurd. [2] If Rios proved adept at serving as one of Perkoff's primary side-kicks in toying with the tourists, he also impressed his fellow poets with an imaginative sensitivity that belied his youthful transgressions as a stick-up man in New York. One of his best-known poems at the time was "The Ball Poem," which had been written in 1954, when he was still living the life of a *poete maudit* (though apparently without any awareness of the tradition). Unlike Newman and Boyd, however, Rios has managed to gather his poems into a full-length collection, ""Memoirs of a Street Poet," in which the dedications encompass a considerable number of the most prominent members of this community (Rios 1994).

Rios, in fact, is one of the few poets of the Venice West scene who is still alive and active as a poet. He has steadfastly maintained the practice of his foundational cluster of poets of burning a poem in honor of "the Lady," the muse-force from whom all poems flow, at least within the self-mythology of the Venice West scene. His adamant requirement ran into equally obstinate institution regulations when he gave a memorable reading at the Los Angeles County Museum of Art in September, 2014. This reading was meant to be a formal, public occasion during which to celebrate and call attention to the exhibition of Edward Biberman's mural of Venice, California. Rios resolved the impasse by holding up a poem and then tearing it up into bits and flinging the bits towards the audience.

The fourth person is Eileen Aronson Ireland, who was one of the last arrivals to become part of the initial core group of Venice West poets. She was born in Brooklyn and moved to Los Angeles and Venice in the late 1950s. She was an active member of the poetry workshop that was founded by Thomas and led by Perkoff. In his journals, Perkoff acknowledges her as a fine poet, but as was the case with her peers in Venice West, she had little interest in circulating her work for publication. According to a conversation tape-recorded by Lawrence Lipton, in fact, he was unable to cajole her into submitting her work for publication (Lipton N.D.). The one time she did submit and had her poetry accepted ended badly, with the publication returning the work with no explanation. In her first major publication of her poetry, in 2015, she has included an homage to the most important poet of Venice West, Stuart Z. Perkoff. She, too, is still alive and writing.

Best Priest
for Stuart Z. Perkoff

hammer voice poet
swinging stinging mass in *holy* workshop
preaching how St. Ezra said
  get out and wait for rain
preparing us to conceive hosts
and praising Eisenstein's patch filmed litanies
and catechizing true to
  low ball adjectives
  skip Latin traps
  love grip-clip

angle-sax

even chanting of a friend had seen *the Lady*
  was all in white *our Muse*
so just for you Best Priest
  we offer up this handle
  even with adjective

Keeping all of the above people in mind, it is now worth presenting a chart that will give some sense of the growth of this community of poets. Since poets moved in and out of the scene, these dates are meant to be approximate markers of their face-to-face contact with each other. Boyd, for instance, had moved back to San Francisco in the late 1950s, but not only moved back to Venice in the early 1960s, but was able to rent his old residence on Carroll Canal again.

1955	1956	1958	1960
Charley Newman	Stuart Z. Perkoff	Stuart Z. Perkoff	Stuart Z. Perkoff
Julia Newman	Suzanne Perkoff	Saul White	Tony Scibella
Stuart Z. Perkoff	Saul White	Tony Scibella	Frank T. Rios
Suzanne Perkoff	Tony Scibella	Frank T. Rios	Lawrence Lipton
Bruce Boyd	Lawrence Lipton	Lawrence Lipton	John Thomas
	Charles Foster	Charles Foster	Eileen Ireland
	Bruce Boyd	Bruce Boyd	Maurice Lacy
	Charles Newman	Alexander Trocchi	Bruce Boyd
			James Ryan Morris
			William Margolis
			Milton Bratton
			Harold Norse
			Steve Richmond

This list primarily features individuals who contributed to the development of Venice West as poets and fiction writers, but several visual artists also were significant members of Venice West, including George Herms, Art Richer, Ben Talbert, Jim Shaw, and Mad Mike Magdalani, and various jazz musicians also took part in performances, readings, and private experiments. Because Stuart Z. Perkoff has generally been regarded as the most significant poet of Venice West, his journals and letters provide a compelling survey of its core membership. [3]

The attention given in this article to John Thomas, Bruce Boyd, Frank Rios, Charles Newman, and Eileen Aronson Ireland as representative figures of a Beat bohemia in Los Angeles should not be taken as an intended divergence from the need for much more critical attention to be given to the poetry of Stuart Z. Perkoff. As I pointed out in *Holdouts* (2001), he is the author of the first long, experimental poem in the United States about the

Holocaust. There is nothing in American literature that in any way begins to compare with "Feasts of Death, Feasts of Love" for breaking the engulfing silence about the shoah after World War II in this country, while at the same time raising new questions in poetics about the relationship of poetry and prose. The fact that such an important poem could be published in the most significant anthology of American poetry published in the past 75 years and yet still be unrecognized within the world of Helen Vender-Marjorie Perloff-Adam Kirsch is nothing short of an astonishing lapse in critical knowledge.

The national notoriety of Venice West, through the publicity it received from Lipton's *The Holy Barbarians* as well as *Life* magazine's coverage, no doubt all but ensured that the countervailing idealism of the poets of Venice West would come to naught. That this bohemian scene produced enduring poetry that still cannot be accorded the slightest recognition in contemporary canonical anthologies remains a confounding testament to its genuine vitality. Bohemia in this case was not a chrysalis with a fragile butterfly. Those who visit Venice, California now and see only the travesty of its gentrification might assume that nostalgia is the only possible emotional response. Quite the opposite. The intellectual challenge to accord the writing of the poets of Venice West its proper place in the canon of twentieth-century poetry remains an ongoing project that is not likely to be resolved in the near future. This was a bohemia destined for a long migration.

Endnotes

[1] For purposes of avoiding redundancy, I have omitted any commentary on Bruce Boyd, who remains the most enigmatic and tantalizing figure in the Venice West community. See the chapter on Venice West, "I Cannot Imagine the Extent of their Aloneness," in *Holdouts* for biographical details in the footnote on Boyd as well as consideration of his best-known poem, "Venice Recalled," in which he compares Venice West with the Beat communities in San Francisco. His decisive evaluation in favor of Venice West as a more organic and propitious gathering of poets remains a startling judgment, especially in light of the fact that he lived in both communities. In fact, he was born in San Francisco, went to UC Berkeley, and was part of Jack Spicer's inner circle. Given that background, it is almost impossible to believe that he would not have been overwhelmingly predisposed to prefer the northern California community, yet the bohemian milieu of Venice West proved to have the greater draw.

[2] Perkoff, Rios, and Scibella garnered such a public image with their water-pistol antics (noted by Perkoff in one of his own poems about "stooging it" on the Venice Boardwalk) that John Thomas a quarter century later wrote a six-line elegy for "Baza" (Bob Alexander, one of the founders of Temple of Man) in which he assigns Baza the role of being the guide to bring all the Venice West poets back from the dead. "You'll / be wearing elaborate disguises, / of course, but the water pistols and the / squirting carnations will give you away" ("Who Do You Think You're Kidding?" in *Thomas* 2011:57).

[3] *The Selected Poems and Prose of John Thomas* (2011) contains prose sketches of some of the people named in the above columns, such as Perkoff and Milton Bratton, as well as others who were simply joyous comrades of the community, such as Gary O'Brien and the flautist Roscoe. The brief portrait of Perkoff in Venice in late 1960 (Thomas 2011:109-10) focuses on Perkoff's attempt to write a poem about the Warsaw Uprising, an ongoing project that serves as evidence that "Feasts of Death, Feasts of Love" was not simply a one-time exercise in Holocaust poetry.

Laurel Canyon

"I Think That Maybe I'm Dreaming": Southern California Gives Birth to the Renaissance Pleasure Faire

Rachel Rubin

The Faire brought the lefties, the artists, the longhairs and the eccentrics out of the woodwork to play together under the trees.

—Alicia Bay Laurel (email to author, Dec. 7, 2009)

A frequently stated goal of a Renaissance faire, since the first one was staged in Los Angeles in 1963, is symbolically to take visitors out of the time and space they normally occupy (Rubin 2012). Above all, of course, this goal encompasses the faire's explicit organizing principle: to portray, with varying degrees of attention to historical authenticity, aspects of Renaissance-era society in Europe. But the temporal and geographic work of the faire means more than that, too: the new "time and place" these events establish also signify a respite from visitors' jobs (where someone else "owns" their time), freedom from social judgments and stratifications (about what constitutes "normal" or "beautiful" or who should associate with whom), desire to live "off the grid," or the celebration of non-conformity. Indeed, the most devoted visitors have even developed a vocabulary to express the disconnect between their lives outside the gates, which they call their "mundane" life, and their lives inside the gates, in that special place called "faire." As California's Renaissance Pleasure Faire developed into a central institution of the 1960s and 1970s counterculture, both patrons and workers have declared that this disconnect was what they loved most about the faire. For instance, the mime Robert Shields, who began his career at the Southern California Renaissance Faire and went on from there to become famous as half of the mime duo Shields and Yarnell, described to me his youthful reaction to the faire by comparing the world *outside* to the television show *Mad Men*. By contrast, *inside* the faire gates, said Shields, "Everything was 'yes!'" (personal communication with the author, June, 2009).

But the Renaissance Faire was itself rooted in a particular place and time. Further, what might be described as its useful and pleasurable "placelessness" could not have come from anywhere else. In the twenty-first century, spread across the United States (and beyond), mounted now in every state in the nation, the faire *as institution* still carries a very particular dateline: southern California, 1963. Fifty years later, the stamp of that first setting continues to make itself known in ways large and small wherever the faire is held. Like the base coat that allows you to paint a house a variety of colors, southern California at the outset of the counterculture remains lurking just below, emerging fully now and then if the surface is deliberately scratched—or just as part of normal processes of aging and weathering.

When the faire's founders, Phyllis and Ron Patterson, got the idea for the faire, they were relatively new residents of Laurel Canyon, a neighborhood long known by then for its bohemian, artistic character (Walker 2006). Among their talented neighbors there they met the people who would help them develop the particularities of what a Renaissance faire would entail (in twentieth-century America, that is). Together, they had the artistic vision to imagine the performances, staging, and marketplace that constituted the Renaissance Pleasure Faire, and also the practical skills to mount it (from recruiting acts, to building booths, to procuring or creating costumes). They had a shared politics that made them want to contribute to Pacifica Radio, the nation's first listener-sponsored radio, for which the first several faires were mounted as a benefit, and even a major, historical crisis facing some of Laurel Canyon's residents—the anti-Communist black lists of the Cold War era—played a role in pushing the faire along its path.

The influence of the Red Scare on the faire was multifarious. First of all—and most practical—is that some of the faire's key creators were available to donate their creative energies because their employment possibilities were constricted by the black list. Second, the politically repressive environment (the time and place those Californians sought to leave "outside the gates") shaped the parodies and humor of the music and drama performances in a way that is lasting today; in Pacifica's live broadcast of the very first faire, for instance, a "Pacifica Crier" announces, "Puritan agitation broke out in Leeds today. Rev. William Penn, leader of the East Middlesex Christian Leadership Conference, was arrested for leading a sit-in demonstration at

Leeds Cathedral. Mastiffs were released against those holding signs saying 'We shall not be removed' and 'Ban the Longbow' " ("Fairest of the Faire" 1963). Finally, a lasting vocabulary and practice was established for bashing the faire—leading, in the 1960s, to public hearings, media excoriations of the "leftists," "hippies," and "weirdies" that supposedly populated it, and even once to the closing of the faire following agitation on the part of a conservative group that coalesced around Ruth Brennan, wife of character actor Walter Brennan, who was, by this time, well-known for his conservative politics. Radio talk-show host Joe Pyne, a pioneer of the confrontational style of interviewing, took to the radio waves to warn about the "Reds wearing red tights," as Phyllis Patterson recalled (Interview with author, Aug. 11, 2009).

Local newspapers covered the attacks on the faire. The *Oxnard Press-Courier* rather humorously captured the claims the faire's critics made: "Right-wingers said the fair . . . attracted hippies and left-wingers" ("Pleasure Faire on Today" May 4, 1968). But despite its naysayers, not only did the faire grow and thrive, but also it became a major engine for the emergence of the early counterculture as a significant constituent of California life in the 1960s. Much of this sense of wonder and possibility, of social and cultural alternative, can be heard in a song the Byrds (Laurel Canyon residents themselves a scant few years into the faire's life) wrote about the sights, sounds, and smells of the faire (and from which my title is taken):

> I think that maybe I'm dreaming
> I smell cinnamon and spices
> I hear music everywhere
> All around kaleidoscope of color
> I think that maybe I'm dreaming
> ("Younger than Yesterday")

This song, titled "Renaissance Fair," was recorded early in 1967; by then the faire had been mounted only four times but had already audibly and visibly shaped southern California's counterculture. Indeed, musician Robb Royer, before he settled into the musical act (Bread) that would make him famous, first borrowed the faire's name for a "sunshine pop" act, Pleasure Fair, hoping that this name would automatically bestow the group with countercultural cachet (interview with author, Aug. 20, 2010). As the faire opened up first in a second California location and then in other states, young people who were coming to be called "hippies" by a disdainful media began to follow its seasonal path to work, marrying the countercultural value of traveling light with the communal living and handicraft-based, alternative economy the faire offered. A number of long-time faire workers hitchhiked across the country and ended up at the faire. Soon, the faire located itself firmly in its time and space in yet another way, as Vietnam veterans found their way there, assuring one another that they had found a place that was "safe" for those bearing the various scars of their time in the war.

In this way, southern California peopled the early faire, creating what came to be known as "Rennies": faire workers who followed the seasonal circuit. Once these early Rennies, these important cultural activists, encountered one another inside the gates, new cultural formations resulted that constituted some of the faire's greatest gifts to the world outside—even if the Renaissance-faire pedigree has retreated from sight in some cases. The faire was once a notable early contributor to an important craft revival during the 1960s, for instance, which in turn led to a new kind of attention as reporters and critics began to watch closely what was being sold there (not to mention pointing the faire out as an employment possibility for fine crafters).

The faire was also able to draw upon southern California's cultural wells—music programs in the extensive state university system, beatnik coffeehouses, the decades-old entertainment industry, early iterations of bohemian or communal living arrangements, the sensory lessons learned from the acid tests—to became central to a generation of Americans' discovery of multiple musical forms, but especially early music and "world" music. The perspective of historical hindsight shows the faire bringing Renaissance instruments out of the narrow scope of the classroom, and acting as a precursor to the experimentation with "ethnic" musical forms and instruments that would become a hallmark of popular music in the 1960s and 1970s; it contributed significantly to the popularity of Middle Eastern dance and music in the U.S., to an appreciation of music from the British Isles—even to the rediscovery of klezmer music. The faire's musical role was complex: first, it supported the musicians financially, thereby allowing them to carry out their musical explorations. Second, the geography of the faire, in which different performances happen on different stages and all over the faire site simultaneously, encouraged the kind of mixing and hybridity of musical traditions that became notable in the music of the period. Third, the faire life-style encouraged communality, which, in the context of music, meant musicians were swapping songs, instruments, riffs, and styles in fascinating and productive ways.

These native California building blocks—Hollywood's adroitness with fantasy, the country's first public radio, west coast communes and crash pads, a history of bohemian, experimental culture—gave "Renaissance" a doubled meaning where the early faire was concerned. Certainly, many talented people worked hard, with a great deal of creative success, to invoke Europe during the fourteenth-seventeenth centuries. But from a historical perspective, it's just as interesting to think of the faire as contributing to a California-born artistic and performing renaissance—one that would spread across the country and come to dominate the way what we now call "the sixties" are remembered. In doing so, the Renaissance Pleasure Faire effectively combined values of "place" with those of "placelessness."

Because of the early faire's community orientation and homespun aesthetic, turning to oral history—presenting a selection of the voices the Byrds tried to capture in their song about the faire—to tell its story seems fitting. The three participants whose interviews follow became involved with the Renaissance Pleasure Faire when its creators were still figuring out what it could and should be, and for whom. The faire was at its most experimental in those years, and, arguably, at its most ecstatic. Each of the three interviewees carried lessons from the faire to future performance and teaching careers, further establishing the faire as a lasting cultural wellspring.

David Ossman (born in Santa Monica in 1936) is best known now as a member of the seminal comedy group *Firesign Theater*. The group, which got its start at the southern California Renaissance Pleasure Faire, recorded more than twenty albums, characterized by political satire, surrealism, psychedelic and layered narrative structure, pop-culture references, and stream-of-consciousness presentation. Ossman was working for Pacifica Radio's Los Angeles station, KPFK, when the 1963 faire was mounted as a fund-raiser for the station. He was one of a team of radio DJs live-broadcasting the event, and 50 years later still describes himself as being quite "taken aback" by how quickly visitors turned into active participants; an example he gives is that patrons showed up on the second day of its two-day run in homemade, cobbled-together costumes. Ossman himself became a performer at the faire in subsequent years (and his daughter was to become a faire costumer). He points to much of his prominent performing career, in the Firesign Theatre and beyond, as indebted to the faire's role in southern California's nascent counterculture.

Interview with author, Feb. 15, 2015

Rubin: The first Renaissance Faire was a fund-raiser for Pacifica radio, which in 1963 was still a fairly new experiment with listener-sponsored radio (Hopkins 1966). What was your involvement with Pacifica?

Ossman: I was in New York City in 1959. I had been an acting manager at Columbia University, and one of my teachers called me up and said there was an opening at FM radio station for an announcer, a summer replacement, and asked if I wanted to apply. I did and got the job, at WBAI. It was a commercial station then, but about six months later, at the beginning of 1960, it became the third station in the Pacifica chain. (The first one was, of course, in Berkeley, KPFA and then KPFK in Los Angeles). I stayed on staff there for about two years and then moved back to California and got job at KPFK.

Rubin: How did Pacifica come to mount the faire?

Ossman: Well, the Pattersons were neighbors of ours in Laurel Canyon. They came around to the station and pitched a fundraiser for KPFK, this event they were calling the Renaissance Faire and May Market. It was going to be at a nearby day camp for kids, not too far away at all [from KPFK]. I can remember that it was well underway in its organization, so we knew exactly what she planned to do, so the way it came alive completely was a surprise to everyone! There were Hollywood actors there; there were people in costume—I was completely taken aback. I was there to broadcast it live for the whole day. I arrived nattily attired in a suit. Phyllis Patterson took one look at me and said, "No, no, no, take that off," and she put me into a Renaissance faire costume.

Photo 1: David Ossman poses in faire costume–known to devoted participants as "garb"–at the third Renaissance Pleasure Faire. (1964, courtesy Ossman Archive)

Rubin: What do you think was important about the faire's costuming?

Ossman: The fact that people showed up in costumes right at the very beginning was quite meaningful. This was 1963. People were still dressing conservatively, and suddenly there is explosion of blousey shirts and colors and low-cut bodices. For the men of the faire, it was the first opportunity to really dress up, go outside and have fun with their neighbors. It was a discard of the restrictive conventions of the 1950s, and those costumes at the early faire became the basis of the whole wardrobe of the late 1960s. I think that kind of fancy dress would have been impossible in the United States without the Renaissance Faire kind of breaking through.

Rubin: A lot of record covers by a range of musicians picture the artists wearing very Renaissance Faire-influenced clothing: the Byrds, the Isley Brothers, Kaleidoscope . . . Of course, a huge number of popular musicians in the 1960s went to the faire.

Ossman: The Byrds, Crosby, Stills & Nash, Buffalo Springfield, Mamas and Papas, the Monkees . . .

Rubin: Besides the clothing people wore to the faire, what other "rules" did you see the faire as breaking?

Ossman: It circumvented the ordinary markets by creating its own marketplace, its own economy—hand-made crafts, all sorts of food, no mass production . . .

Rubin: Your broadcast of the very first faire makes a lot of references to the headlines of the day in a very amusing way. How aware were people of current events as they created this new project?

Ossman: To start with, KPFK had spoken out at that time very strongly for civil rights and against the war in Vietnam. We had teach-ins on those issues very early on, and Pacifica really was a pacifist organization. I think right from the very beginning the performers at the faire wanted to use current events, but mask them in Elizabethan language. There were a lot of very clever pieces that were written and performed that had to do with what was going on in the war but were presented through period language, which functioned as a kind of an underground methodology. It was euphemistic, but everybody got it, and it still fit with the language of the faire.

Rubin: Can you make a connection between the faire's values you've spoken of—including aesthetic values, political values, community values, and so forth—and the work you went on to do in the Firesign Theater?

Ossman: By the time the faire got rolling on its third, fourth, fifth year everyone had their job to do in the faire, and there was still a very populist and radical edge to what was going on. I mean, remember what we did, our show at the faire; it was about King Arthur's court, knights going out on the quest for the drug that they were using at the time, so it was an extended drug joke, and people laughed there, but the people who are afraid didn't know what we were talking about. We were both very critical of hippie culture and a clear part of it. This allowed us to be productively irreverent.

Like David Ossman, Judy Kory was involved in the Renaissance Pleasure Faire from its inception. As a cast member, she played several roles over the years, ranging from the mayor's wife to a wandering fruit vendor. Kory speaks of the faire as having a transformative effect on her, bringing her out of a socially imposed shell of sorts; before the faire, she says, she was a "prim housewife." But within three years, she was handing flowers to cops at the Great Underground Arts Masked Ball and Orgy (GUAMBO), a celebration of the second anniversary of the *Los Angeles Free Press* (Hopkins 1966). The faire was deeply involved with this signature countercultural event. The *Free Press,* often cited as the first underground newspaper of the 1960s, itself got its start at the faire in 1964, when founder Art Kunkin handed out the paper's first edition, dubbed the *Faire Press* for the occasion, and filmmakers Les Blank and Gary Taylor showed their "beautiful Pleasure Faire Film" [1] at GUAMBO (Hopkins 1966).

As well as shaping Kory's character, the faire shaped her career trajectory: she subsequently became an expert on Living History, an educational practice seeking to give both participants and observers a sense of having entered another period of time. Kory's association with the Living History Center in Novato, California, spanned from 1975 to 1996. She has played historical characters in a variety of settings, ranging from schools to museums, and has taught performance skills to both children and adults.

Interview with author: Feb. 20, 2015

Rubin: How did you come across the faire in the first place?

Kory: Phyllis Patterson, the founder of the faire, was in a room at KPFK, and I walked in there. I had been making dolls for a left-wing bazaar. She was writing down people's names on a whiteboard opposite the contributions they were going to make to the faire, and she said to me, "What do you do?" I said, "I make dolls." "How many dolls have you made?" "Oh," I said, "I could make one a week." She said, "All right, you could be a fruit seller." That's when I started. I dealt in apples.

Rubin: What about that first faire really made a lasting impression on you?

Kory: I was a little prim housewife at that time. I was married to a mathematician. I was carrying a basket of apples for sale, walking around. I had a coin purse in my bodice. I was looking up at the sky because I was too shy to look anybody in the face. I was singing, [sings] "Apples, fresh apples, come buy one from me. Try my cold, juicy fruit, picked off me own tree." I saw in front of my face a quarter, so I took the quarter with my right hand, took the little coin purse out of my cleavage with my left hand, put the quarter in and took out a dime with my right hand, put the coin purse back in my cleavage—all without looking at the guy. I reached to get an apple, handed him the apple, still without looking at him, and he said to me, "I don't want an apple." Then I looked at him, and he said, "I just wanted to see you make change." At that point, it's like I woke up! I saw that this is a game, and I can have fun! It's ok. I don't have to be the princess!

Rubin: Yes, play can be so serious! What would you say were the artistic priorities of performance at the faire?

Kory: Oh, improvisational theater. We learned from Rachel Rosenthal. [2] I met Rachel at the faire. Then I learned about her company. Ron [Patterson, co-founder of the faire] and I did a workshop with her, and Rachel gave us a structure in which we could improvise. Rachel was so important to our performance! That structured improvisation gave us tremendous freedom, and I never felt that that people might be difficult to bring up on stage to perform with us. Ron and I became an improvisational duo. We had lots of fun! I remember one of the nicest things that happened was when the MGM movie star Marsha Hunt, who was with UNESCO at the time, saw us perform, and we made her laugh. We just made her laugh!

Because of the faire's lessons and experiences, faire performers were also able become street performers, to go out on the street and perform among people and make good money.

Rubin: Thinking about the various roles you played as a faire cast member—which, among other things, meant you walked around the faire site and interacted in character with faire patrons—do you see a connection between the improvisational nature of faire performance and rule-breaking, particularly when it came expectations for behavior based on identity?

Kory: Well, I was taught to cross my legs when seated, and wear white gloves and matching shoes and handbags. I was generally closed-mouth. I was able to be more expressive. Yeah, it certainly influenced the freedom to be as you are, and to be authentic when you are talking.

Rubin: Did you have wishes for what audience members would receive as a result of the faire's bohemianism?

Kory: One of the things I wanted was for people to be able to speak about sex in a relaxed, normal manner, and not to have to carry out prim conversations. You couldn't say "pregnant" on television! [At the faire] I could use the word for a weapon to mean a body part and then tease somebody about it. I could do a lot of things that I couldn't otherwise do. I think that to be able to express yourself like that, freely, without any punishment . . . I wanted people to be able to do that. At the faire we were free to play, to be expressive, to improvise, without any prurient or puritanical judgment attached to it. The faire's *permission*, then the self-permission you've gotten from having taken part, that's probably the main thing that people come away with: permission.

Will Spires, who was born in 1944 in San Diego, is a gifted multi-instrumentalist who started performing at the Renaissance Pleasure Faire in 1964, when he was 21 years old. Spires entered the faire though Los Angeles's Beatnik-inflected coffeehouse scene, which he describes himself as "dropping out of high school" to join (Interview with author, Mar. 28, 2011). That is where Spires met the late Bob Thomas, a key figure in the early faire's musical performances and development. Before long, law enforcement had found ways to shut down many of the coffeehouses, and, in the words of Thomas, "Afterward, the only place you could gather with people of your own stripe was the midnight movies at Melrose Avenue near sunset, and then . . . there was the faire!" (Brown 1979). Both Thomas and Spires sketch out a direct continuity between the gatherings and bohemian cultural practices of the coffeehouses and the cultural energy of the early faires.

Spires recalls that Thomas—later to become well-known for his close association with Grateful Dead sound engineer Owsley Stanley, A.K.A. "the Acid King"—recruited him for the faire by telling him, "You'll see everyone you know!" At first, Spires says, he, Thomas, and Thomas's wife, Julia, would show up with as many as 30 different instruments and decide what to play in the moment. Financially, they were buskers; Spires recalls that they earned a gratifying amount of money that first time, and donated half of it to KPFK. Over the course of his involvement with the faire, Spires notes many structural changes: the configurations and aesthetic priorities of the musical groups, compensation of the musicians, the move to more formal, on-stage performance. These performances at the Renaissance Pleasure Faire also led to performances in other venues in both southern and northern California.

Interview with author, Feb. 22, 2015

Rubin: You did most of your performing at the faire as part of band Bob Thomas led called the Golden Toad. How would you characterize its repertoire?

Spires: Well, the Toad could do two things. First, we had to meet certain requirements that the faire set in terms of playing period music. That was mostly using drums and trumpets to announce things that were going on, when they opened the faire, for instance, or when major shows on the main stage were starting. When we had our *own* stages at the faire—the let us set up our own stages for several years—then we'd just do whatever we pleased. Very typically Bob Thomas and I would play fiddle and bagpipe music. Bob was playing some Portuguese bagpipes, and I played fiddle with his Portuguese and Spanish music. Then Ernie Fischbach joined us. Ernie had been studying the *sarod* at the Ali Akbar Khan school up in Marin, and he'd play *ragas*. We played some medieval music, largely on fiddles of different kinds. Bob Thomas's tastes were much more wide-ranging than my own; we explored something new every year. He played music from Morocco and Algeria; he played different string instruments that he was interested in at that time.

Photo 2: The Golden Toad, c. 1967. Left to right: Don Brown, Ron Patterson, Lisa Phillips, Robert D. Thomas, Will Spires. (Courtesy Will Spires; photographer unknown)

Rubin: Did the period of the Renaissance have much to do with it?

Spires: Sure . . . but blended and bent insofar as many people were able! The earlier faires were much more free-ranging. As I recall, there was a shift from "the Renaissance" in general to a specific emphasis on Elizabethan England that was pushed in about 1974-75. At that point there were workshops on language, costume, period, etc., and entertainers and even servers at ale stands had to attend these workshops as a precondition of employment.

Rubin: Which other musicians or styles were central to the faire's development?

Spires: There was a large group of people that played flamenco, and they were very serious and did not play anything else. The person I remember most in that category is the late Chris Carnes; he had, he gone Spain to live for years, and he studied and played with some of the most serious gypsy flamenco artists of the 1960s, or really of the twentieth century. He was the personal student of guitarist Diego Del Gastor, who was at the center of a group of singers and dancers and guitarists in a part of Spain called Maron de La Frontera. Carnes learned Diego's repertoire, much of it note for note: that's very, very serious, personal study with the master.

The other people in the flamenco troupe were also very, very serious dancers and guitarists. Sol Feldthouse, from Kaleidoscope, played with the flamenco group. [4] Patricia Farber

was a dancer and choreographer. She studied Balkan dance and particularly folk dance from North Africa. There would be at least thirty women dancing and singing and wearing traditional costumes, many of which were antique textiles from Patricia's collection. She was a costume designer and a textile artist as well as a collector of textiles.
Some of the performances were very deeply rooted in careful research and personal study. We felt that we had to go to the source of that music and present ourselves to the people who had been playing in the first place and see what kind of reception they gave. We did that with Irish music with the Irish community in San Francisco. I went to Louisiana and Mexico to study with people I admired tremendously. Bob Thomas went to England and studied Moorish dance and English piping and developed a repertoire. Eric Thompson went to West Ireland and learned a great deal of music there as well as in London where there was expatriate Irish music. I think we had high standards for ourselves and wanted to double -heck our efforts with the real people. We had to learn to listen more carefully.

Rubin: Solomon Feldthouse, whom you've just mentioned, is often credited with bringing Middle Eastern and North African instruments and influences into American popular music, especially through Kaleidoscope. Did the early countercultural music scene that seemed to thrive in and around the faire get picked up by the music industry often?

Will Spires: Most of us didn't listen to much popular music. One thing that happened fairly often particularly from, say, 1966 through 1968, was that there were talent scouts from record labels out. They would see us at the faire, or they would see us playing street music. Then these people would come up and flash their business cards at us. One of them would say in these very words: "Do you have any original material?" and we just smiled and laughed and said, "No, we don't write original material. We're just playing traditional music."

Rubin: It does seem that liberating your artistic selves from that sort of corporate structure is something the faire allowed you to do (for a while, anyway). Actually, "liberation" was a word that would come to characterize 1960s discourse (women's liberation, black liberation, gay liberation, and more). What else was liberating about the early faire?

Will Spires: I think it was liberating to see ourselves in volume, to see the size of our community . . . not in coffeehouses or art cinemas, but hundreds and later thousands of us outdoors in the daylight, en masse. It was also a very important place for gay people to be out, although there was a great deal of tension within the faire crews themselves about gay men. I think I heard some of the most homophobic language I ever experienced in my life from the work crews at the faire.

Rubin: Why do you think the faire's opposition found it threatening?

Will Spires: The sheer size of the thing must have been confounding and scary to conservatives. The sexuality, the drug use, the color, the mockery of straight culture, and the enthusiastic response to all of this may have seemed like a slap in the face, and it didn't go away! It came back every year.

The Renaissance faire has, by now, long moved well beyond California, and while handicrafts are still for sale and satirical (sometimes off-color) performance still holds sway, it has become a corporate-owned form of entertainment. In the twenty-first century, the best description of the faire, what Raymond Williams called a "cultural formation," has evolved from "counterculture" to "subculture." The most common insults leveled at its workers and its active participants have shifted as well; instead of "hippies" and "leftists," it's now common to hear about "nerds" and "rednecks." (The faire's openness to queer expression has been consistently mocked throughout the faire's 50-year history, often focusing, unsurprisingly, on the notion of men in tights.) But the evolution of the terms with which the faire is mocked demonstrates that as a cultural institution it continues to act as the "slap in the face" that Will Spires described above, and the artistic paths of Ossman, Kory, and Spires—all of whom have continued explore, experiment with, and share new performance forms and content—demonstrate that the faire gates were perhaps not such a dividing line after all.

Endnotes

[1] Hopkins is referring to an unreleased film Les Blank shot in 1964, when he was a film student. Blank would go on to be an important

documentarian, particularly known for his films about American musical forms.

[2] Rachel Rosenthal is a multi-disciplinary performance artist and theatrical pioneer. In 1955 she founded Instant Theater in North Hollywood, which focused on interactive and improvisational performance. Instant Theater became well-known for its "happenings"—gatherings that became iconic to representations of the 1960s artistic and countercultural "scene."

[3] Kaleidoscope was a psychedelic folk band known for its introduction of instruments and musical elements from various traditional ethnic musics. In the late 1960s, the band recorded four albums for Epic Records. Interestingly, there was an English psychedelic rock band of the same name active during the same period, pointing to a broadening aesthetic and cultural significance of experimentation with perception-altering drugs *and* the mixing of musical traditions.

References Cited

Archival Abbreviations:

AAA - Archives of American Art, Smithsonian Institution at Huntington Library.
CRC - Civil Rights Congress Los Angeles Chapter Records, Southern California Library for Social Studies and Research, Los Angeles.
DHP - Dorothy Healey Papers, Special Collections, California State University, Long Beach.

Abrams, Brett L. (2008). *Hollywood Bohemians: Transgressive Sexuality and the Selling of the Movieland Dream.* North Carolina: McFarland.

Ackerman, Carl, director. (1999). *Doc Ball: Surfing's Legendary Lensman.*

Allen, Donald, ed. (1960). *The New American Poetry*. New York: Grove Press.

Anderson, Benedict R. (1983). *Imagined Communities: Reflections on the Origin and Spread of Nationalism*. London: Verso.

Anderson, Ida Frances. (1909). *In Love's Garden, and Other Verses*. Los Angeles: Arroyo Guild Press.

Anon. (1931). "Riders of Sunset Seas." *Los Angeles Times Sunday Supplement,* Jan. 18.

Anon. (1968). "Pleasure Faire on Today Despite Zone Board Delay," *Oxnard Press-Courier,* May 4, 10.

Apostol, Jane. (1992). *Olive Percival: Los Angeles Author and Bibliophile*. Los Angeles: Department of Special Collections, University Research Library, University of California, Los Angeles.

_____. (1994). *El Alisal, Where History Lingers*. Los Angeles: Historical Society of Southern California.

______. (1996). "Margaret Collier Graham: First Lady of the Foothills," *Women in the Life of Southern California: An Anthology Compiled from Southern California Quarterly*. Los Angeles: Historical Society of Southern California, 162-91.

______. (1997). *Painting with Light: A Centennial History of the Judson Studios*. Los Angeles: Historical Society of Southern California.

Arms, L. L. (1942). "Humper!" *Christian Science Monitor Magazine*, Nov. 7.

Arnar, Anna Sigridur. (2011). *The Book as Instrument: Stéphane Mallarmé, The Artist's Book, and the Transformation of Print Culture.* Chicago: The University of Chicago Press.

Austin, Mary Hunter. (1932). *Earth Horizon*. Boston: Houghton Mifflin.

Baigell, Matthew. (2006). *American Artists, Jewish Images.* Syracuse: Syracuse University Press.

Ball, John Heath, photographer. (1995). *Early California Surfriders: A Collector's Edition of Rare Photographs Covering Classic California*

Longboard Surfing in the Thirties and Forties. Ventura, CA: Pacific Publishing (first published as "California Surfriders," 1946).

Banham, Reyner. (1971). *Los Angeles: The Architecture of Four Ecologies*. Berkeley: University of California Press.

Baretta. (2006). *Topanga Beach Snake Pit: Volume 1*. Los Angeles: Brass Tacks Press.

Barker, Nicholas, ed. (1982). "Jake Zeitlin at Eighty." *The Book Collector*, 31, Autumn, 283-92.

Bartlett, Lanier. (1938). "Movie Memories" ms. 330, box 195, Federal Writers' Project of California Records (Collection 306), Department of Special Collections, Charles E. Young Research Library, University of California, Los Angeles.

Bay-Laurel, Alicia. (2009). Email to author, Dec. 7.

Beach, Christopher. (1999). *Poetic Culture: Contemporary American Poetry between Community and Institution*. Evanston: Northwestern University Press.

Becker, Howard. (1982). *Art Worlds*. Berkeley: University of California Press.

Benjamin, Walter. (1973). "The Boheme," in *Charles Baudelaire: A Lyric Poet in the Era of High Capitalism*, trans. Harry Zohn. New York: New Left Books, pp. 11–34.

Bingham, Edwin R. (1955). *Charles F. Lummis: Editor of the Southwest*. San Marino: The Huntington Library.

Blake, Tom. (1935). *Hawaiian Surfboard*. Honolulu: Paradise of the Pacific Press.

Blue Juice. (1979). "Inside-Outside Boogie." *The Best of Blue Juice*. Malibu: J. Murf (distributed by Brass Tacks Press).

Bowron, Fletcher. (1945). Fletcher Bowron, remarks at Declaration of INTERdependence celebration, July 4, file "Remarks July-Dec. 1945," box 34, Fletcher Bowron Papers, Huntington Library.

Bourdieu, Pierre. (1995). "The Conquest of Autonomy: The Critical Phase in the Emergence of the Field," in *The Rules of Art: Genesis and Structure of the Literary Field*, trans. Susan Emanuel. Stanford, CA: Stanford University Press, pp. 47–112.

Brooks, David. (2000). *Bobos in Paradise: The New Upper Class and How They Got There*. New York: Simon and Schuster.

Browne, Clyde. (1932). *Olden Abbey San Encino: A Tale of Its Building and Purpose, with Some Idea of the Difficulties of Its Burgeoning and Fruition, as Set Forth Chronologically by the Master Printer Clyde Browne, Who Strove Amain for Ten Long Years Upon Its Walls*. [Garvanza]: Abbey San Encino.

Brunner, Francis. (1925, 2000). *Southern California's Prettiest Drive: Topanga and Las Flores Canyon Stages*. Reprinted by the Topanga Historical Society.

Bukowski, Charles, et al., eds. (1972). *Anthology of Los Angeles Poets*. Los Angeles: Laugh Literary.

The Byrds. (1967). "Pleasure Fair," *Younger than Yesterday*. Columbia 7.

Campbell, Robert. (2002a). "Rodeo Grounds Last Spark of Eden," in *Idlers of the Bamboo Grove: Poetry from Lower Topanga Canyon*. Los Angeles: Brass Tacks Press.

_____. (2002b). "The Rebirth of the Frustrated Artist," in *Idlers of the Bamboo Grove: Poetry from Lower Topanga Canyon*. Los Angeles: Brass Tacks Press.

Candida-Smith, Richard. (1995). *Utopia and Dissent: Art, Poetry, and Politics in California.* Berkeley: University of California Press.

Carl Oscar Borg Personal Papers and Newspaper Clippings. (1906-1948). Ms. 677, Braun Research Library Collection, Autry National Center, Los Angeles.

Carpenter, E. H. (1948). "Clyde Browne – Master Printer," *Quarterly News-Letter*. San Francisco: The Book Club of California, Summer, 56-61.

Capra, Pablo, ed. (2002). *Idlers of the Bamboo Grove: Poetry from Lower Topanga Canyon*. Los Angeles: Brass Tacks Press.

_____. (2004). "Topanga Ranch Motel Residents Get 30-Day Notice," *Topanga Messenger*, July 29.

Captain Beefheart & His Magic Band. (1967). "Electricity," *Safe As Milk*. New York City: Buddah Records.

Chidester, Brian. (2008). "A Short History of L.A. Bohemia." Accessed at http://www.myspace.com/beatnikbeach/blog/405582609.

Chiacos, Elias. (1994). *Mountain Drive: Santa Barbara's Pioneer Bohemian Community*. Santa Barbara: Shoreline Press.

Citizens' Committee to Outlaw Entrapment. (1952). "An Anonymous Call to Arms," open letter, file 5, box 2 (CRC).

Civil Rights Congress. (1952a). Leaflet for meeting, Jan. 22, folder 19, box 12 (CRC).

_____. (1952b). Leaflet for meeting, Mar. 28, folder 19, box 12 (CRC).

Clark, Tom. (1991). *Charles Olson: The Allegory of a Poet's Life.* New York: Norton.

Cleary, Bill. (1963-1965). *Surf Guide* magazine. Los Angeles.

Clements, Grace. (1968?). – *but is it ART?* Unpublished memoirs, David W. Forsberg Papers, Reel 4048 (AAA).

Clover, Samuel T. (1914). "Millard and His Books." Reprinted from *The Los Angeles Graphic*, Nov., 2.

Cloonan, Michele V. (2006). "Alice Millard and the Gospel of Beauty and Taste," *Women in Print: Essays on the Print Culture of American Women from the Nineteenth and Twentieth Centuries*. Wisconsin: University of Wisconsin Press, 159-78.

Clyde Browne and the Abbey Press Collection (ND). William Andrews Clark Memorial Library, MS.2007.016. University of California, Los Angeles.

Coates, Paul. (1953). "Well, Medium and Rare," *Los Angeles Mirror*, Mar. 12, file "Mattachine Society: Early 1950s," ONE Institute and Archives, University of Southern California.

Cotter, Holland. (2011). "When Art Happened to L.A: A Review of *Rebels in Paradise* by Hunter Drohojowska-Philp," *New York Times*, Aug. 19.

Courtney, Robert. (ND). "The Coffee House Craze." Private publication.

Damon, Maria. (1993). *The Dark End of the Street: Margins in American Vanguard Poetry*. Minneapolis: University of Minnesota Press.

Davies, David W. (1982). *Clyde Browne: His Abbey & His Press*. Pasadena: The Castle Press.

_____. (1985). *Scott E. Haselton and His Abbey Garden Press*. Los Angeles: Dawson's Book Shop.

Drohojowska-Philp, Hunter. (2001). *Rebels in Paradise: The Los Angeles Art Scene and the 1960s*. New York: Henry Holt.

Duncan, Michael, and Kristine McKenna. (2005). *Semina Culture: Wallace Berman & His Circle*. Santa Monica: D.A.P./Santa Monica Museum of Art.

Easton, Malcolm. (1964). *Artists and Writers in Paris: The Bohemian Idea, 1803–1867*. London: Arnold.

Ellingham, Lewis, and Kevin Killian. (1998). *Poet Be Like God: Jack Spicer and the San Francisco Renaissance*. Hanover, NH: Wesleyan University Press/University Press of New England.

Everson, William. (1976). *Archetype West: The Pacific Coast as Literary Region*. Berkeley: Oyez.

Fairweather, Andrew. (2007). "On The Origins of Bohemia." (Accessed Jan. 31, 2014). https://andrewfairweather.wordpress.com/essays-stories/essays-2/on-the-origins-of-bohemia/.

Feigel, Bob. (2014). *A Personal History of Surfing's Gold Years*. www.surfwriter.net.

Feitelson, Lorser. (1941). "What is Postsurrealism?" *Spanish Village Art Quarterly*, Spring.

_____. (1950). Letter to Millier. June. Lorser Feitelson and Helen Lundeberg Papers, Roll 1103 (AAA).

Fiske, Turbese Lummis, and Keith Lummis. (1975). *Charles F. Lummis: The Man and His West*. Norman, OK: University of Oklahoma Press.

Fox, Howard. (2006). "SoCal: The Big Picture," in Catherine Grenier. (2006). *Los Angeles 1955-1985: The Birth of an Artistic Capital*. Paris/San Francisco: Centre Pompidou.

Florida, Richard. (2002). *The Rise of the Creative Class: And How It's Transforming Work, Leisure, Community, and Everyday Life*. New York: Basic Books.

Frankenheimer, John. (1966). *Seconds* (motion picture). Los Angeles: Paramount Pictures.

Goffman, Erving. (1986). *Stigma: Notes on the Management of Spoiled Identity*. New York: Simon and Schuster.

Goldstein, Laurence. (2014). *Poetry Los Angeles*. Ann Arbor: University of Michigan Press

Gordon, Dudley. (1972). *Charles F. Lummis: Crusader in Corduroy*. Los Angeles: Cultural Assets Press.

Gornick, Vivian. (1977). *The Romance of American Communism*. New York: Basic Books.

Graham, Margaret Collier. (2005). *Sage Bloom and Water Rights: Stories of Early Southern California*. Intro. Michele Zack. Pasadena: Many Moons Press.

Grenier, Catherine. (2006). *Los Angeles 1955-1985: The Birth of an Artistic Capital*. Paris/San Francisco: Centre Pompidou.

Griffiths, David B. (1998). *Beach and Temple: Outsider Poets and Artists of Western America*. San Francisco/London: International Scholars Publications, 1998.

Gruen, John. (1972). *The Party's Over Now*. New York: Viking Press.

Harbach, Dennis. (2015). *Charles Lummis' Home: El Alisal's Remarkable Visitors*. Private publication.

Hay, Harry, et al. (1951). "Mattachine Society Missions and Purposes," in Harry Hay. (1996). *Radically Gay*. Boston: Beacon Press.

Healey, Dorothy. (2000). Personal Interview by Daniel Hurewitz, Silver Spring, Maryland.

Heimann, Jim, ed. (2004). *Icons: Surfing: Vintage Surfing Graphics*. Los Angeles: Taschen.

Henderson, Jaime. (2014). *The Bohemian Brownes of Arroyo Seco*. (http://www.kcet.org/socal/departures/columns/history/the-bohemian-brownes-of-the-arroyo-seco.html).

Herny, Ed, et al. (2008). *Berkeley Bohemia: Artists and Visionaries of the Early 20th Century*. Salt Lake City: Gibbs Smith.

Hertz, Richard. (2003). *Jack Goldstein and the CalArts Mafia*. Ojai: Minneola Press.

_____. (2009). *The Beat and the Buzz: Inside the L.A. Art World*. Ojai: Minneola Press.

Higgins, Winifred Haines. (1963). "Art Collecting in the Los Angeles Area, 1910-1960," Ph.D. diss. Los Angeles: University of California, Los Angeles.

Hobbs, Stuart. (1997). *The End of the American Avant garde*. New York: New York University Press.

Hopfengart, Christine, and Michael Baumgartner. (2013). *Paul Klee: Life and Work*. Bern: Hatje Cantz.

Hopkins, Jerry. (1966). "GUAMBO Is an Act of Love-Mothers, Happenings, Dancing." *Los Angeles Free Press*, July 29.

Hopps, Walter. (1996). *Kienholz: A Retrospective*. New York: Whitney Museum of Art.

Hubert, Renée Riese. (1988). *Surrealism and the Book*. Berkeley: University of California Press.

Hurewitz, Daniel. (2007). *Bohemian Los Angeles*. Berkeley: University of California Press.

Hyde, Robert (Bobbie). (1960). *Six More after Sixty*. New York: Doubleday.

Ireland, Eileen Aronson. (2015). "Splints and Splinters." *Spot Literary Magazine*, 8, ed. Susan Hansell. Tucson, AZ.

James, David, ed. (1996). *Power Misses: Essay across (Un)popular Culture.* London: Verso.

_____. (2003). *The Sons and Daughters of Los: Culture and Community in L.A.*

Philadelphia: Temple University Press.

James, David E. (2005). *The Most Typical Avant Garde: History and Geography of Minor Cinemas in Los Angeles*. Berkeley: University of California Press.

James, Don. (1996). *Surfing San Onofre to Point Dume, 1936-1942.* Santa Barbara: T. Adler Books.

James, George Wharton(1906). *The Wonders of the Colorado Desert (Southern California) Its Rivers and Its Mountains, Its Canyons and Its Springs, Its Life and Its History, Pictured and Described; Including an Account of a Recent Journey Made Down the Overflow of the Colorado River to the Mysterious Salton Sea*. Boston: Little, Brown.

_____, ed. (1909). *Arroyo Craftsman*. Los Angeles: Arroyo Guild Press.

Johnson, Anne Beckwith. (2001). *Home is Where the Bus Is*. Santa Barbara: John Daniel & Company Books.

Jordan, David Starr. (1922). *Days of a Man, Being Memories of a Naturalist, Teacher and Minor Prophet of Democracy*. Yonkers-on-Hudson, NY: World Book Co.

Kampion, Drew. (2003). *Stoked! A History of Surf Culture.* Salt Lake City: Gibbs Smith.

Kaufman, Alan. (1999). *The Outlaw Bible of American Poetry*. New York: Thunder's Mouth Press.

Kelley, Robin. (1990). *Hammer and Hoe: Alabama Communists during the Great Depression.* Chapel Hill: University of North Carolina Press.

Kohner, Frederick. (1957). *Gidget: The Little Girl with Big Ideas.* New York: Bantam Books.

Kollwitz, Käthe. (1979). Jake Zeitlin Bookshop and Gallery, 1937. Long Beach: Art Museum and Galleries, California State University, Long Beach.

Kory, Judy. (2015). Personal Interview with Rachel Rubin. Los Angeles.

Kroeber, Theodora. (1964). *Ishi: The Last of His Tribe*. Berkeley, CA: Parnassus Press.

Kubernik, Harvey. (2009). *Canyon of Dreams: The Magic and Music of Laurel Canyon.* New York: Sterling.

Kuenzli, Rudolf, and Francis Naumann, eds. (1990). *Marcel Duchamp: Artist of the Century.* Cambridge: Massachusetts Institute of Technology Press.

Kurth, Peter. (2001). *Isadora, A Sensational Life.* Boston: Little, Brown.

Kurtzworth, Harry Muir. (1937). "Art Comment," *Saturday Night*, Jan. 2.

Larson, Roger Keith. (1991). *Controversial James: An Essay of the Life and Work of George Wharton James*. San Francisco: The Book Club of California.

Lasar, Matthew. (2000). *Pacifica Radio: The Rise of an Alternative Network.* Philadelphia: Temple University Press.

Leland, John. (2015). "Dennis Hopper's Drugstore Camera Photo," *New York Times*. Apr. 27.

Lettner, Natalie, and Werner Hanak. (2006). *Malibu Song*. Vienna, Austria: Eurotrash Productions.

Levin, Joanna. (2010). *Bohemia in America: 1859-1920*. Palo Alto: Stanford University Press.

Lewitzky, Bella. (1985). "Los Angeles in the '40s," lecture, San Francisco, Mar. 29, tape recording. (AAA).

Lipton, Lawrence. (ND). Los Angeles: The Lawrence Lipton Archives, Special Collections, University of Southern California.

_____. (1959). *The Holy Barbarians*. New York: Julian Messner.

Los Angeles County Communist Party Educational Department (LAED). (1950). "Session Seven: The Negro Nation," "Study Outline Negro Liberation," Jan 1-4. Box 69d. (DHP).

Lovas, Paul, and Pablo Capra. (2011). *Topanga Beach Experience: 1960s-70s*. Los Angeles: Brass Tacks Press.

Lueras, Leonard. (1984). *Surfing: The Ultimate Pleasure*. New York: Workman International.

Lummis, Charles Fletcher. (ND). Diaries. Los Angeles: Lummis Papers, Braun Research Library Collection, Autry National Center.

_____. (ND). El Alisal House Book. Los Angeles: Lummis Papers, Braun Research Library Collection, Autry National Center.

_____. (ND). Scrapbooks. Los Angeles: Lummis Papers, Braun Research Library Collection, Autry National Center.

_____. (1895). "Tenderfoot College," *Land of Sunshine*. Mar., 2, 71.

_____. (1898a). *Land of Sunshine*. Nov., 11, 369

_____. (1898b). "The New League: For Literature and the West," *Land of Sunshine*. Apr., 13, 214.

_____. (1899). *Land of Sunshine*. Nov., 11, 369.

_____. (1901). "In Western Letters," *Land of Sunshine*. May, 14, 392.

_____. (1901). "A Sage-Brush Oasis," *The Land of Sunshine*. Jan., 14, 28.

_____. (1909). *Out West*. 31, 992.

_____. (1929). *Flowers of Our Lost Romance*. New York: Houghton Mifflin.

_____. (2012). *Birch Bark Poems* [keepsake]. Los Angeles: The Historical Society of Southern California.

Lynch, Gary, and Malcolm Gault-Williams. (2001). *Tom Blake: The Uncommon Journey of a Pioneer Waterman*. Corona Del Mar, CA: Croul Family Foundation.

Marcuse, Herbert. (1955). *Eros and Civilization: A Philosophical Inquiry into Freud*. Boston: Beacon Press.

Marquis, Alice Goldfarb. (1981). *Marcel Duchamp: Eros, c'est la vie: A Biography*. Troy, NY: Whitston Publishing Co.

Macdonald-Wright, Stanton. (1944). "Art," *Rob Wagner's Script*. October 21. Beverly Hills, CA: Wagner Pub. Co.

Markoff, John. (2005). *What the Dormouse Said: How the Sixties Counterculture Shaped the Personal Computer Industry.* New York: Penguin.
Masheck, Joseph. (1971). "Letter to the Editor," *ArtForum,* 9, Jan., 71.
Mathers, James. (2002). "A Village on Cracking Stilts," *Idlers of the Bamboo Grove: Poetry from Lower Topanga Canyon.* Los Angeles: Brass Tacks Press.
May, James Boyer. (ND). Fullerton, CA: Archive (1932-1972). Editorial papers, *Trace* magazine. Special Collections, California State University, Fullerton.
May, Kirse Granat. (2002). *Golden State, Golden Youth: The California Image in Popular Culture 1955-1966.* Chapel Hill: University of North Carolina Press.
Maynard, John Arthur. (1991). *Venice West: The Beat Generation in Southern California.* New Brunswick, NJ: Rutgers University Press.
McCrackin, Daisy Duck. (2002). "In the Canyon," *Idlers of the Bamboo Grove: Poetry from Lower Topanga Canyon.* Los Angeles: Brass Tacks Press.
McWilliams, Carey. (1967). "Jake," *A Garland for Jake Zeitlin, On the Occasion of His 65th Birthday & the Anniversary of His 40th Year in the Book Trade.* J.M. Edelstein, ed. Los Angeles: Grant Dahlstrom & Saul Marks, 3-5.
Meltzer, David. (1971). *The San Francisco Poets.* New York: Ballantine.
Miles, Malcolm. (2014). "Cities of the Avant Garde," *The Cambridge Companion to the City,* Kevin R. McNamara, ed. New York: Cambridge University Press, pp. 153-62.
Milk, Harvey. (2003). "Tired of the Silence, June 25, 1978," in *Ripples of Hope: Great American Civil Rights Speeches,* ed. Josh Gottheimer. Cambridge, MA: Basic Civitas Books.
Mohr, Bill. (2011). *Holdouts: The Los Angeles Poetry Renaissance 1948-1992.* Iowa City: University of Iowa Press.
Moure, Nancy Dustin Wall. (1978). *Dictionary of Art and Artists in Southern California before 1930.* Los Angeles: Privately published.
Murphet, Julian. (2001). *Literature and Race in Los Angeles.* Cambridge: Cambridge University Press.
Naison, Mark. (1983). *Communists in Harlem during the Depression.* New York: Grove Press.
Novak, Estelle Gershgoren. (2002). *Poets of the Non-Existent City: Los Angeles in the McCarthy Era.* Albuquerque: University of New Mexico Press.
Ossman, David, prod., ed. (1963). "Fairest of the Faire." Radio broadcast, KPFK, North Hollywood, California, Aug. 25.
_____. (2015). Personal Interview with Rachel Rubin. Los Angeles.
Overton, Grant. M. (1918). *The Women Who Make Our Novels.* New York: Moffat, Yard & Co.
Parry, Albert. (1933). *Garrets and Pretenders: A History of Bohemianism in America.* New York: Dover.

Patterson, Karin Gaynell. (2007). "Expressions of Africa in Los Angeles Performance, 1981-1994." Ph.D. diss., University of California, Los Angeles.

Peabody, Rebecca, et al., eds. (2011). *Pacific Standard Time: Los Angeles Art, 1945-1980*. Los Angeles: Getty Research Institute.

Perkoff, Stuart. (1998). *Collected Poems: Voices of the Lady,* ed. Gerald Perkoff. Orono, ME: National Poetry Foundation.

_____. (ND). Stuart Z. Perkoff Papers. Los Angeles. Special Collections. University of California, Los Angeles.

Phillips, Lisa. (1996). *Beat Culture and the New American, 1950-1965*. New York: Whitney Museum of American Art.

Plagens, Peter. (1999). *Sunshine Muse: Art on the West Coast, 1945-1970*. Berkeley: University of California Press.

Powell, Lawrence Clark. (1950). *Recollections of an Ex-Bookseller*, published to mark the anniversary of the new bookshop of Zeitlin & Ver Brugge. Los Angeles: Plantin Press.

_____. (1954). *The Alchemy of Books and Other Essays and Addresses on Books and Writers*. Los Angeles: Ward Ritchie Press, 143.

_____. (1959). *Heart of the Southwest: A Selective Bibliography of Novels, Stories and Tales Laid in Arizona and New Mexico & Adjacent Lands*. Los Angeles: Dawson's Book Shop.

_____. (1967). "Memo to Jake Zeitlin," *A Garland for Jake Zeitlin, On the Occasion of His 65th Birthday & the Anniversary of His 40th Year in the Book Trade.* J.M. Edelstein, ed. Los Angeles: Grant Dahlstrom & Saul Marks, pp. 35-38.

Pritchard, Jane, ed. (2010). *Diaghilev and the Golden Age of the Ballets Russes 1909-1929*. London: V & A Publishing.

Rachmuhl, Sophie. (2015). *A Higher Form of Politics: The Rise of a Poetry Scene, Los Angeles, 1950-1990.* Trans. Mindy Menjou and George Drury Smith. Los Angeles: Beyond Baroque Books/Seismicity Editions.

Rensin, David. (2009). "Miki Dora: Topanga Days," *Malibu Magazine*. Apr. 1.

Rios, Frank T. (1994). *Love from the Darkside.* Los Angeles: Sawbone/Temple of Man.

Ritchie, Ward. (1967). "The Forgotten Street of Books." *A Garland for Jake Zeitlin, On the Occasion of His 65th Birthday & the Anniversary of His 40th Year in the Book Trade.* J.M. Edelstein, ed. Los Angeles: Grant Dahlstrom & Saul Marks, pp. 49-59.

_____. (1980). "Illustrations by Paul Landacre," *Westways,* 72, 16-19, 77-78.

_____. (1982). "The Jake Zeitlin I Knew Fifty Years Ago," *The Book Collector,* 32, Autumn, 293-97.

_____. (1987). *Fine Printing: The Los Angeles Tradition.* Washington, D.C.: Library of Congress.

_____. (1995). "Alice Millard as I Remember Her," *AB Bookman's Weekly*, 95, 7, 648-66.

_____. (1996). *A Southland Bohemia: The Arroyo Seco Colony as the Century Begins*. Pasadena: Vance Gerry/The Weather Bird Press.

Rohloff, Chris, and Pablo Capra. (2009). *Topanga Beach Snake Pit: Volume 3*. Los Angeles: Brass Tacks Press.

Rosenthal, Robert. (1985). "Los Angeles & Chicago: Two Cities, Two Bibliophiles," in *A Bibliophile's Los Angeles: Essays for the International Association of Bibliophiles.* Los Angeles: William Andrews Clark Memorial Library, pp. 3-27.

Rosenzweig, Roy. (1983). *Eight Hours for What We Will: Workers and Leisure in an Industrial City, 1870-1920.* New York: Cambridge University Press.

Rossinow, Douglas. (1998). *The Politics of Authenticity: Liberalism, Christianity, and the New Left in America*. New York: Columbia University Press.

Rubin, Rachel. (2012). *Well Met: Renaissance Faires and the American Counterculture.* New York: New York University Press.

Ruby, Jay. (2012). *Coffee House Positano – A Bohemian Oasis in Malibu – 1957-1962.* Boulder: University of Colorado Press.

_____. (2014). *The Property: Malibu's Other Colony.* [http://www.jayrubyworld.com].

Russell, Ron. (1993). "Going for Broke to Battle Blaze," *Los Angeles Times*. Nov. 11.

Sahlins, Marshall. (1972). "The Original Affluent Society," *Stone Age Economics*. Chicago: Aldine-Atherton.

Schneider, Nina. (2014). "Under the Sign of the Sagebrush: Idah Meacham Strobridge and the Southland's Bohemia," *California State Library Foundation Bulletin*, 109, 2-11.

Schrank, Sarah. (2009). *Art and the City: Civic Imagination and Cultural Authority in Los Angeles.* Philadelphia: University of Pennsylvania Press.

Scibella, Tony. (2000). *The Kid in America.* Los Angeles: Black Ace Books/Passion Press.

Scott, A. O. (2014). "The Paradox of Art as Work." In Cross Cuts, *New York Times*, May 9.

Shelton, Suzanne. (1981). *Divine Dancer: A Biography of Ruth St. Denis*. New York: Doubleday.

Sherman, Miriam. (2000). Personal interview by Daniel Hurewitz, Los Angeles.

Sherrell, Jean, ed. (1992). "Carl Oscar Borg," *The Californians*, 10, 3, 12.

Sides, Josh. (2006). *L.A. City Limits: African American Los Angeles from the Great Depression to the Present*. Berkeley: University of California Press.

Smith, Richard Candida. (1995). *Utopia and Dissent: Art, Poetry, and Politics in California.* Berkeley: University of California Press.

Solnit, Rebecca. (1990). *Secret Exhibition: Six California Artists of the Cold War Era.* San Francisco: City Lights.

Solomon, Mark. (1998). *The Cry Was Unity: Communists and African-Americans, 1917-1936*. Jackson: University Press of Mississippi.

Sontag, Susan. "1973," *On Photography*. New York: Delta.

Spires, Will. (2015). Personal Interview with Rachel Rubin. Los Angeles.

Starr, Kevin. (1985). *Inventing the Dream: California through the Progressive Era*. New York: Oxford University Press.

_____. (1989). *The Rise of Los Angeles as an American Bibliographical Center*. Sacramento: California State Library Foundation.

_____. (1990). *Material Dreams: Southern California through the 1920s*. New York: Oxford University Press.

_____. (1996). *Endangered Dreams: The Great Depression in California*. New York: Oxford University Press.

State Education Committee, Communist Party of California (SEC). (1946). "The Fight for the Freedom of the Negro People: Material for Club Discussions in Connection with the Anniversaries of Lincoln and Douglass and Also in Relation to the Communist Position on the Negro Question." Feb. 12, box 69c. (DHP).

Steinbeck, John. (1945). *Cannery Row*. New York City: Viking Press.

Stern, David H., and Bill Cleary. (1963). *Surfing Guide to Southern California*. Los Angeles: The Fitzpatrick Publishing Company.

Stern, Jean. (ND). "The Great Bohemian Migration" (accessed at http://www.kcet.org/socal/departures/highland-park/arroyo-culture/plein-air.html).

Stern, Jean, and William H. Gerdts. (2002). *Masters of Light: Plein-Air Painting in California, 1890-1930*. Irvine, CA: The Irvine Museum.

Stevens, Konrad . (1977). Interview by John D'Emilio, Los Angeles, Jan. 5, tape 00405, International Gay Information Center Collection, New York Public Library.

Stevens, Mark and Swan, Annalyn. (2004). *De Kooning: An American Master*. New York: Alfred A. Knopf.

Stewart, Katherine. (2007). "Mountain Drive: Santa Barbara's Experiment in Living," *Santa Barbara Magazine*.

Strausbaugh, John. (2013). *The Village: A History of Greenwich Village*. New York: Harper Collins.

Terry, Walter. (1976). *Ted Shawn, Father of American Dance*. New York: The Dial Press.

Thomas, John. (1972). *John Thomas*. Red Hills Press.

_____. (2011). *Selected Prose and Poetry of John Thomas*. Los Angeles: Raven Productions.

Thompson, E. P. (1967). "Time, Work-Discipline, and Industrial Capitalism," *Past and Present: Journal of Historical Studies*, 38, 56-97.

Thompson, Kathleen Dakin. (1975). *Twenty-Seven Boxes Full of Paper: The Zeitlin & Ver Brugge Archive*. Los Angeles: specialization paper in partial fulfillment of MLS, University of California, Los Angeles.

Thompson, Mark. (2001). *American Character: The Curious Charles Fletcher Lummis and the Rediscovery of the Southwest*. New York: Arcade Publishing.

Timmons, Stuart. (1990). *The Trouble with Harry Hay: Founder of the Modern Gay Movement.* Boston: Alyson Books.
Tool. (2007). *Topanga Beach Snake Pit: Volume 2.* Los Angeles: Brass Tacks Press.
Turner, Fred. (2006). *From Counterculture to Cyberculture.* Palo Alto: Stanford University Press.
Vangelisti, Paul, ed. (1998). *L.A. Exile: A Guide to Los Angeles Writing 1932-1998.* New York: Marsilio.
Walker, Michael. (2006). *Laurel Canyon: The Inside Story of Life in L.A.'s Legendary Rock and Roll Neighborhood.* New York: Faber and Faber.
Warner, Simon. (2013). *Text and Drugs and Rock and Roll: The Beats and Rock Culture.* New York: Bloomsbury.
Warren. Beth Bates. (2011). *Artful Lives: Edward Weston, Margrethe Mather, and the Bohemians of Los Angeles*. Los Angeles: The J. Paul Getty Museum.
Whiting, Céclie. (2006). *Pop LA: Art and the City in the 1960s*. Berkeley: University of California Press.
Ward Ritchie Papers. (ca. 1930-1978). Los Angeles: William Andrews Clark Memorial Library, University of California, Los Angeles.
White, Minor, ed. (1973). *Edward Weston: Fifty Years.* New York: Aperture.
Wiley, Sharyn. (2003). "Messages from the Promised Land: Bohemian Los Angeles, 1880-1920." Ph.D. diss., University of Colorado.
Wilkins, Thurman. (1936). "At the Sign of the Petrel," *VO Magazine* 4, Mar., 38-39, in file 16, box 12, Paul Landacre papers, William Andrews Clark Memorial Library, University of Californa, Los Angeles.
Wilson, Elizabeth. (2000). *Bohemians: The Glamorous Outcasts*. New Brunswick, NJ: Rutgers University Press.
Winter, Robert W. (1998). *The Arroyo Culture*. Pasadena: The Clinker Press.
Young, Jock . (1971). *The Drugtakers: The Social Meaning of Drug Use*. London: Paladin.
Young, Noel. (1973). *Hot Tubs: How To Build, Maintain & Enjoy Your Own*. Santa Barbara: Capra Press.
Zahn, Thomas C. (1954). "Surf Boarding from Molokai to Waikiki," *Paradise of the Pacific*, Mar. 26, quoted in Lynch and Gault-Williams, 184.
Zeitlin, David. (1997). Personal Interview by Genie Guerard. Los Angeles.
Zeitlin, Jake. (ND). Interview by Joel Kugelman. Los Angeles, KPFK.
_____. (1926-1987). Jake Zeitlin Papers (collection 334), Charles E. Young Research Library Special Collections, University of California, Los Angeles.
_____. (1927). *Unofficial Map of Booklovers' Lane & Environs.* Los Angeles: Jake Zeitlin.
_____. (1965). "Who Shall Silence All the Airs and Madrigals?" *Library Journal,* 90, 11, 2479-83.

_____. (1972). *Small Renaissance, Southern California Style.* First published in the *Papers* of the Bibliographical Society of America, 50, first quarter (1956). Reprinted for the author, Los Angeles: Richard Hoffman.

_____. (1980). Interview by Joel Gardner in *Books and the Imagination Oral History Transcript: Fifty Years of Rare Books.* Oral History Program, University of California, Los Angeles.

_____. (1983). "Recalling Paul Landacre." Landacre, Paul, and Phil Freshman. *Paul Landacre, Prints and Drawings*. Los Angeles: Ahmanson Gallery, Los Angeles County Museum of Art, 5-6.

Contributors

Pablo Capra is a writer and publisher of Brass Tacks Press. From 2006 to 2011, he edited and co-wrote a series of *Topanga Beach* books. The most recent one was *Topanga Beach Experience: 1960s-70s* with co-writer Paul Lovas. He manages a *Lower Topanga Photo Archive*, which is hosted on the Brass Tacks Press website, www.lifeasapoet.com.

Genie Guerard, Manuscripts Librarian, is a native Angeleno who has worked in the UCLA Library Special Collections since 1998 as a digital archivist, and as curator of manuscripts and archival collections since 2000. Her curatorial responsibilities are in the areas of the visual arts, book arts, dance, and literature, including archives of individuals and organizations that have built Los Angeles's history, politics, and culture. She received a B.A. in art, majoring in painting and drawing, from California State University, Northridge, and her M.L.I.S. from UCLA in 1998. Her previous work experience was as a production artist, production manager, and researcher for Los Angeles design offices.

Richard Hertz was Director of Graduate Studies at Art Center College of Design from 1979 until 2001. Previously, he taught for six years at Cal Tech and for five years at CalArts. His books *Jack Goldstein and the CalArts Mafia* (2003) and *The Beat and the Buzz: Inside the L.A. Art World* (2009) are well known for their exploration of the "messy back story" of contemporary art history. Hertz's family, which includes the physicists Heinrich Hertz, the discoverer of electromagnetic waves, and Gustav Hertz, winner of the Nobel Prize in physics in 1925, emigrated from Germany in 1937. He is currently writing a book about his family titled *MegaHertz: The Hertz Family in Exile.*

Jessica Holada is currently the Director of Special Collections and Archives at California Polytechnic State University, San Luis Obispo, and actively developing their teaching collections of artists' books and the graphic arts. From 2006 to 2013, she was the Poster Librarian at the Margaret Herrick Library, Academy of Motion Picture Arts and Sciences. In 2012, she guest-curated the Occidental College exhibition *Where Bohemians Gathered: Print Culture on the Arroyo Seco, 1895-1947.* Over one hundred books, pamphlets, photographs, and pieces of ephemera highlighted Occidental's extensive holdings, enhanced with loans from UCLA, the Autry National Center, and Scripps College. The exhibition complemented a symposium co-sponsored by the Southern California Chapter of the American Printing History Association where Jessica serves as Membership Chair. She received her Master of Library Information Studies from the University of California, Los Angeles, and a Bachelor of Arts in Art History from Loyola Marymount University.

Daniel Hurewitz is an associate professor of history at Hunter College, CUNY. His scholarship focuses on the development of twentieth-century U.S. gendered and sexual identities, the emergence of LGBT politics, and the resistance that movement generated. His first book, *Stepping Out* (1997), traced a history of LGBT life across Manhattan, presented as a series of walking tours. His second book, *Bohemian Los Angeles and the Making of Modern Politics* (2007), focused on the communities of L.A. artists, leftists, and gay activists who helped give birth to the American gay rights movement and identity politics more broadly. His more recent work attempts to shape a history of American homophobia, and a current book project analyzes how the homophobic policies of the 1930s were put into action at the local level, and given meaning by police forces, district attorneys, and judges.

Kristin Lawler is Associate Professor and Chair of the Sociology Department at College of Mount Saint Vincent in the Bronx. Her first book, *The American Surfer: Radical Culture and Capitalism*, was published by Routledge in 2011 and examined the politics of American surf culture during the twentieth century. She is a member of the editorial collective of the journal *Situations: Project of the Radical Imagination*; her work has been published there as well as in several edited collections, *Z Magazine*, and the digital forum of the Social Science Research Council. Dr. Lawler received her Ph.D. from the CUNY Graduate Center, and she is currently at work on a book on slacker culture and the labor movement.

Bill Mohr's poems, prose poems, and creative prose have appeared in over five dozen magazines, including *Antioch Review, Blue Mesa Review, Caliban (On-line), Santa Monica Review, Sonora Review,* and *ZYZZYVA.* Individual collections of his poetry include *Hidden Proofs* (1982) and *Bittersweet Kaleidoscope* (2006). In March, 2015, Bonobes Editores in Mexico published a bilingual edition of his poem, *Pruebas Ocultas.* His account of West Coast poetry, *Holdouts: The Los Angeles Poetry Renaissance 1948-1992*, was published by the University of Iowa Press in 2011. Mohr has a Ph.D. in literature from the University of California, San Diego, and is currently an Associate Professor at CSU Long Beach.

Harry Polkinhorn, born and raised in southern California, is a psychoanalyst in private practice, President of the Board of the San Diego Psychoanalytic Center, and emeritus professor of English and Comparative Literature at San Diego State University. For 10 years he edited and published the underground magazine *Atticus Review* and was a founder of Atticus Press, which issued books and broadsides, some printed by hand-operated letterpress. He is the author of over 40 books of poetry, fiction, translations, and edited collections. His current scholarly interests focus on the Latin American avant-gardes, as well the intersections of psychoanalytic theory and the creative arts.

Naima Prevots is Professor Emerita, American University, Washington, D.C., where she was Chair, Department of Performing Arts, and Director of Dance. Her degrees are as follows: B.A., Brooklyn College; M.S., University of Wisconsin; Ph.D., University of Southern California. Her writings include three books: *Dancing in the Sun: Hollywood Choreographers, 1915-1937* (UMI Research Press, 1987); *American Pageantry: A Movement for Art and Democracy* (UMI Research Press, 1990); and *Dance for Export: Cultural Diplomacy and the Cold War* (Wesleyan University Press, 1990). She has written numerous monographs and refereed journal articles; published dance criticism and book reviews; and commissioned several reports. Her awards include six senior Fulbright fellowships and an N.E.H. fellowship. She currently teaches on-line courses for the National Dance Education Organization.

Rachel Rubin is professor of American Studies at University of Massachusetts, where she also serves as Director of the Center for the Study of Humanities, Culture, and Society. Rubin has published widely on subjects ranging from gangsters in modernist literature, to country music and working-class culture, to Asian Americans and cyberculture; her most recent book is *Well Met: Renaissance Faires and the American Counterculture* (2012). She is currently working on a study of the Patrice Lumumba People's Friendship University in Moscow. Rubin regularly appears on Boston-area public radio as a popular culture commentator.

Jay Ruby is a UCLA graduate and an emeritus professor of anthropology at Temple University in Philadelphia. He has been exploring the relationship between cultures and pictures for the past 40 years and is considered a leader in the field of visual anthropology and multimedia ethnography. His research interests revolve around the application of anthropological insights to the production and comprehension of photographs, film, and television. A founding member of the Society for the Anthropology of Visual Communication, past president of International Film Seminars, Ruby holds advisory and board memberships in a number of national and international organizations. Since 1960, he has edited a variety of journals on American archaeology, popular culture, and visual anthropology. For the past three decades, he has conducted ethnographic studies of pictorial communication in Juniata County, Pennsylvania, Oak Park, Illinois, and Bohemian Malibu (see astro.temple.edu/~ruby/ruby/)

Katherine Stewart is an American journalist and author. Her work has appeared in *The Nation, The Guardian, The New York Times, Reuters, The Atlantic, Bloomberg View, Religion Dispatches, Newsweek*

International, Rolling Stone, The New York Observer, The Nation, AlterNet, The Daily Beast, Santa Barbara Magazine, and others. Her most recent book, *The Good News Club* (2012), focuses on religion and public education. She has also published two novels, and she co-wrote a book about the musical Rent.

Mark Thompson, who currently resides in Philadelphia, writes about law, history, and food, among other topics. He has contributed to dozens of newspapers and magazines including the *Atlantic Monthly, New Republic, Wall Street Journal* and *Los Angeles Times*. His first book, *American Character: The Curious Life of Charles Fletcher Lummis and the Rediscovery of the Southwest*, was honored by Western Writers of America in 2002 with a Spur Award for best biography. He has also written *Vintage California Cuisine: 300 Recipes from the First Cookbooks Published in the Golden State* and *Vintage Vegetarian Cuisine: Early Advocates of a Vegetable Diet and Some of Their Recipes, from 1699-1935*. Thompson is a graduate of Columbia University Law School.